Salvations

p. 219

Orientational plism

vs

Inclusivist plism

FAITH MEETS FAITH

An Orbis Series in Interreligious Dialogue
Paul F. Knitter, General Editor
Editorial Advisors
John Berthrong
Julia Ching
Diana Eck
Karl-Josef Kuschel
Lamin Sanneh
George E. Tinker
Felix Wilfred

In the contemporary world, the many religions and spiritualities stand in need of greater communication and cooperation. More than ever before, they must speak to, learn from, and work with each other in order both to maintain their vital identities and to contribute to fashioning a better world.

FAITH MEETS FAITH seeks to promote interreligious dialogue by providing an open forum for exchanges among followers of different religious paths. While the Series wants to encourage creative and bold responses to questions arising from contemporary appreciations of religious plurality, it also recognizes the multiplicity of basic perspectives concerning the methods and content of inter-religious dialogue.

Although rooted in a Christian theological perspective, the Series does not endorse any single school of thought or approach. By making available to both the scholarly community and the general public works that represent a variety of religious and methodological viewpoints, FAITH MEETS FAITH seeks to foster an encounter among followers of the religions of the world on matters of common concern.

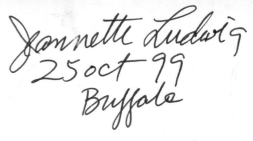

FAITH MEETS FAITH SERIES

Salvations

Truth and Difference
in Religion

S. Mark Heim

ORBIS BOOKS

Maryknoll, New York 10545

Second Printing, February 1997

The Catholic Foreign Mission Society of America (Maryknoll) recruits and trains people for overseas missionary service. Through Orbis Books, Maryknoll aims to foster the international dialogue that is essential to mission. The books published, however, reflect the opinions of their authors and are not meant to represent the official position of the society.

The cover design of *Salvations* is by Miriam Haas. Figures (from the top proceeding clockwise) are a thirteenth-century figure of Christ crowning the Virgin taken from the Rheims Cathedral; an Ife (Nigerian) bronze head; a third-millennium B.C.E. Neo-Sumerian Goddess; the third-century B.C.E. Greek Koré of Euthydikos; and the third-century B.C.E. Ibero-Phoenician Lady of Elché. Artwork adapted from photographs in André Malraux, *The Voices of Silence*, trans. Stuart Gilbert (Garden City: Doubleday & Company, 1953), pp. 242, 544, 76, 79, and 23.

Library of Congress Cataloging in Publication Data

Heim, S. Mark.
    Salvations : truth and difference in religion / S. Mark Heim.
        p.   cm.   —   (Faith meets faith)
    Includes bibliographical references and index.
    ISBN 1-57075-040-8 (alk. paper)
        1. Christianity and other religions.   2. Religious pluralism.
    3. Religious pluralism—Christianity.   I. Title.   II. Series.
    BR127.H42   1995
    261.2—dc20   95-20401
                                                                      CIP

For
David Jacob Heim
Beloved by hundreds as their "Pastor David"
and by his family as husband, brother, father,
for his wisdom, goodness, joy, and faith.

Contents

PART II

SALVATIONS

Preface

This book has been longer in the making than I expected or desired. The compensation—and frequently the challenge—over this period has been the variety of persons who have educated or incited me. I can make only a representative attempt at gratitude.

The members of the study group on Responses to Religious Pluralism in the Faith and Order Commission and the members of the Interfaith Working Group, both of the National Council of Churches of Christ in the USA, have been significant conversation partners. For some years I was also privileged to serve as a member of the Committee on Christian-Muslim Relations of the National Council of Churches. The Commission on World Mission and Evangelism of the World Council of Churches and its director, Christopher Duraisingh, have been most gracious in allowing me to participate in several of its study consultations. I am especially thankful for the opportunities for interreligious encounter which have come to me through these various relationships. Colleagues at the United Theological College in Bangalore, South India, particularly Principal E. C. John and professors Somen Das, Eric Lott, O. V. Jathanna, and Fred Downs, offered gracious hospitality as well as patient answers to many questions during a sabbatical leave there in 1986-87 and on subsequent visits.

Earlier versions of several portions of this work appeared in journals, and the responses to those articles have been very useful. I thank the editors of *Modern Theology*, *Religious Studies* and *First Things* for that opportunity and for permission to include here portions from those articles.

Here in Boston, several congenial groups have meant a great deal to me. The regular meetings of the Boston Theological Society have provided many opportunities to rehearse the issues treated here. I offer special thanks to Owen Thomas, whose own writing in this area alerted me to the work of Nicholas Rescher. In recent years, the Society for Comparative Theology, under the leadership of Francis Clooney, S.J., and John Berthrong, has been a consistent source of new ideas, new references, and chastened formulations of my thoughts. Francis Clooney's friendship and his scholarly example in this area are both gifts that I value highly. The "Divine Plenitude Group," organized through Boston University by Peter Berger and John Berthrong, has embarked on an interdisciplinary and wide-ranging exploration of religious pluralism, in which exploration it has been a pleasure to participate.

Still closer to home, I thank the students at Andover Newton Theological School who have enlivened my classes on world religions and Christology and religious pluralism, and my faculty colleagues who have both encouraged and challenged, especially Max Stackhouse and Gabriel Fackre. Sadly, some colleagues have been removed from that circle of conversation by death. Before his tragic illness, Orlando Costas's too brief tenure among us brought to me in an Hispanic idiom a striking fire both for missiology and for dialogue. A primary reason I wish this book had been completed earlier is that George Peck would still have been alive to read it. It was his passion for India, his commitment to Christian witness, and his delight in Hinduism that first set me on this path. With regard to these matters his spirit could be well summarized: "I have committed my life to Jesus Christ; *therefore* I am open to other religions." I hope I share some of that same spirit.

I am only one of many who can testify to Paul Knitter's stimulation and encouragement. He and Bill Burrows have nudged this book toward greater clarity, a service readers could appreciate only if they saw what they had been spared! They both have made it a pleasure to work with Orbis Books.

Melissa Lewis Heim's work as a historian has dealt with interactions between American missionaries and Indians in South India during the nineteenth century. Her emphasis on the concrete texture of such relations—issues of language, childhood development, household management, gender relations, social customs, political and economic power—has always been a welcome dimension in our discussions. It does not value her scholarship less to thank her more for her support and partnership in the mundane schedules of our shared life, for the joy of that life is far more to me than her books or mine. As for Sarah and Jacob, who were hardly oblivious to the work that occupied me, my main hope is that it constitutes one of the more minor of their memories of their father from these years.

Salvations

ıntroduction

"Those who know only their own religion, know none." This familiar maxim of religious studies tells part of the story. Until we see our own faith could have been otherwise—and this requires awareness of actual alternatives—we can hardly grasp its distinctive shape. In this sense, knowledge of other people's religion and knowledge of our own arise simultaneously. If I do not recognize my faith tradition is one among many, I am ill-prepared to understand others or myself.

There is a complementary truth of equal scope: "Those who are not decisively committed to one faith, know no others." The faith that makes me different from others is the primary instrument I have for appreciating their differences. The extent to which I know my religious convictions and experience condition my approach to virtually every question is the same extent to which I can recognize the depth of an alternative. I have no resource so crucial for grasping the encompassing nature of a neighbor's faith as the encompassing nature of my own. Nor can anything enable me to appreciate my neighbor's faith in its integral otherness so much as awareness of my own status as an "other." The particularity of my own tradition prepares me to grasp the meaning of specificity in another. Though I may learn much that is entirely new to me, I have nothing to learn it *with* save what has come to me through my own religious life.

The attempt to deal fruitfully with religious pluralism is in large measure the struggle to balance these insights. It is a struggle that is spiritual as well as intellectual, theological as well as moral.

We are in the midst of an explosion of literature on religious pluralism. This current high level of interest in religious diversity stems from a series of specific historical events. Its primary roots lie in the European enlightenment, the modern Christian missionary movement, and the explosive expansion of Western economic systems and colonial power. Out of this nexus the familiarity with various religious traditions, the acquaintance with (even to some extent the construction of) their texts and practices, and the experience of cultures shaped by them have reached a critical mass. The claim that this awareness of religious diversity is historically unparalleled is itself parochial. It ignores Christian communities outside Europe, for instance, which have long lived side by side with neighbors of various traditions. But the importance of this diversity remains.

There is a vast contemporary scholarly encyclopedia describing specific faith traditions, their sub-groups, texts, practices, beliefs, leaders, and histories. For the most part these materials seek sympathetic access to the internal vision, the self-understanding of the religion in question. A literature nearly as extensive seeks to interpret the religions in some set of unifying categories. The philosophy of religion, for instance, explores the cognitive content and coherence of various beliefs. Much work in religious studies uses social theory or psychological analysis to judge the effects of lived faiths on individuals or societies. Responses to religious diversity from within particular traditions employ their own specific categories, the "theology of religions" being a Christian example.

In this last field, a number of outstanding Christian theologians have turned their energy toward pluralistic theologies of religion. They call for a Copernican revolution, an unequivocal denial of Christian uniqueness. They find Christianity (and other traditions as well) infected with a virulent exclusivist virus: the affliction of imagining its religious truth superior to others and its path to salvation the only one. This sickness is similar to and often reinforced by racial and cultural prejudice, so that devaluation of non-Christian religions goes hand in hand with devaluation of the culture and humanity of persons who participate in them.

Advocates of such pluralistic theologies maintain the only antidote to this disease is a consistent reconstruction of the fundamentals of Christian faith and, similarly, of all faiths. They insist theology must now take the religious experience of all humanity as its ground and avoid claiming a unique religious value for any tradition. At first this challenge focused on criticisms of Christian exclusivism but offered little by way of an alternative account of religious diversity. That has changed decisively. Now several significant constructive theories embody these concerns, calling forth a growing number of responses.[1]

The pluralistic challenge is a crucial one. The questions that these writers have pressed upon theology—often against strong resistance—are real. If their diagnosis is convincing, we should steer by their course. If their accounts of religious diversity are seriously wanting, then they need not be rejected only in favor of unruffled traditionalism. Instead we may learn from them and search further.

This book seeks to do just that. It addresses an odd paradox in contemporary discussions, one that seems to me a key to future developments. The paradox is this: the most insistent voices calling for the af-

---

[1] Among the most constructive statements are John Hick, *An Interpretation of Religion*; W. C. Smith, *Towards a World Theology*; Paul Knitter, *No Other Name?*; Raimundo Panikkar, *The Trinity and the Religious Experience of Man* and *The Intrareligious Dialogue*. For a range of responses, see Gavin D'Costa, ed., *Christian Uniqueness Reconsidered*.

firmation of religious pluralism seem equally insistent in denying that, in properly religious terms, there is or should be any fundamental diversity at all. The assertion that major faith traditions are independently salvific means, in its most common forms, that they are equivalently effective in achieving a single human end. This conclusion undermines the distinctive value that can be attributed to the particulars of the actual faith traditions, though respect for these traditions is ostensibly its cardinal premise.

These theories also oddly seem to provide little reason why an adherent of one faith should value or require the thick descriptions of another religion's character which we increasingly take for granted. There is a tension between pluralistic theories of religion and studies of specific traditions not unlike that between Christian theology and biblical studies in the modern period. The first tends to approach details as exemplifications of principles already known while the second tends to insist that interpretations must be consistent with the particulars retaining their stubborn particularity. This tension is magnified many times, however, by the fact that unlike the documents of the Bible, the religious traditions do not claim a common identity or source.

Pluralistic theologies see themselves as the remedy for a toxic exclusivism in which one religious tradition views others as materially different and therefore fruitless. For many, the issue is fundamentally a moral one. We can be hostile or at best patronizing to faiths other than our own, with consequent strife and oppression. Or we can definitively recognize they are as true and effective in every relevant respect for their adherents as ours might be, resulting in mutual respect and social harmony. The only morally defensible choice, they contend, requires a "move away from insistence on the superiority or finality of Christ and Christianity toward a recognition of the independent validity of other ways" (Knitter 1987b, viii).

I want to point out that the "finality of Christ" and the "independent validity of other ways" are not mutually exclusive. One need not be given up for the sake of the other unless we insist there can be only one effective religious goal. One set of ways may be valid for a given goal, and thus final for that end, while different ways are valid for other ends. I suggest that the various traditions cannot be put on a single scale and the discussion limited to the question of how much of some single human possibility each one can achieve. The faiths are cross-woven in a variety of dimensions and even to place one entirely on the evaluative matrix of another yields no simple verdict. There are likely to be, for instance, a number of views among Buddhists on what to make of Christianity, on purely Buddhist grounds.[2] This rightly complicates, but does

---

[2] See for instance the variety of views expressed in Part III, "Buddhist Perceptions of Christianity in the Twentieth Century," in Paul Griffiths, ed., *Christianity Through Non-Christian Eyes*, 135-190.

not abolish, the possibility of vulnerable judgments made from within one tradition. What in my view is incoherent is any supposition of a neutral "meta-theory," of judgments made from above the religions rather than among them.[3]

A widely accepted typology of approaches to religious pluralism provides for three categories: exclusivism, inclusivism, and pluralism (Race 1982). The typology has been developed within Christian theology, but applied analogously to other faiths. Exclusivists believe the Christian tradition is in sole possession of effective religious truth and offers the only path to salvation. Inclusivists affirm that salvation is available through other traditions because the God most decisively acting and most fully revealed in Christ is also redemptively available within or through those traditions. Pluralists maintain that various religious traditions are independently valid paths to salvation.

These distinctions serve some purposes, but seriously mislead us as the definitive map of our options. The typology is fully coherent only on the assumption that salvation is an unequivocal, single reality. Given that assumption, it distinguishes between the limitation of salvation to one group, its qualified availability to all, or its full achievement by parallel, distinct paths. This a priori limitation of the religious possibilities is dubious, and the usefulness of the typology hinges on that limitation.

Its categories treat religious traditions as reified, single entities which "sit still" for people to make the kind of global judgments that the types represent. Yet the very same tradition, viewed in different lights, can require each of these judgments. If we take religions in their thickest historical, empirical description then exclusivist or "one and only" judgments appear inevitable, almost tautological. In this life, the only way to Buddhist fulfillment is the Buddhist way; the only way to Jewish fulfillment is the Jewish way; and so on. The impetus for study of religious diversity is the realization we cannot assume we already know what it is like to be a Sikh or a Sufi. The only way to find out is to approach that tradition and its adherents directly. If we do so, we discover a unique complex of elements, interlocking patterns of life, which cannot be descriptively equated to anything else.

---

[3] This is a different point than the question of whether it is legitimate to make second-order judgments about religion, judgments that do not agree with the self-understandings of adherents. It is legitimate. Wayne Proudfoot's *Religious Experience* makes the case for such second-order judgments while W. C. Smith argues in *Towards a World Theology* that in principle second-order and first-order accounts should agree, that no observer should reach a judgment about a religious tradition that its devotees cannot endorse also. My point here is simply that "meta-theories" are in no different position than religious judgments made on another tradition; such judgments do not have to accept as final that tradition's account of itself.

We may speculate about convergences on a metaphysical plane between, say, Buddhist "saints" and Jewish "saints." We may be able to specify some similarities in the effects of their practices. However, the premise of the whole discussion is that we have no difficulty generally distinguishing between them to begin with, for they are embedded in communities, practices, images, and doctrines that are distinct. If we leave aside for the moment salvation as a postmortem or transhistorical state, it would seem that religious traditions are simply, descriptively exclusivist. To know one is not to know the others. Each is a "one and only"; their salvations are many.

There are of course interesting cases of the combination of religious traditions: cases where people may follow both Buddhist and Confucian paths, for instance. This only reinforces the point. Were they not exclusivist, there would be no need to follow two ways, since the same range of ends could be achieved in either alone. Both are practiced because each constitutes a unique pattern yielding distinct fulfillments, fulfillments in this case regarded as compatible and complementary.

By contrast, if we view religious traditions as composites of their constituent elements, it seems we must be inclusivists. As an aggregated sum of practices, doctrines, and injunctions, no faith is without duplication elsewhere. If it is a Christian virtue to honor one's parents or to keep a sabbath, then these are realized in and through other religions as well. Truth or benefits that attach discretely to these elements in one faith must also attach to them in another. These truths are available in more than one tradition. But it is also true that the traditions are obviously not completely congruent: each has individual practices and beliefs not found in others.

Yet again, if we choose to view the religions from the standpoint of certain analytical disciplines, we certainly must be pluralists. If our test is the ability to organize and sustain major cultures or civilizations, then the world religions all meet it. They can be judged formally equivalent in fulfilling this function, no one uniquely successful or the hidden cause of the success of the others. If the test is the cultivation of selected generic moral attitudes (purposely leaving out any that might be distinctive of one or some traditions rather than others), then despite the daunting difficulty of controlling for the different contexts in which the faiths have worked, one may plausibly argue for a rough parity among the traditions on that score. There are many religious ways to address effectively certain basic needs of human life.

To be an exclusivist for any one of the three categories requires that we ignore or discount the importance of the other two perspectives. Just so, traditional exclusivists have tended to downplay parallels between Christianity and other faiths and to argue that cross-tradition comparisons, if properly carried out, indicate the univocal superiority of Christian norms and practice. Just so also, the most prominent contemporary pluralists relegate specific individual elements in a tradition and its concrete historical texture to secondary status; these are the culturally variable forms in which we encounter what is truly ultimate for religion. Their truth or falsity, their integral uniqueness, are both beside the point. Classical inclusivists analogously deemphasize both the integral unity of other traditions—out of which they lift individual elements that can be threaded together to form an incognito approximation of their own faith—and the possibility of finding significant *separate* religious truths there.

These three dimensions cohere in each tradition, and one does not exclude the others. If "salvation" means the achievement of *some* desired religious aim, then we can—like pluralists—affirm that a number of paths lead to salvations: there is an "any way" sign at many forks on the religious journey. If "salvation" means a religious fulfillment of some determinate nature, then we may—like exclusivists—affirm that it is constituted by certain features to the exclusion of others: there is an "only way" sign at many turnings. In either case we must—like the inclusivists—acknowledge that all these paths link with each other, that "cross-traffic" is a real possibility. Many roads are also connecting routes and bear travellers over the same ground toward different destinations.

I contend that it does make sense to speak of salvation in the plural—hence the title of this book. My aim is to make the case that this is not only defensible but preferable on many counts to current options. The book is set up primarily as a critical conversation with pluralistic theologians, and my view is significantly shaped by their concerns. Like their proposals, mine requires significant rethinking of traditional Christian theology.[4] But, in fundamental disagreement with their proposals, I argue there is a real diversity of actual religious ends.

One of the reasons I am led to propose this alternative is a desire to keep the interpretation of religion in some recognizable contact with careful description of religion. Many today maintain that all the empirical and phenomenal elements of a faith tradition are extrinsic to its true core or meaning. This belief comes in several versions. It may claim some transhistorical knowledge of the religious ultimate, which can be used to relativize all the actual religious traditions. It may stress exactly the opposite: that our categories are entirely conditioned and limited and therefore the empirical faiths must be seen as each alike inadequate attempts to grasp what cannot actually be known at all. It may instead

---

[4] The crucial question posed for Christian theology by my thesis is how it is to incorporate the realization of religious ends other than its own. This is outlined in chapter 6, but it is a subject I hope to take up more fully on another occasion.

define a social function religion should serve, impartial as to the concrete features any tradition may employ to fill the bill.

Whatever its form, the cost of this conviction is extremely high. It means that the painstaking attempt to become acquainted with and in some measure to understand the distinctive features of other peoples' faiths—precisely what makes them other—has, literally, no religious meaning. At best it has an exemplary meaning: in learning the particulars of another religion we learn nothing of substance except the formal fact that there *are* other ways. For those with a meta-theory of religion, pluralism is real but superficial. The cultural and historical means are different but the actual religious end—transcending self, or relating to the ultimate—is the same. For those who stress the ineffability of the divine, religious pluralism is deeply significant, but it can signify only one thing. Each specific religious difference tells us the same sublimely simple dogma over and over again: the divine is mystery. Our categories do not apply. And those who judge religions in terms of social effects clearly want existing pluralism severely winnowed to leave only those variations that instrumentally support full justice as they understand it. Such principles of "pluralistic theology" have the odd similarity of denying precisely any pluralism of authentic religious consequence. The specific details of the faiths seem to become irrelevant.

This is so strikingly contrary to the practice and exhortation of most pluralistic theologians, who stress exactly the necessity for theology to take religious diversity seriously, that it calls out for exploration. If I am assured that my own religious path leads inevitably to the same end as that of other traditions, does so independently of them, and that in any event the empirical features of none of our traditions are integral elements of that religious fulfillment, what have the Athens and Rome of meta-religious theory to do with the Jerusalem or Benares of actual faiths?

I would suggest that the hypothesis of multiple religious aims, salvations, turns out to provide the strongest ground for each of three elements that conventionally are not thought compatible: the religious significance of careful study of faith traditions, the recognition of distinctive and "saving" religious truth in religions other than one's own, and the validity of witness by one faith tradition of its uniqueness and superiority in relation to others.

In what follows, then, I argue for a true religious pluralism, in which the distinctness of various religious ends is acknowledged. Although this allows the validity of religious witness, it is also, I suggest, at the same time the only basis on which one can suppose there is significant distinctive truth in traditions other than one's own. Where witness can have no meaning, it is dubious if dialogue may either.

The argument proceeds in two parts. The first is a critical discussion of major types of pluralistic theology. This seeks to outline a "job description" for another approach to religious diversity that would be less liable to the objections I note. The second is a positive statement of my "more pluralistic hypothesis." Here I try to describe that position and to deal with some major criticisms of it.

Part One considers three major contributory streams of pluralistic theology, three broad avenues by which different writers have advanced toward similar conclusions.[5] Pluralistic theories have philosophical, historical, and ethical dimensions. We do an injustice to the scope and power of this perspective if we limit discussion only to one of these dimensions. There is a cumulative effect to the three types of argument we should not evade, although I hold that this broader context also illuminates some fundamental failings of the pluralistic agenda.

Chapter 1 deals with the philosophical dimension of the question, particularly the issue of religious knowledge. Here the focus is on John Hick's "pluralistic hypothesis," arguably the most extensive and detailed case yet made for a pluralistic account of the religions, as Hick is undoubtedly the single most influential writer in the contemporary discussion. Chapter 2 turns to another aspect, that of religious history. Here the primary dialogue partner is Wilfred Cantwell Smith, whose case for a pluralistic theology looks not so much to philosophical theory but to the history of religions. Chapter 3 considers how the imperative of social justice figures in the discussion. Paul Knitter has articulated this focus on "orthopraxis" with special cogency, and in dealing with his thought we encounter the broader moral case for a pluralistic theology. Chapter 4 attempts to draw together the critical elements in the first three chapters into a summary of the difficulties with pluralistic accounts generally.

Part One takes up what I think are the most extensive and consistent cases for "pluralistic" interpretations of religious diversity. The decision to focus on Hick, Smith, and Knitter follows this logic, since one could hardly find three writers more prominent or influential in advancing the pluralistic perspective. All three are Christian Westerners, natives of the United Kingdom, Canada, and the United States respectively. There are some other significant Christian voices, notably Raimundo Panikkar, Aloysius Pieris, and Stanley Samartha, who speak out of Asian cultures. I find them to be on somewhat different wavelengths than my three primary subjects, despite their own willingness to be identified in some way as "pluralists." Panikkar particularly has been

---

[5] These correspond roughly to the three "bridges" by which one may cross over into pluralism suggested by Paul Knitter in "Introduction," Hick and Knitter, *The Myth of Christian Uniqueness*, ix.

suggestive to me in developing my own view. To put it in a self-interested way, where these writers differ from the three I examine, I tend to think these differences are quite consistent with my own thesis; where they agree, I think them liable to the same criticism and drawing on identical sources. To the objection that "pluralistic theory" is discussed here largely as an intra-Western affair, my response is that the theories I discuss are in fact exactly that, much more thoroughly so than generally acknowledged.[6] As I indicate in Chapter 4, I find an underlying similarity in Hick, Smith, and Knitter which has very much to do with liberal Christianity's appropriation of modernity. One of the aims of this book is to draw out this genetic particularity of pluralistic theologies and to question claims that it has been transcended.[7] Panikkar has raised this caution quite explicitly and both Samartha and Pieris also recognize it.

In Part Two I turn to a statement of my thesis. I present this in three stages, mirroring the structure of Part One. Each chapter describes one dimension of my perspective and seeks to test it against the valid questions raised by pluralistic theologies. Chapter 5 presents a "more pluralistic hypothesis" and tests it philosophically. This discussion draws particularly on the work of Nicholas Rescher and the conversations in contemporary philosophy over relativism and objectivity. Chapter 6 expands the same thesis in terms of the historical and sociological dynamics of religious life and makes an empirical case for its validity. Chapter 7 reviews the implications of my view for religious diversity and justice, facing the moral test. Chapter 8 offers a conclusion and summary view of the possible implications of this argument.

I stress, by anticipation, that my thesis has a triangular shape, with three sides which I have tried to distinguish clearly and which the reader needs to bear in mind. On one side is an argument about the *status* of theories of religious diversity. On another is an argument for a particular *type* of theory of that diversity as against others. And on yet a third side there is a particular *instance*—a Christian instance—of what I regard as a legitimate type. I can briefly summarize these three stages as follows. My view of the status of meta-theories of religious diversity is non-exceptionalist: such theories stand among and not above religious accounts of the world. Second, I argue in favor of the class of such theories that recognizes an authentic pluralism of alternative religious

---

[6] The point has been eloquently made by a number of authors, particularly Lesslie Newbigin in *The Gospel in a Pluralist Society*.

[7] See in this connection Kenneth Surin, "A `Politics of Speech': Religious Pluralism in the Age of the McDonald's Hamburger," in D'Costa, *Christian Uniqueness Reconsidered*, 192-212, and Tom F. Driver, "The Case for Pluralism," in Hick and Knitter, *The Myth of Christian Uniqueness*, 204-206.

aims. Third, among Christian theologies of religion, therefore, I argue in favor of such types of inclusivism as also recognize the reality of alternative religious ends.[8] Obviously these three elements are closely linked. Indeed, one of the primary recommendations of my hypothesis is that I believe it offers the most consistent account of all these levels.

Though much of my argument is made without extensive explicit theological reference, it is rooted in a Christian perspective. This confessional commitment does not compromise the argument, since I have maintained that there are no neutral meta-theories that offer a different order of knowledge about the religions. But it is equally appropriate according to my argument that others should test it by their own particular religious standards. Insofar as such tests show the theory consistent with faithfulness to their own traditions, this will reinforce both their proper standards of judgment and the universal intent of Christian theology.

---

[8] My earlier book, *Is Christ the Only Way?*, is an instance of the kind of inclusivist Christian view of the religions for which this work tries to provide a much broader grounding. The framework I commend legitimates inclusivist perspectives such as that expressed in my earlier book, in various religious traditions, recognizing that such broad frameworks are grounded in just such particularist commitments and their claims to universality.

PART I

Pluralisms

1

Adjusting to the Real

John Hick and the Pluralistic Hypothesis

For two months of Sunday afternoons we had met together, a group of Muslims, Hindus, and Christians, to listen to presentations and discuss them in small groups. The college campus where we gathered was an oasis of calm in the crowded bustle of this city in South India. This particular afternoon, a group of us walked in the gardens and talked with the monastic head of a local vaishnavite ashram who had addressed us on the meaning of *moksha*, "release" or "liberation," for Hindus. In his presentation he had stressed a favorite metaphor for this state of fulfillment: waking up.

When we are in it, a dream can be extremely vivid, he told us. We feel its objects, we move in its world. Yet in the instant of awakening we realize completely that the dream was but a veil for our actual place and being. Just so will our present world appear when we achieve moksha. One of the Muslim students frankly shared his puzzlement. If this world is like a dream, he asked, then what are we to you, or you to us? Are we illusions, figments of each other's imagination? The monk adjusted his robes with a smile. "We are dreams, talking to dreams." He was silent for a moment, while we savored the peculiar beauty of this image. "But of course," he went on, "you will ask me 'Who is having this dream?' And I will tell you that it is Brahman who is having this dream, and it is Brahman who each of us is when we wake up." As we walked on and he answered our questions with the same amused concreteness I seemed to glimpse, unsteadily and only for a few moments, what it might be like to be in a world constituted as he suggested it was. A similar experience could come from regular attendance at temples or simply from increased familiarity with the city's many funeral processions. With time it was possible to be at least a bit infected with the perspectives through which my neighbors approached these things. Small glimpses, but glimpses none the less.

Our conversation meandered further into the well-worn dialectics of the great Hindu philosophers and their distinction between the faces of Brahman clothed with the appearances of our world—Brahman with qualities—and Brahman without qualities, on which such appearances have no purchase. To read of these things in a textbook is one thing. The reader can at least clearly sense there the deeply subtle intelligence of this particular part of Hindu tradition. But it is another thing to see and hear these elements expressed winningly in the concrete constitution of a life or a community. I do not believe that those of us in this band came away with much in the way of new information. I know that I came away with a vision new to me of what that information might mean.

Such stories are hardly unusual. They make up one important strand in our religious experience. This strand is not just the experience of other people's religion as something that we are exposed to as observers. It includes a fragile dimension of insight into, we might say of tentative participation in, a small slice of that experience itself. What are we to make of such experiences in our own religious terms? What is their moral? This is not a new question, but it is receiving newly insistent answers.

Wilfred Cantwell Smith, for instance, has long affirmed that the major religious traditions share in equal measure the potential to mediate God's grace and salvation. He observes that the most painful thing for him has been the way other Christians have received this claim. "They might well have heard the report joyously, yet be held back through fear that it might not be true. Instead, many reacted by rejecting the new vision with a fear lest it be true" (Smith 1988, 373). This picture of Christians, anxious that God might find a way to redeem humanity without membership in their club, is both comic and sad. It leads easily to Smith's conclusion: to question God's full revelatory action in all the religious traditions is theologically and morally wrong. Those who do so are "disloyal to Christ and...are blaspheming God" (Smith 1988, 267).

This passionate statement, which oddly itself takes the form of religious condemnation, summarizes the challenge for a dramatically new approach to religious pluralism. Smith poses that challenge pointedly to his own community, but it can be replicated for others as well. Christian pluralistic theologies of religion in similar vein have flowered in recent years. John Hick, W. C. Smith, and Paul Knitter offer what I take to be among the most extensive and cogent examples.[1] All three have

---

[1] Raimundo Panikkar's work, which is every bit as extensive and which reflects even broader scope, is not included here because in my judgment he literally breaks the mold which pluralistic theology has set for itself. Despite participating in the pluralistic manifesto *The Myth of Christian Uniqueness*, Panikkar's own critique of pluralistic theology contained in that piece and other writings makes him a figure who points us beyond the exclusivist-inclusivist-pluralist typology altogether. We will return to this question in chapter 6.

played significant roles in bringing religious diversity to the center of theological discussion.

Pluralistic theology is by no means a homogenous movement. These theologians unite in a call to "cross the Rubicon" from exclusivism and inclusivism, which they see differing only in the degree of imperialism, to pluralism. But they make the crossing themselves in various ways.[2] In Hick's case pluralistic theology is cast in a primarily philosophical form, while Smith argues mainly in historical terms and Knitter in ethical ones. Close consideration of their proposals will provide us several maps of the country on the far side of the Rubicon and a fuller appreciation of the motives and means for making the trip. This chapter will consider Hick and the philosophical case for a pluralistic outlook. Subsequent chapters will cover the historical and ethical arguments. In chapter 4 I will suggest some common roots and problems of all three approaches.

THE PLURALISTIC HYPOTHESIS

John Hick is the best-known interpreter of the pluralist position. His Gifford Lectures, *An Interpretation of Religion*, provide the mature statement of a thesis evolved over some twenty years of intense work in this area. There he summarizes the "pluralistic hypothesis" this way. An "infinite Real, in itself beyond the scope of other than purely formal concepts, is differently conceived, experienced and responded to from within the different cultural ways of being human" (Hick 1989, 14). The great world faiths embody different responses to the Real from within these variant cultural ways of being human. In each tradition that "transformation of human existence from self-centeredness to Reality-centeredness is taking place" by which humans find ultimate fulfillment.

Given this premise, Hick asks if there are criteria by which to judge different religious traditions as totalities. He concludes that "the basic criterion is soteriological; and the salvific transformation is most readily observed by its moral fruits, which can be identified by means of the ethical ideal, common to all great traditions, of agape/karuna (love/compassion)" (Hick 1989, 14). There is then an ethical test for how well each religion is realizing the common religious end they all seek.

Past approaches to faith diversity, Hick says, have either been confessional, where those within one tradition evaluate others in its terms,

---

[2] For the argument of a self-identified exclusivist see Harold Netland, *Dissonant Voices*. For a variety of strong inclusivist views, see D'Costa, *Christian Uniqueness Reconsidered*. The typology "exclusivist-inclusivist-pluralist" is described originally in Race, *Christians and Religious Pluralism: Patterns in the Christian Theology of Religions*.

or reductionistic, where religions are explained entirely in terms of some constituent dynamic: psychological, social, biological. He proposes to break this impasse. His thesis is a "religious view of religion" which affirms religious views of the world as valid (over against naturalistic accounts) but does not privilege any particular religious view above others (over against all confessional views). Pluralistic theology as Hick presents it is primarily a philosophical hypothesis. It grounds the cognitive and experiential cores of the great religious traditions in one common object and one common salvific process, whose character Hick describes. He provides a meta-religious perspective which accounts for the religions' specific beliefs, practices, and objects as culturally variant versions of the reality and process he posits.

Hick's *An Interpretation of Religion* is a multifaceted work, woven from theses of different types that are compacted in this brief summary. One of the impressive features of the book is the clarity of these theses and the care with which Hick presents arguments which appear to oppose them. A fuller exposition is necessary to appreciate the several lines of thought which are united in his argument.

First we can note Hick's working definition of religion as "belief in the transcendent," and his specific focus on the "post-axial age" world religions which are distinguished from earlier world-maintaining faiths by their concern with "salvation/liberation as the realization of a limitlessly better possibility" (Hick 1989, 12). He denies that these elements— transcendence and salvation/liberation—are the essence of religion, for he renounces any essentialist definition. He favors a "family resemblance" approach. There is no set of characteristics every faith has, but a continuum of resemblances similar to those between activities we call "games." Some games use balls; some do not. Most have rules; a few don't. Just so, religions can be grouped in terms of close as well as more distant relations. Hick says he chooses to focus upon belief in transcendence as a feature present in most religions.

In the past, he suggests, argument about transcendence was always conducted in reference to some specific formulation of it, say an Islamic one or a Vedantic one. But this is no longer appropriate in our pluralistic world. We are now able to recognize in full the human projection involved in all these specific notions of transcendence and to pose the question in terms of a mysterious reality behind them (Hick 1989, 9). The defense of any specific notion of transcendence is always liable to criticism with regard to its historical conditioning. The pluralistic approach turns this around and stresses the consistency of some belief in transcendence across many times and cultures. This leads us to an important set of epistemological questions.

Hick argues for what he calls the "religious ambiguity of the universe." Here he draws upon work that he has done previously as a Christian theologian in relation to the question of theodicy, regarding "epistemic distance" (Rowe 1991, 111-137). Were God immediately present to our experience, we would effectively be unable to be autonomous persons, unable to respond to God freely. The power and mercy of God would literally overwhelm us, leaving us no choice whether to believe in God's existence or to trust God's characteristics. Therefore humans are held at an "epistemic distance" from the divine in order to have their own creaturely freedom. This veil at the same time protects us from and denies our access to certainty about God's existence or nature.

The philosophical argument between naturalists and believers, then, is a tie. The evidence is inconclusive and can legitimately be weighed differently by different observers. In support of this contention, Hick argues that all conscious experience is "experiencing as." That is, the cultural categories we bring to our experience of the world permeate and constitute that experience thoroughly. This constructive dimension increases in scope as we move from our perception of the physical world to our perception of other persons to our perception of the whole. It is in the religious realm that this dimension has widest play. So Hick concludes that "both religious and naturalistic ways of construing the world arise from a fundamental cognitive choice, which I call faith, which is continuous with the interpretive element within our experience of the physical and ethical character of our environment" (Hick 1989, 13).

The issue between religion and naturalism is "ultimately a factual one in which the rival world-views are subject to eventual experiential confirmation or disconfirmation" (Hick 1989, 13). This recalls Hick's earliest work in philosophical theology where he defended the cognitive meaningfulness of religious beliefs on the grounds of eschatological verification. In response to objections that faith predicted no specific state of affairs in distinction from another and so was empty, Hick maintained there were future conditions in which certain religious expectations would be confirmed or refuted: "eschatological verification" (see Hick 1964, 253-279). Religious statements are meaningful even if the conditions to decide them do not yet exist.

Within his pluralistic hypothesis, Hick continues to argue strenuously against non-realist interpretations of religion, however practically useful some such interpretations may find faith or however readily such approaches might support harmony among the traditions. He is committed to affirming the various traditions as *religiously* valid. He insists that religious faith involves a cognitive content. Both in the propositional affirmations they make and in the tacit premises of their key practices, religious traditions contain content that cannot be translated without remainder to naturalistic terms.

Given the religious ambiguity of the universe, and the constructive element in interpreting its data, Hick concludes that it is rationally appropriate for those who experience their lives in relation to a transcendent to trust that experience and to "proceed to believe and to live on that basis" (Hick 1989, 13). The same of course is true for those whose "faith" is a rejection of all transcendence. Both groups are epistemologically justified but both are running a risk, for only one is right.

These then are the terms of the problem of religious diversity as Hick constructs it. He turns away from several easy paths toward religious comity. By insisting that it is rational for believers to trust their religious experience and by further arguing that religion has distinctive cognitive content he sharpens the expectation that pluralism must mean contradiction, since the varying forms of religious experience seem to justify contrasting sets of beliefs.[3] Each of the faiths offers coherent world-views entailing verifiable expectations. So, as Hick says, "have we not, in showing the fact-asserting character of the plurality of religious options, thereby established their radical incompatibility?" (Hick 1989, 188).

There is justified religious belief in Agni as well as Allah, in dharma as well as Demeter. At this point it may seem most reasonable to conclude either that religions are not cognitive in character at all, or that only one or some mutually consistent subset of these differing justified beliefs can eventually prove to be true. Hick has already rejected the first, and he claims there is no ground for preferring one justified belief over another save the entirely arbitrary one that it happens to be mine.

Instead, the fact that varying religious beliefs are epistemically justified, particularly when joined with Hick's assumption that some kind of salvific process is underway in each tradition, suggests to him that these apparently contrasting faiths "constitute different ways of experiencing, conceiving and living in relation to an ultimate divine Reality which transcends all our varied visions of it" (Hick 1989, 235-236). The key element here is the postulate of a radical Kantian disjunction between this Reality in itself and as it is humanly thought and experienced.

Since Hick's defense of religious faith rests upon the epistemological legitimacy of trusting religious experience, it is a difficulty that the Real in itself is clearly not a direct object of experience. To know the Real solely as a postulate of the reason, as Kant understands religious knowledge, is not acceptable to Hick. Whereas Kant sharply distinguished sense perception and moral or religious knowledge, Hick wishes to see them continuously, in the same categories. He acknowledges that the Real *is* a postulate advanced to account for religious experience, but also insists that it is more than a postulate: the Real is actually encountered in religious experience "in, with, and under" the particularities of that experience. These particularities are the product not of immutable

---

[3] In fact Hick draws a number of careful qualifications around this "right to believe." What one accepts on the basis of religious experience must be both important and possible, among other things (see Hick 1989, 219).

a priori categories of human understanding but of variable historical and cultural "equipment" in contact with the Real.

There is a strong apologetic cast to Hick's thought that should not be overlooked. His vision of the religious traditions is one in which it is no longer possible to doubt any specific religion per se. It rules out both arrogance and fallibility at once. If one epistemically defensible faith is true, all are. The religions are validated together or necessarily all hang separately. In a single swoop, the apologist's task is greatly simplified. One can enter a religious tradition with no concern that any other actual alternatives existed, with the confidence that though there are many and even apparently conflicting religions, this is no reason to doubt the validity of your own or of religion generally. The variety of religions, used as a perennial reproach to the claims of any one, is now turned into testimony in support of all.

Hick defends his postulate of the Real in explicitly apologetic terms. He insists it is the simplest hypothesis that can account for the plurality of religious experience while saving the ultimate validity of the various traditions. Without this postulate the ultimates of the traditions are in irremediable conflict, and hence some invidious judgment must fall at least on some. With the postulate, all the traditions can be seen to image the absolute in ways that allow appropriate response. They can be recognized to be in order as they stand.

A further dimension of the pluralistic hypothesis involves the soteriological criterion as a pragmatic test of religious traditions. Hick deploys this in two main ways. On the one hand it supports his decision to turn away from the possibility of conflict among faiths. If moral development is our guide to gauge whether salvific transformation is taking place within a faith, then in Hick's view a rough and unprejudiced survey indicates something near parity among the major (and most other) traditions. This does not seem consistent with the notion that only one or a few of them can be valid. If there is one fundamental empirical basis upon which Hick builds, it seems to be this contention that a single salvific process, as measured morally, is advancing at a similar pace in each of the religions.

The soteriological criterion serves also to avoid the completely relativistic conclusion that any religious faiths or practice whatsoever must be affirmed. To Hick it is "self evident, at least since the axial age, that not all religious persons, practices and beliefs are of equal value" (Hick 1989, 299). Using the ethical test, it is possible sometimes to conclude that salvific transformation is *not* taking place to any meaningful extent in a particular group or practice and hence that this is not true response to the Real. The pluralistic hypothesis still distinguishes true from false religion.

Where does this ethical standard of judgment come from? Hick states that "self-sacrificing concern for the good of others" is the basic ethical

principle of the great traditions (Hick 1989, 325). In fact it antedates
these traditions and as a basic human insight has been a standard by
which great teachers like the Buddha or Muhammad have been accepted
and recognized as authentic mediators of the Real. At the same time, the
resultant traditions have purified and extended the principle. Thus it
constitutes a valid norm by which to judge religions in their entirety as
well as to judge specific elements within any tradition. Hick is at pains
to point out that the application of this norm across different traditions
and their different cultural and historical contexts is a very complicated
matter. For the purposes of his hypothesis, only the broadest general
conclusions are suggested.

Hick sees the situation this way. Believers within different religious
traditions have equal epistemological justification for trusting their religious experience. Applying the ethical test for salvific transformation,
Hick gives the great traditions similar aggregate scores—within a broad
margin of error. These two strands then suggest, though they do not
demonstrate, a kind of parity among faiths. Hick's defense of religious
belief as intrinsically realistic implies some irreducible cognitive content in each faith. The postulate of a single noumenal ultimate—the
Real—conceived differently in various traditions offers a way to pull
these elements into a coherent whole. If it once is granted that there is
such an absolute, then Hick's stress on "experiencing as"—the inevitable constructive aspect of all perception—may plausibly explain why
that absolute would be described in such varied, even contradictory ways.

The cognitive content of religion is validated by the fact that there
truly is a transcendent referent for its belief and it is in relation to this
object that human transformation toward a "limitlessly better possibility" actually takes place. This is what each religious tradition can be
taken to affirm through its historically contingent terms. Here Hick leans
crucially on his view of "mythological truth," which he has applied also
in extended treatments of Christology (Hick 1977). Any language within
a religious tradition which intends to be about the Real in itself—as
opposed to the effects or marks of the Real in human life—can only be
mythological.

We can and do use literal and analogical language about our experience of the Real's manifestation *as if* we were referring to the Real in
itself. And the value of such statements is that they effectively express
the practical meaning of the Real "by evoking in us an appropriate dispositional response" (Hick 1989, 351). Mythological truth has to do
with the attitude persons adopt under the myth's influence, not its content. To take the Christian example, this means that to view Jesus of
Nazareth as representative of God's way with humanity is itself one
appropriate way to relate to the Real and so is religiously true, quite
apart from any factual determinations which might apply to particular

elements of the myth like "Jesus" or "God."[4] Certain attitudes and actions on our part are appropriate dispositions toward the Real, while others are not. Mythological language evokes and regulates just such dispositions in us. It is a crucial imperative of Hick's hypothesis that all religious traditions should recognize and accept this understanding of their own practice.

None of our religious language can be applied appropriately to the unexperienceable Real. Thus all the ultimates of the faiths—God, Brahman, Sunyata—are themselves myths. They are the *personae* and *impersonae* of the Real. The Real is the "noumenal ground of the encountered gods and experienced absolutes witnessed to by the religious traditions" (Hick 1989, 246). The only accurate statements that can be made about it are purely formal ones which attribute no concrete qualities.

The pluralistic hypothesis attempts to hold together two fundamental elements: all major religions are salvifically effective and all have real cognitive content. The key to reconciling the two is to find some shared cognitive content and a way of interpreting the apparent contradictions. The shared formal substance of religions is postulated to be their affirmation of the realization of a limitlessly better possibility by centering on the Real rather than the self. The solution to apparent contradictions among faiths is to insist these conflicts all fall into one of two categories. Either they are only apparent conflicts (having to do with mythological truths which may contradict each other literally but whose actual religious function is to evoke equivalent dispositions in believers) or they are true differences but have to do only with historical forms associated with the Real (whose empirical truth or falsity is finally irrelevant).

This thesis does allow for a nuanced approach to various elements within each religion. There is a cognitive propositional core which each tradition can be taken to assert implicitly through the confession of its particular forms. That core states there is an ultimate noumenal Real and through appropriate human response to this Real a transformation toward a limitlessly better possibility takes place. Most of the explicit statements and beliefs in a religious tradition are mythological in nature: they commend and exhibit some of *our* appropriate dispositional stances in relation to the Real. Insofar as they have any religious cognitive content at all, it is identical to the "core" just stated. Religious "one and only" claims show up from this perspective as "love language," similar to a wife's affirmation that her husband is the kindest man in the world. This should not be heard, and is not truly intended, as a literal

---

[4] This is an approach whose conclusions Hick believes overlap those of George Lindbeck's treatment of doctrine (cf. Hick 1989, 360 n. 4).

comparative claim. It truthfully expresses the disposition of the speaker toward her husband.[5]

On the other hand, Hick recognizes that in their varied responses to the Real the traditions may make assertions that are truly factual in nature. The Qur'an's testimony about certain events in the life of Muhammad might be a case in point; the beliefs of some faiths in reincarnation may be another. Whether relating to historical events like the *hjira* or transhistorical ones like reincarnation, there may be instances where such assertions in different religions directly contradict each other. In these cases he is quite willing to allow that eschatologically some will turn out to be true and others false.

Thus Hick says there are some real contradictions among religious claims, real open questions which will eventually be decided in favor of one side or another, though we currently have no way of doing so. But we can safely be agnostic about such issues: nothing of salvific importance depends on them. For instance, it may turn out to be decidably true or false that Jesus rose bodily from the dead or that there are heavenly Buddhas. "May," because these statements might be entirely mythical in character, lacking factual reference but truly evoking the proper

---

[5] I will not have occasion below to treat this analogy extensively. It appears widely in discussions of pluralism today. It will suffice here to point out a few of its more serious difficulties. First, even should full weight be given to the comparison, it cuts in the opposite direction to what is suggested. If a wife's confession that her husband is the kindest man in the world represents a kind of "dispositional adjustment" on her part toward him, it represents just such an adjustment toward that particular man among and in distinction from all others, not a disposition toward "The Man." Even if the statements are not meant literally, they literally and decisively commit the speaker to one among many. The only way to avoid this conclusion is to suggest that one spouse's love for another is not truly for the sake of that other person but is an instrumental means to relate to something for which that person is only a secondary form.

Second, if each religion could have but one adherent, the analogy would be a good deal more telling. As it is, I recognize other people appropriately love different persons than I do precisely because we are living different lives, with different specific qualities and aspirations, and because the fulfillment of those lives will consist in the realization of different ends. If we were to assume that "marital happiness" was one univocally recognized and sought thing, then we could well expect mass conflict over those individuals best suited to provide it to any applicant of the opposite sex. Indeed, if we think of love in a sense broader than that of marriage covenant we realize that some persons are much more widely loved than others, and for sound reasons.

Third, "My husband is the kindest man in the world" and "My husband is the richest man in the world" may both be hyperbolic, dispositional statements. It is hardly true that they carry no affirmation of content, or that this content does not truly differentiate both the person described from others and the fulfillment sought by the speaker.

disposition toward the Real. Not only do we not know certainly now whether these statements are true or false, we don't know whether they belong in the category of mythical or factual assertions, and so whether they are *eligible* to be true or false. But as no particular element in either category can be essential for salvation, our inability to know the applicable category is also of secondary importance. Whatever opinion one holds or whatever practice one takes up in relation to these differences will presumably not affect one's relation with "the Real" and the achievement of salvation/liberation, provided the mythic structure of which they are a part serves to evoke an appropriate disposition in us. Hick puts it this way:

> Such beliefs concerning matters of trans-historical fact vary in importance within the belief system to which they belong; and at the top end of the scale they may be indispensable to a given doctrinal structure. It does not however follow that that structure is itself indispensable for salvation/liberation. On the contrary, it suggests otherwise: for it seems implausible that our final destiny should depend upon our professing beliefs about matters of transhistorical fact concerning which we have no definitive information. It seems more likely that both correct and incorrect trans-historical beliefs, like correct and incorrect historical and scientific beliefs, can form part of a religious totality that mediates the Real to human beings, constituting an effective context within which the salvific process occurs (Hick 1989, 369-370).

I trust this is a fair, if all too brief, summary of Hick's argument. Its scope is impressive, its facets complex. Serious opposition to it, so the author tells us, stems only from parochial egotism (Hick 1989, 377). Is the hypothesis right?

WHAT'S NOT PLURALISTIC
ABOUT THE PLURALISTIC HYPOTHESIS?

Hick's thesis rests on two sweeping assumptions, each questionable: a metaphysical dogma that there can be but one religious object, and a soteriological dogma that there can be but one religious end. Together they lead to conclusions which are even shakier.

The first assumption postulates that the realm of ultimate reality consists of a single, noumenal element which Hick calls "the Real." Hick makes this assumption though he acknowledges the realm of noumenal reality might itself be plural, might correspond more closely to the description given by one or more particular tradition than to his account, or might simply be such as to support the realization of several kinds of ultimate religious fulfillment (Hick 1989, 248). The observation that various religious traditions speak of ultimates which are in significant measure ineffable cannot legitimately lead to the conclusion that there is but one identical ineffable ultimate of which all religions speak (Ward 1990, 5).

Hick's postulate of "an infinite Real" as the single, true referent in all religious practice depends on acceptance of the Kantian world of things in themselves. He appeals frequently to those strains in various religious traditions which assert the ineffability of God, or nirvana, or moksha or Sunyata. But these apophatic accents in the traditions generally assert ineffability of their religious referent in contrast to other objects in the world, which can be known more simply as they are. Hick stresses the gap between subject and object in all knowing which has marked modern Western philosophy. The Real is an instance of this general principle. Hick enthusiastically pursues Kant's move to sacrifice knowledge to make way for faith.

Even mysticism, which is sometimes claimed as evidence of the identical unitive destiny of all religions, is not in Hick's view actual contact with the Real. It remains experience in the categories brought by the believers from their historical traditions (Hick 1989, 295). Thus mystical truth also remains mythological truth, in the sense described above; it exhibits a human disposition toward the Real. But a literal reading of its affirmation of undifferentiated experience is no more in order than a literal reading of other particularistic claims. Even in the "profoundest unitive mysticism the mind operates with culturally specific concepts" and what is experienced is a manifestation of the Real, not the Real itself (Hick 1989, 295). Nevertheless, as we have seen, Hick claims mysticism like other expressions of religion does have some real cognitive content because it generically asserts the existence of the Real and the possibility of transforming relation to it. And Hick presumes this tacit formal assertion is eschatologically falsifiable.

Our review of Hick's hypothesis noted the argument he mounts for granting religious experience validity as a true source of knowledge. He moves from the assertion that the faithful in different traditions have justified grounds for holding their beliefs to the hypothesis that there must be a common noumenal object beyond their conditioned, conflicting, yet epistemically defensible views. Having argued that there is justification for conflicting religious beliefs, he considers only two alternatives: reject them all as delusory or affirm one or some to the exclusion of others. He rejects the first alternative in rejecting naturalistic accounts of religion. The second he rejects because he says any such choice among similarly justified religious beliefs could only be arbitrary, based on personal prejudice or location. Ruling out these options, Hick sees his hypothesis as the reasonable sequel: the rough parity of justification corresponds to an equality of essential religious truth regarding a noumenal Real and the salvific process centering on it, though this truth may be expressed in religious totalities which include conflicting claims of fact and apparently conflicting mythological forms.

This hardly follows.[6] Hick's argument leans heavily on the implicit suggestion that all beliefs that are similarly epistemically justified ought to be presumed to be similarly true (or false). This is plainly not the case, and Hick recognizes it eloquently when he contrasts naturalistic and religious views. He holds that both of these are epistemically justified interpretations of experience. But he insists one must be wrong and the other right. In this case, if two people are justified in believing contradictory things they are each also justified in thinking the other mistaken.

This is an equally reasonable conclusion regarding differences among religions, and would not require that one and only one religion will prove to be true nor in itself decide how many of the traditions are salvifically effective. From such a perspective, it is appropriate for people justifiably holding contrasting religious beliefs to recognize their fallibility, to assume that the other's belief contains truth as well as error, and to strive to assimilate that truth up to and including the possibility that the two could be discovered to have some deeper unity. But each may also rightly continue to regard the other as mistaken in fundamental respects. Insofar as Hick's argument from the epistemic justification of religious belief suggests any conclusion, it would seem to suggest this approach more consistently than his pluralistic hypothesis.

Hick stresses that epistemically justified belief may have as its object false assertions. But even these false assertions (as well as purely mythological ones, to which truth and falsity do not apply in the same way) are the means by which a "religious totality" mediates the Real to humanity. Just as the present epistemic justification of belief is not affected if some or all of these beliefs eventually turn out to be wrong, so the religious ultimate which Hick hypothesizes each religion mediates is not called into question if specific religious expectations turn out to be false.

But it is only the *current* justifiability of holding a belief which is unaffected by its future falsification. Under some future conditions, such religious belief might no longer be justified. Hick slides too easily from a diversity of views which are currently epistemologically defensible to an assumption that these views should turn out to be equally true (or false) as regards a single ultimate religious content. He does not present this hypothesis itself as a belief provisionally defensible among other alternatives, pending circumstances which will decide its validity, but apparently as a belief justified under *any* set of future circumstances.[7]

---

[6] I am indebted to Keith Ward, who has made this point cogently (see Ward 1990, 12-13).

[7] Should a naturalistic account of religious belief prove in some way to be eschatologically verified—abstracting for the moment from how that might be done—then Hick might allow this as refuting his hypothesis. For the purposes of my argument, however, this can be left aside. I am concerned with the differentiation of Hick's hypothesis from any other religious belief.

That is, it is justified not only if some specific religious expectations or all of them should prove to be false, but also if a particular set of them should prove true! This is a point we will explore more fully below.

The second sweeping assumption in the pluralistic hypothesis is that if real human transformations are taking place in various religious traditions—identified by moral behavior—then in fact one identical salvific process is taking place in them all.[8] Hick maintains the major "post-axial" faiths are all distinguished by concern for some kind of salvation/liberation, as opposed to earlier traditions which he says were more concerned with the world-maintenance of crop harvests, fertility, and social stability. "Religion" then for Hick is by definition a "post-axial" tradition or something analogous to such traditions, and "salvation" is presumed to be the main concern of all religions. Hick further assumes that one and the same salvation is taking place in each religious tradition and no other sort is possible. Since salvation or at least the process that leads to it is not noumenal, it can be known concretely enough to serve as the primary criterion in assessing actual religious traditions: how well is each doing at what all are about?

Hick sharply condemns any group which asserts those who follow its path are more likely to attain a religious good than those following another path. This condemnation is not relaxed even for those who profess there is in principle no barrier at all to those in other traditions finally attaining this end also. Hick's anathema seems specially directed toward the assertion within one religious tradition that its end or religious fulfillment is *distinct* from those in other traditions.

The fundamental question is not about the limits on access to any particular religious tradition's salvation, though he certainly condemns those who would place such limits. Even should the limits be eliminated, Hick rejects any inclusivist approach which understands outsiders' access to a religious fulfillment to be on the terms of the "home" tradition or by exclusive means of the realities it confesses. He holds that each tradition has access on its own terms, but access to an end which is everywhere the same.

Though Hick believes there are real differences among religions, he denies these differences have any important bearing on the soteriolgical function of each religion as a whole. It seems to be a paradoxical axiom in his hypothesis that anything about which it is possible to differ religiously cannot be *religiously* significant, to the extent of leading toward a different religious fulfillment than others. By means of your religious tradition you achieve religious fulfillment. But absolutely nothing which is distinctive in your tradition, in the life of faith that you lead, can be integral to that fulfillment itself. This is a curious conclusion for

---

[8] For a critique of the validity of this test see Rebecca Penz, "Hick and Saints: Is Saint Production a Valid Test?," 96-101.

one like Hick, who has so strongly stressed "experiencing-as." If religious ends are, even in part, *human* states, then it would seem historical and cultural elements must be a constitutive aspect of them. Hick himself argues as much about mystical experience.

So what is the nature of this salvation which Hick claims is identical for all, achieved via many different paths and yet bearing the indelible mark of none of them? It is a transformation toward a "limitlessly better possibility" through centering on the Real rather than the self. Hick believes we can crudely measure *that* this transformation is happening by the moral behavior of believers involved. Those who manifest compassion for others and respect certain moral standards are presumed to be involved in an appropriate relationship with "the Real."

But what this transformation is like for the person, what the better possibility itself may be like, what the Real is like, and even what the self one transcends is like are all experientially given in the concrete texture of different traditions. Hick uses the word "salvation" in a univocal sense, but this usage makes of it a purely formal abstraction. It is as if one were to say that the differences in concrete study among various trade, professional, and graduate schools were "not vocationally significant." Each of these schools forms people with some kind of discipline, to practice some kind of skill, in relation to the same physical universe. And one can plausibly claim that success in any of them requires some similar types of human transformation: attentiveness, self-criticism, honesty. Is the fact that there are people from all these schools who are employed, efficient, and happy proof that there is, at base, only one human vocation? Plainly not. Yet Hick presumes a similar progression to formulate his "soteriological criterion." At issue at the moment is not whether moral behavior is the best test for the realization of a religious end, but whether it can be simply posited as the index of the achievement of only one religious end. Hick's attempt to validate this kind of argument must lean heavily on eschatological expectations, to which we will turn later.

It is important to be clear about Hick's view: *that* you have adopted some one among all of the mythological and perhaps conflicting traditions is salvifically significant because without some such vehicle you cannot center on the Real. To relate to the Real directly is impossible. But to choose one tradition over another or to side with one against another on a specific religious matter and to live concretely on that basis cannot in Hick's view be determinative with regard to the nature or the possibility of salvation.[9]

---

[9] I leave open the possibility that such a choice might in Hick's view have some significance for salvific efficiency in a strictly biographical sense—that for a given person at a given time certain religious options and not others would allow him or her to proceed most expeditiously in the salvific process. This would not alter my point.

Hick holds that all the concrete historical features that distinguish one faith from another or constitute its practices are determined by large-scale cultural variables or small-scale psychological ones. As such, "religion" in the sense that most historians or anthropologists or believers would identify it is for Hick a functional vehicle of religion in the true sense. It may be that people are free to make a choice for or against religion generically (on this, more in a moment) but any choice *among* religious options must be without substantive religious motives or consequence.

Since for Hick differences over factual matters (such as whether Jesus was crucified or Muhammad travelled from Mecca to Medina) or commitments to differing mythic truths do not deflect people from realization of the same salvation/liberation, it is worth inquiring whether any differences at all are relevant. We have already seen that Hick believes certain ethical failings would indicate one is not progressing well toward salvation. However, unless salvation is simply identified with certain ethical behavior—something Hick rejects—we do not have a convincing reason to presume that this ethical behavior occurs in association with the realization of only one religious end.

Leaving moral behavior aside for the moment, are there any other religious differences that would affect the attainment of salvation? Most particularly, is the difference between naturalistic and religious beliefs itself one that is soteriologically significant? Hick speaks of this difference as a momentous one, of a choice either way running the risk of being very importantly mistaken, profoundly deluded (Hick 1989, 210). It might seem then that this is an option with real religious import.

But apparently it is not.[10] To side with one religious tradition against another on what may prove to be a matter of fact is to run the risk of being mistaken, but not "importantly" mistaken, since this has no bearing on salvation. If naturalistic explanations turn out to be correct, this certainly does have a bearing on salvation. It is not possible, in Hick's terms. All religion would then be "profoundly deluded." However, if Hick's generic religious truth holds, a single salvation is not only possible but apparently necessary. Could it be that holding naturalist convictions regarding the facts impedes or even precludes salvation, while adhering to any "post-axial" religion assures it? To say so would run Hick afoul of his own strictures against exclusivism, so it seems safe to conclude that he rejects this possibility. In fact in a recent essay Hick makes this clear. He affirms that humanists and Marxists may be "responding to the Real without knowing that they are doing so" ("Reply" in Hewitt 1991, 83). This, he says, is an "entirely appropriate inclusivism,"

---

[10]C. Robert Mesle indicates in his review of *An Interpretation of Religion* that Hick has confirmed this reading of his position.

even though he is ordinarily quite scornful of the equivalent inclusivist mode when deployed by specific religious traditions.

Even if they hold false beliefs on what Hick regards as the most momentous question that faces humanity, and have built their lives concretely on such assumptions, Hick concludes this would not affect naturalists' achievement of the religious fulfillment they deny and resist. Indeed, it seems consistent with his pluralistic hypothesis to maintain that it is precisely through their naturalism that they would be "saved." Hick writes, "It seems implausible that our final destiny should depend upon our professing beliefs about matters of trans-historical fact concerning which we have no definitive information" (Hick 1989, 369-370).[11]

Hick can be criticized here for falling away from the pluralist principles he has expounded: if the humanist "faith" in toto is salvifically effective, why insist that its tenets are false and Hick's are true, that humanism's salvific effect is, so to speak, parasitic on the truth of religion? Hick surely condemns such a claim from one religion to another. Would it not be more consistent with Hick's general approach to say that, like the *persona* and the *impersona* of the Real, naturalistic and religious views are two equally good ways of relating to a great unknown?

Or Hick can be criticized for revealing that despite protests to the contrary he is actually an inclusivist through and through, one who in-

---

[11] Arguments like this lead some of Hick's critics to maintain that he bases his hypothesis that all religions mediate the same salvation implicitly on the theistic ground of a loving God who will not disadvantage any. He has dismissed these critics as narrow dogmatists who think Christians are the only ones who know of the love of God. See for instance, John Hick, "Straightening the Record: Some Response to Critics," 1990, 188-190, 194. This rather evades the main point, which is that if Hick insists the Real is beyond personal or impersonal characterization, how can he reach normative conclusions based on its personalistic "fairness"? Hick's whole point here hinges on the assumption that human destinies are administered in some way. If the Real were viewed, as Hick argues it can be with equal justice, as an impersonal order or structure, it does not seem "implausible" at all that our final destiny might depend on convictions about transhistorical reality concerning which we do not have definitive information. An impersonal structure would be under no obligation, or have no means, to make it otherwise. The "implausibility" Hick appeals to can only derive from some kind of agency on the part of the Real. And he has gone to some lengths to assure us that "agency" is only a mythic description that does not touch upon the Real in itself. Why then should Hick side definitively against an impersonal Real, which could not be supposed to arrange things so humans have definitive information regarding a religious end? His attempt to fall back on an appeal to a general "cosmic optimism" of post-axial religions is not much help, since this optimism was always based on the availability and power of some one of the specific religious realities Hick regards as mythic.

sists that those of other religious convictions can only be saved by means that he understands and they do not. Then it would be consistent for Hick to view humanists as he does, since in fact he views all religious believers as also responding to the Real without knowing that they are doing so: they think they are relating to God or the dharma or some such mythological form. Hick may respond convincingly to one of these criticisms, but hardly to both.

Hick's approach does seem to be the classically inclusivist one he otherwise rejects when it is a Muslim arguing the Hindu's moral virtue is ultimately rooted in Allah, or a Buddhist arguing the Jew's ethical integrity is anonymous participation in the dharma. He exempts himself from the charge of being an inclusivist because he relativizes the ultimates of particular faiths not in favor of one among them, but in terms of something above and beyond them all: the Real. Of course, all religious inclusivists also believe that the object of their faith is above and beyond the particularities of other religions—and often their own as well. Hick is thus hardly unique in the kind of religious object he imagines.

His thesis is distinctively a meta-theory of religion, like those derived from Freud or Marx. Its plausibility depends on the claim to transcend the frame of reference of the religions, to speak not from among them but from above them. When such a theory is naturalistic, it sees the "true meaning" of the faiths in some social or psychic dynamic which has been cloaked by metaphorical language. Hick attacks these interpretations as reductionistic. His own meta-theory is by contrast a friendly reductionism, which sees a true *religious* meaning of the faiths obscured by metaphorical language. He asserts that the real truth of religion—the existence of an infinite Real toward which various cultural religious forms allow us to orient ourselves so as to transcend self—is explicitly grasped only in his meta-theory. He argues the faiths grope toward this truth in their own conditioned, particular manners; like all inclusivisms, his comes to fulfill and not to destroy.

Hick's recruitment of naturalists as "anonymous religionists" reflects the extremity to which he presses both the noumenalism of the Real and the singularity of salvation. When dealing with the various religious traditions, Hick says that false and accurate views on factual matters as well as constitutively differing mythical structures can all be salvifically effective because of the disposition toward the Real they evoke. In regard to naturalism, he seems finally to say that a considered and conscientious attempt to deny any religious ultimate and to avoid any disposition, let alone a positive one, toward it can actually constitute an appropriate response to that ultimate. Thus when Hick says religions evoke dispositions "appropriate to the Real" this phrase tells us literally nothing about the disposition in question. That disposition could perfectly well be described functionally as one which does not absolutize the self and which observes some common moral injunctions, dispensing entirely with reference to "the Real."

Hick contends that no purposeful relation to "the Real," in its generically philosophical form or in its cultural forms as "God," "Brahman" or "Dharma," is necessary for appropriate relation to it. Salvation then does not require intentional relationship with the Real in any of its forms, and is not affected by varying concrete human religious goals. It is approached and realized wherever humans strive for ends larger than their narrow interests and incorporate in that striving some skeletal moral principles. To be laggard in pursuing the rigors of some such commitment can stall one's salvific process, but cannot affect the end in view. The one clearly *ineffective* salvific path, it appears, is that of pure egotism.

It is instructive to compare the way Hick treats conflict between naturalistic and religious views and among religious views themselves. In both types of conflicts he believes the people on either side are epistemically justified in their beliefs. As we have seen, he holds all these forms of belief are salvifically effective for serious adherents. The difference seems to be that religious believers differ over matters whose truth or falsity makes no difference to true religion. Naturalists and religious believers differ over matters whose truth or falsity is crucial. This last statement requires modification however. There is really only one matter here Hick regards as crucial: whether religious faith has one irreducible referent which makes possible one limitlessly better possibility. When naturalists and believers argue, as they usually do, over specific religious affirmations (Does a personal God exist? Is karmic doctrine nonsense?), they are really replaying the irrelevancies of conflict *among* the religions over the forms of the Real. It is only naturalists' attempt to deny the significance of *all* of the forms at once which amounts to a denial of the Real as a religious object, and thus to a difference over something that is crucial. But, as we have seen, this denial—though having to do with a matter whose truth is crucially important—is itself a conviction that can also effectively mediate salvation as well. Therefore the naturalist's denial that there is any substance to Hick's thesis has no more salvific significance than conflict among various religious forms. All things considered, one cannot say that per se it is more—or less—conducive to salvation than the alternatives.

There is an interesting passage in the first chapter of *An Interpretation of Religion*. After stating that he will focus on religion as characterized by belief in the transcendent (though he notes that only "most forms" of religion affirm a salvific reality which transcends our world) Hick goes on to note a benefit flowing from that choice. He says this focus does not make the discussion a controversy between believers and unbelievers, religion and irreligion, but precisely a controversy among the religious. In a growing contemporary debate it has become "a vital *reli-*

gious question whether religion requires or can on the contrary dispense with belief in a transcendent reality. In focusing upon this issue we shall thus be addressing what is both the most momentous and the most contested issue in religious discourse today" (Hick 1989, 6).

Having made this comment, Hick immediately passes on to other matters. He is certain that religion cannot dispense with belief in transcendent reality, since it is this belief (in its varied mythological forms) which he regards as the valid cognitive core in all religion. Hick's hypothesis takes on the character of a defense not only of religion against naturalism but specifically of *true* religion against distortions that "dispense with belief in a transcendent reality." If belief in such a reality is rejected or devalued we will be thrown back to regarding religious differences as religiously significant or to regarding all religion as illusion. That is, if religious language and experience do not point to a reality which completely transcends their categories and texture, then those categories and texture remain indicative of truly disparate claims. We would be back in a realm of significant religious choice.

Any tradition without affirmation of radical transcendence, any religious movement that regards its object as fully immanent in the world is very problematic for Hick. In such a case, since religious fulfillment or "salvation" is understood to be entirely within the historical frame, that fulfillment would partake of historical conditioning and have a thoroughly concrete nature. Religious objects would retain to the end their own distinctive character: a situation fatal for Hick's hypothesis. The radical Kantian dualism he insists on heightens the absolute transcendence of the divine, its noninvolvement and nonidentity with our categories. Such dualism is sharply attacked by many theologians today, as an alienation of religion from earthly concerns. Certainly process theologians and many feminist theologians would make this point. This is the intra-religious controversy to which he refers.

Here is a point of tension between Hick and those equally enthusiastic about a pluralistic theology of religions who want to ground it not in a noumenal transcendent, but in the struggle to realize an immanent order of justice (see, for example, Knitter in Hick and Knitter 1987). On the one hand, it seems Hick should be committed to treat practical differences over matters of justice and morals in the same way he treats other religious differences: they can be of no soteriological significance. Yet he tells us clearly they are of soteriological significance in one crucial way. Moral transformation of a highly general sort is used by Hick as an indicator *that* the salvific process is underway: the "soteriological criterion." Hick believes moral evaluation of persons or specific ethical teachings can tell us to some extent which are "further along." He has firm confidence in his own ability to make such cross-cultural and cross-traditional moral judgments. These judgments serve as an index, a "thermometer" which indicates that the salvific reaction is underway.

But Hick resolutely resists any suggestion that the religious object or the religious end *consists* in a certain moral order or behavior. No concrete notion of justice can be identified with salvation on his terms. This would veer dangerously toward an exclusivist faith, distinguishing the true religion, with its beliefs and coordinate practices, from all other false religions (even if this true religion did not correspond to a single, historical tradition). Morality is a marker, testifying to the presence of salvific effectiveness. Its importance rests in the fact that it is within the range of our measurement, while for Hick the true object and human end of religion are by definition beyond our conception. It is ironic, then, that for all his consistent insistence on the necessity of the transcendent, even the super-transcendent, as the true and only religious referent, Hick's own treatment of the Real seems to make it finally dispensable—his definition of mythological truth amounting to "that which evokes other-centeredness" (Mesle 1990, 714).

The reason Hick stresses the religious-naturalist divide so strongly is ultimately one having to do with salvation. Because the naturalist's understanding of human fulfillment fixes it firmly within the historical plane, that fulfillment necessarily retains a conditioned and particular quality. This is precisely the quality Hick insists salvation must *not* exhibit. It must be understood as unrestricted and eschatological, otherwise its concrete features would align it more with one faith's account than another's. Second, in explaining why he rejects non-realist though ostensibly "religious" interpretations of religion, Hick makes it clear that it is not because they are false (this can't be demonstrated) but because they are "cosmically pessimistic" and hence "cannot credibly claim to represent the message of the great spiritual traditions" (Hick 1989, 208). They are pessimistic because they are not "good news for all"; the millions of persons dead and unfulfilled in history are lost forever on such views. For such non-realists the better possibility religion may image is entirely a historical project. It may have been realized by some for a time in the past. Their religious hope is that it may be realized by many in the future, in a world of more justice, peace, and happiness. But for Hick this vision of a more fortunate posterity living with increased justice and equality is not really salvation at all. He has defined salvation as a limitlessly better possibility for human beings (Hick 1989, 12). The humanist's melioristic future is not a *limitlessly* better possibility even for the minority of individuals fortunate enough to participate in it, and it is not a possibility at all for the vast majority of persons in history. For Hick, non-realist religious outlooks are not authentically religious, not so much because they explain religious belief and behavior in a reductionist way as because they lack a sufficiently unrestricted hope for human transformation.

It is Hick's view of salvation, more than any other element, which determines the structure of his pluralistic hypothesis. He assumes there can be only one actual religious end and goes on to presume that similar moral behavior is a reliable indicator that this end is being realized. But moral similarities might equally be by-products of quite different human vocations, as one might observe generically similar expressions of loyalty and selflessness in a member of a criminal organization, a member of the armed services, and a parent. Since Hick is convinced there can be no such substantial diversity of religious aims, he feels no need to consider this possibility.

Because Hick insists that the one true religious end must not be proximately more consistent with the claims of one tradition than another, he removes that end to extremes of eschatological distance and philosophical generality. In pursuit of a single, universal system equidistantly above all the traditions Hick is willing to limit sharply the extent of the truth value he could otherwise grant to particular traditions. For instance, since he is committed to the conclusion that the religions are all talking about "the Real" and about the same identical ultimate human destiny, he is committed to the assumption that everything the faith traditions say or do which points to another conclusion is fundamentally mistaken, requiring reinterpretation in Hick's terms. There is no personal, agent "God" such as Muslims imagine, nor any concrete "Dharma" such as Buddhists profess. Such believers are in error through and through in their convictions about such specifics; they are correct only in the disposition which Hick perceives within their faiths and in the object he hypothesizes behind their forms. Ironically, were Hick not so intent that the traditions should express the same truth, they would have more room to be simultaneously accurate in their concrete description of varying religious paths and aims. If God and the Dharma are each real, for instance, then the Muslim and Buddhist traditions are both much more concretely correct than Hick would allow. Because of the practical benefits he sees in the assumption of an identical religious end, Hick is willing at this crucial point to opt for a religious truth that brooks no rivals because it defines away all alternatives.

But salvation also becomes the most strained part of Hick's hypothesis. In his system Hick has pressed a Kantian dualism extraordinarily hard. He pushes "the Real" far into the noumenal realm to protect it from any characterization which might compromise its neutrality among the traditions, at the same time making it virtually dispensable. He pulls everything in the traditions themselves radically within the cultural forms of "experiencing-as." It is only salvation which bridges this gap, since it involves "centering" on the Real, connecting the many and the one.

Desiring to affirm the many religious ways, Hick hones them to a highly abstract point of identity—salvation—and locates their validity at that point. The result is that the concrete historical traditions are affirmed functionally as ways to this formal ultimate, but any truth or differential experiential content in them is cut away as irrelevant or even pernicious insofar as it might stimulate parochial thinking. Since he admits that the "soteriological criterion" can only be applied by selecting out certain similar aspects in what are empirically *different* concrete forms of religious life, it is crucial to ask whether he provides convincing grounds to presume that there is but one end of all the faith paths and that he has described it more adequately than any existing tradition.

THE PLURALISTIC HYPOTHESIS: MEANING LESS THAN MEETS THE EYE?

Hick maintains that religious convictions are meaningful because there are conditions under which evidence sufficient for determination of their truth or falsehood will obtain. As he says, an eschatological postmortem experience of communion with a personal God and the saints may not—since it is still the experience of a human subject—be able to rule out conclusively all possibility that it is illusory. It might not even conform in any specific details to widespread types of expectation (for angels or robes). Yet he acknowledges that such an experience would verify the Christian theistic religious expectation beyond any reasonable doubt (Hick 1989, 179). Therefore, although there are no possible current tests that could adjudicate the claims made by Christians about eternal life, those claims are meaningful.

However, the sole religiously significant cognitive content which Hick allots to the religious traditions—that there is a noumenal ultimate Real impinging upon us, in relation with which humans are transformed by reality-centeredness toward a limitlessly better possibility—must itself be subject to eschatological verification to be meaningful and true. If not, then Hick's tenacious argument for a realistic versus a non-realistic view of religion has the effect of vindicating the truth value of the particular religious traditions but denying it to his own pluralistic hypothesis.

Of course he has said that there are other matters of fact at issue in the various traditions. But he has said 1) that we cannot possibly know now how the truth of these matters is distributed among the religions, and 2) that these are matters about which we can be religiously agnostic, since their determination is of no soteriological significance. For all we know all the facts of this type might turn out to be on the side of one religion. But that would not be of the slightest importance for the religions qua religion. It is only the fact that the religion is one of the historical *personae* or *impersonae* of the noumenal Real that is religiously significant. So the assertion that a single, noumenal Real impinges in all religion and is the source of human transformation to a limitlessly better future must make its own way as a religious claim. It cannot borrow its credentials from the particular traditions it attempts to subsume.

Hick must provide or at least plausibly predict some evidence that would favor the distinctive claims he makes over against or beyond those of the traditions.

Hick says his pluralistic hypothesis is not committed to any particular eschatological prediction. That the human project will have a limitlessly good fulfillment is an expectation Hick abstracts as common to all post-axial religions. This fulfillment could take many forms, he says, "and it is important to insist that the basic expectation of a limitlessly good fulfillment could be correct without any of our present ways of picturing it proving adequate" (Hick 1989, 360 n. 8; also see 180). This is rather beside the point, since the same may be said of any of the specific religious expectations: an eschatological future in communion with God or in the cessation of nirvana might either prove correct without present pictures of them being adequate. The question is whether there is a distinctive eschatological situation that would particularly confirm the terms of the pluralistic hypothesis itself "beyond a reasonable doubt." What specific state of affairs is predicted as confirmatory of the faith that there is a noumenal Real behind the specific religious traditions and that it is in relation to this Real—*instead* of one of the religious ultimates advanced by the faiths—that we are being salvifically transformed to a limitlessly better possibility?

It would seem that the hypothesis is stated in just such a form as to be in principle unverifiable even under eschatological circumstances. First, it is hard to see how any experience of fulfillment could constitute verification of a "limitlessly better possibility." Something that transcended all our hopes and expectations could not be known to be limitless, even if it unequivocally seemed better. Second, whatever experience of beatitude was encountered in such circumstances, the assertion that it is a single noumenal "Real" which is the source of this experience is just what could not be verified. Hick makes a point of saying that even in the most intense mystical experiences of union with the ineffable, there is no unmediated contact with "the Real" but still an experience in and through the form of the ultimate in a specific tradition (Hick 1989, 294-295). He takes this dramatic confirmation of the pervasive role of our concepts in perception as support for his hypothesis. That is, if one were to grant the existence of a single noumenal Real, this incorrigible character of all human perception as "experiencing as" would readily account for the diffraction of that reality into pluriform traditions. But surely this same factor precludes eschatological verification of such a hypothesis; if the Real has *no* contact with any of the categories which are intrinsic to our experience we can hardly specify circumstances under which we would "recognize" the Real when we met it. The purely formal category of "exceeding our categories" will not provide even the limited knowledge Hick needs. If we encounter what is beyond our capacities to conceive, we are not even entitled to presume the literal conclusion that it is one and not many.

Despite the real apophatic strains which Hick finds in the traditions, it is because the various religious traditions insist on characterizing their religious object and their religious end through some conditioned but definitive terms that they qualify as making religious truth claims at all, if we are to take Hick's eschatological test seriously. A theist's experience of communion with God need not in any way be an experience of all the qualities of God or precisely of those beyond our capacity to experience in order for that experience to be confirmatory. Something analogous might be said of the "experience" of nirvana, for instance. But Hick's hypothesis requires some conceivable conditions in which it would be verified by an experience of the noumenal Real, that is, experience of what cannot be experienced. It is not a matter here of doubting that a given eschatological scenario will come to pass, but of a religious claim that corresponds to no differentiated set of circumstances at all. The failure of Hick's pluralistic hypothesis to specify any such set puts its own cognitive status in jeopardy.

Hick might object that any eschatological fulfillment which resembled in specific form one or a combination of those suggested by the post-axial religions would be compatible with his thesis. This is true—if we stress "compatible"—but it only reinforces the suspicion that the hypothesis is empty. If any such spectrum of eschatological fulfillments is consistent with the pluralistic hypothesis, then in principle even an outcome for all humans which conformed in great detail to the terms of only one religious tradition would be consistent with his hypothesis also. That is, Hick is saying that if some people come to communion with God, others attain nirvana, others realize their oneness with Brahman, and yet others (we may suppose) live on only in the natural processes of the universe which give rise to new levels of complexity and being . . . or if all persons reached only one of these ends this would count as a vindication of his thesis about salvation. The fact is that such fulfillments would be powerful evidence for the cognitive validity of the specific religious tradition or combination of traditions in question and their account of themselves, in preference to Hick's account. There would be nothing at all distinctively confirmatory of Hick's hypothesis in such a situation.

There is an important distinction here. The proposition "Reality is such that the human hope for a future condition of presently inconceivable good can be realized" is one that could be confirmed by the realization of any of a number of specific eschatological visions or combination of elements from such visions. The realization of any one of these specific religious hopes would verify the general proposition. It is easy to mistake Hick's hypothesis as being of the same sort. It is not.

If it were, he would in essence be saying that "one or some of the post-axial religions or some combination of their tenets will prove to be true." That is emphatically not what Hick understands himself to be doing, for it would require insisting on the possibility that Buddhists (or any other tradition) may turn out to be correct and all others wrong. His hypothesis states a condition that would have to be additionally true beyond any realization of the hopes of a single religious tradition or any combination of traditions; namely, that it will prove to be the case that a single noumenal Real, beyond description by any of the religious traditions, is operative in each of them to bring about one limitlessly better religious end for all humanity.

If I claim that there are some fish, including trout and bass, in this lake, my observation of a trout and someone else's catching a bass both count as confirmation of the claim. But if my claim instead is that there is a fishy ultimate in the lake, which manifests itself to some as trout and others as bass, but which is beyond characterization as one or the other, neither of these concrete experiences offers any distinctive collaboration of that thesis in preference to the first one. When he speaks eschatologically about the pluralistic hypothesis, Hick blurs this difference. On this score, Hick's hypothesis looks less like the "Copernican revolution" he invokes and more like the old postulate of "the ether"—invisible, imperceptible matter pervading space—as an explanation for motion. If anyone questioned that assumption, the lack of specific evidence is pointed to triumphantly as just what the theory predicts!

That there proved to be postmortem experiences of communion with God, or experiences of additional worldly lives, or both, would confirm theistic beliefs and/or beliefs in reincarnation. They would not of themselves count at all in favor of the proposition that this communion with God and karmic reincarnation were secondary manifestations of a more primordial "Real." Of course, the experience of an increasingly worse possibility would apparently serve to refute Hick's hypothesis, along with some other religious beliefs.

We can imagine an eschatological scenario in which the scales are lifted from our eyes and we all recognize that the same absolute has all along been encountered within the various religious traditions or in some set of them. In fact, each religious tradition itself envisions this possibility very clearly, with "the One" corresponding to that tradition's understanding of the ultimate. But it is such a scenario that precisely cannot take place on Hick's terms, since "the Real" that he is talking about cannot be recognized *an sich*, for as such it is completely noumenal. And if it is recognized through some cultural medium, that form will necessarily have roots in particular traditions.

The best we could do to salvage meaning for the pluralistic hypothesis is to imagine an eschatological situation in which all people found themselves in similar or converging conditions which were unexpected and neutral as regards all their various prior religious expectations. If these persons were able to observe and interact with each other, they might infer that there was some reality at work here different from or transcending that conceived in any of their traditions. This is the only concrete state of affairs that would distinctively correlate with the pluralistic hypothesis. In such a case, the pluralistic belief would not be directly confirmed, but only permitted as a postulate, a highly formal theory of highest generality to cover the known data, awaiting some further specification.

Even to imagine this "best case scenario" for the pluralistic hypothesis we have to change it fundamentally. This scenario necessarily requires the truth of one particular set of religious beliefs—the continuation of personal consciousnesses and relationships—and the falsehood of any others that conflict with them. Therefore the pluralistic hypothesis must be committed to these particular beliefs, contrary to its claims to be neutral on such matters. In order to imagine this scenario we must also suspend what Hick himself affirms to be an integral aspect of all human experiencing, our "experiencing as." There is no reason to suppose that, whatever these unexpected eschatological circumstances were, persons would not continue to interpret them in different ways according to the diverse resources that have previously shaped religious perception (Hick 1976, 415-416).[12]

I would like to pursue this point, since Hick has done so himself in *Death and Eternal Life*. He considers there the possibility, which in his opinion appears to be a probability, that the various religious expectations will turn out to be justified in specific terms.[13] Drawing on the

---

[12]The eschatological vision which Hick himself describes in the conclusion of *Death and Eternal Life*, were it to prove true, would seem to confirm vividly not only the truth and validity of some specific religious assertions over others (a fact that would not itself violate the pluralistic hypothesis) but to confirm the validity of one set of religious expectations concerning the nature and basis of salvation/liberation over others (which would violate the hypothesis). Hick is quite clear that *An Interpretation of Religion* is the definitive statement of his views and in recent comments indicates that at least his characterization of the final unitive state in *Death and Eternal Life* has been superseded. See Hick 1990, 191; see also Hick 1989, 6).

[13]How much of Hick's earlier position in *Death and Eternal Life* he retains is for him to say. In what follows I leave aside any reference to his description of the final unitive state (see note 12 above). If his most recent understanding of this final unitive state regards it as one in which the Real is authentically experienced as both personal or impersonal by different persons, this would only reinforce my argument that specific religious expectations remain experientially confirmed throughout. I address the rest of his eschatological vision because on my understanding of his argument in *An Interpretation of Religion* this vision is compatible with the pluralistic hypothesis and would also seem to be one in which the various religious expectations prove not only to have been epistemically justified but predictively valid, thus maximizing the truth value of all religions. One would think then that this instance is highly favorable to Hick's hypothesis. Obviously the pluralistic hypothesis could be compatible with other visions as well—too many, I suggest!

Tibetan Book of the Dead, Hick surmises that very few if any persons are ready at death to pass directly to a final "unitive state." The great majority may enter upon a postmortem state which Hick suggests is a subjective one of "realistic dreams." What we encounter here depends "largely upon the beliefs and the consequent anticipations of different individuals" (Hick 1976, 415).

A Christian thus may experience a judgment scene drawn from the New Testament, leading to a period of blissful or painful experiences which his expectations might "create for him." For a thoroughly secularized person this subjective state might be experienced as one almost indistinguishable from life in this world. Hick speculates that after an undetermined period in these states of realistic dreaming the eventual sequel is "further embodiment in another world, in another space" (Hick 1976, 417).

My observation is a simple one. What Hick describes here is the eschatological confirmation of various specific religious expectations. He, of course, prejudges the matter by characterizing this as "subjective" experience, though he is tantalizingly reticent on what the locus of this experience is and what "subjective" means in the case of unembodied persons. But certainly if we bracket for a moment Hick's further speculative account, given as it were from the other side of the other side, the experiences he describes could only be taken by those experiencing them as the strongest possible confirmation of their specific religious expectations . . . or non-expectations.

Is there a heaven? Is nirvana actual? If we ask such questions, it seems Hick can answer yes to any number of them. But you can only attain them by being a believer and by striving to follow the way that seeks them in preference to other ends. Hick is quite explicit about this: our immediate postmortem state of "realistic dreams" depends upon the previous beliefs and anticipations developed in various traditions. No one, in Hick's telling, encounters something he or she did not anticipate in some manner. In what way does this differ from more or less exclusivist believers' accounts of their own tradition—that there is only one way to reach their religious end? Nearly all such exclusivists acknowledge there are other possible ends, but regard these as either penultimate or negative. If we stop Hick's film here, as it were, what he has described is the realization of various concrete faith expectations, as claimed by the religious traditions, not confirmation of his own thesis.

Of course this is not the end of Hick's imagined eschatology: people pass on to further embodied lives in other worlds of diverse types and converge eventually toward a single unitive state. Even if we leave aside the fact that this is obviously speculation piled upon speculation—post-eschatology—we must note Hick's serious doubts that the "I" undergoing these subsequent lives retains any meaningful memory or continuity with the "I" preceding them. He thinks this unlikely. If he is correct, then this would only reinforce the conclusion that in the contrasting religious beliefs of different traditions we have *accurate* indications of different eschatological destinies and experiences for those who follow different faiths. As these different faiths shape lives in distinct concrete ways in history, so too would they in the only future life we will know as ourselves. The unitive state which lies on the ultimate horizon, at which point perhaps human beings pass beyond "experiencing as," is the same point at which human beings themselves pass away. If this is meant finally to be the moment that confirms Hick's hypothesis, the hypothesis is on safe ground. By definition there is no one there to know the result.

Once again, the difference that Hick's hypothesis makes seems to be zero. I mean "difference" in exactly Hick's terms of a specifiable kind of experientially accessible future evidence which would count in favor of this hypothesis in preference to others. In Hick's own eschatological vision we find experiences that could count to confirm specific religious expectations, even specific conflicting expectations—since what proves experientially true for one person in the postmortem state may prove different from that for another. Insofar as his scenario is correct, it is the cognitive value of those traditions that is confirmed, not Hick's hypothesis.

That religious expectations other than one's own should be validated by eschatological experience—assuming that those in the eschatological states know this—could be taken by each as consistent with continued affirmation of his or her particular view of the religious ultimate. The theist who experiences communion with God could view the entrance of others into nirvana as a punishment, a freely chosen lesser good, or a stage on the way to eventual reunion with God. The Buddhist could easily view the theist's entrance into heaven as a reward of merit and a stage on the journey to true enlightenment. But any state of affairs that would distinctively correlate to Hick's hypothesis of a noumenal Real behind the apparent religious ultimates and a single limitlessly better possibility would still be wanting. If we look to the "post-eschatological" journey to provide it, we have the Cheshire Cat dilemma that as we wait for any distinctively predicted circumstances to come over the horizon the subject who would be able to do the verifying is, on Hick's supposition, increasingly less "there."

I have not forgotten Hick's contention that his hypothesis is not committed to any particular form of positive eschatological outcome, even his own. The point is not that if Hick's eschatological vision fails, so does the pluralistic hypothesis. It is precisely that if Hick's vision is true it provides no specific grounding for the hypothesis. If this is so for Hick's own vision it seems that it is even more true, as I have argued, for other possibilities.

The difficulty seems to be that given the nature of Hick's pluralistic hypothesis itself, there are only two distinctive experiential circumstances that can be specified as counting in its favor. The first would be direct experience of the naked noumenal Real as the source behind conceptualized religious experience. The second would be set in a kind of "post-eschatology" where we cannot apparently be clear that the relevant experience would any longer have the same subject.

In short, the pluralistic hypothesis is a religious claim which falls afoul of the charge of emptiness against which Hick has fought so valiantly to defend religious claims in general. If x signifies "the existence of a single noumenal Real which impinges in all religious traditions and is the source of human transformation toward a limitlessly better possibility," then according to Hick's definition we could include in the set of possible worlds where not-x was the case any world where the ultimate reality was significantly such as it is described by Buddhism, or by Islam, and so on, or by some combination of elements from these. We could also include in this set of not-x any world in which there was a diversity of religious ultimates.

What set of experientially accessible circumstances, here or eschatologically, would be compatible with x and not with not-x? This is what Hick does not specify, even in his own fullest statement of an eschatological vision in *Death and Eternal Life*. The challenge Hick has set himself is to provide a religious account of religion which is compatible with affirming a substantial common cognitive truth and a single common soteriological result in all the religions. What my analysis suggests is that the attempt to do this is, perhaps necessarily, required to be compatible with so many states of affairs that real cognitive content evaporates. The various religious traditions, in running greater cognitive risk, escape at least this danger.

If I were to say that I am a Christian and that in addition to being a Christian I also hold Hick's hypothesis, what additional meaningful statement have I made? In terms of specifying or predicting a set of distinctive experiential circumstances, it seems I have made none. What the hypothesis does do is to commend a certain set of attitudes on my part and the part of others—attitudes of respect, humility, openness, which can be held also by those who do not affirm this hypothesis. It does exactly what non-realist accounts of religious language contend that language does. As such, unconfused with a religious truth claim, I can see no objection to it.

Hick's pluralistic hypothesis provides an excellent introduction to the wide range of issues involved in an account of religious diversity. No other version of pluralistic theology has reached the same level of breadth, clarity and consistency. He provides a rigorous interpretation of the data of religion from the premises of his hypothesis. There is, however, no compelling reason to accept those premises as true. He acknowledges this by commending the thesis primarily on the grounds that it best serves certain values which are not merely rational ones. Hick claims the pluralistic hypothesis is the most effective way to secure 1) real cognitive content for religion (a non-reductionistic view of religion); 2) substantial parity among the faiths, and thus the elimination of any excuse to privilege some; and 3) a standard that can detect radically dysfunctional religion, and so avoid relativism.

My critical discussion has focused primarily on whether Hick's thesis actually succeeds in fulfilling the terms he sets for it. I have suggested it does not. His desire to affirm a foundational cognitive content for the faiths seems finally to be cancelled out by the purely formal nature of this content, unable even to meet Hick's religiously friendly standard for meaning. Similarly, his claim for a unitary and universal "salvation" in the religions appears incoherent. In later chapters I will turn to an alternative account of religious diversity I believe more effectively achieves much that Hick seeks, but also differs in its views of the proper priorities for an interpretation of religious diversity.

Hick's pluralistic hypothesis leans heavily on philosophical formulations. Issues of epistemology, ontology, and meaning dominate the scene. But this is only one line of approach to pluralistic conclusions. Others would maintain it is neither the most appropriate nor the most powerful. We will turn in the next chapter from the arena of philosophy, with its severe clarity, to the concrete texture of history, with its nexus of interrelations.

2

Forms of Faith

Wilfred Cantwell Smith and the Historical Unity of Religion

The church had been built in a grand British colonial style but was now austere and somewhat dilapidated. Its interior was clean and empty, only a few cushions spread on the marble floor. The group that gathered on this warm Indian evening included Hindus, Muslims, and Christians.

During the first hour or so together the Hindus sang some bhajans in praise of Vishnu and placed flowers around a traditional oil lampstand with its five wicks. Muslims chanted several suras from the Qur'an. Christians sang a hymn, read a psalm and a gospel lesson.

But then all of us settled into silence, the silence of spiritual shadow. For another hour more or less we sat so, unruffled by words or actions, like a little colony of spiders casting our fragile webs across the wide spaces. There is no way of knowing surely what another does with such solitude, or what sets astir those thin filaments of awareness. But there was an undeniable sense of unity as we said our quiet good nights under the brilliant stars. People do not share stillness without some effect.

This particular group was inspired by the example of Swami Abhishiktananda, a French Roman Catholic who devoted his life to spiritual encounter with Hinduism. In his view this encounter must finally look beyond the realm of doctrine and practice. Its true locale is "the cave of the heart," that secret, profound place where each person makes response to the divine, "the place of ultimate encounter, where the spirit of man becomes one with the Spirit of God" (Abhishiktananda 1969, xvi).[1] The attempt to journey to the depths of another's heritage and the attempt to plumb the depths of one's own both lead to this cave of wordless meeting. Here human faith, quiet before/in the transcendent, stills the language of religious difference and recovers its unity.

---

[1] Fr. Bede Griffiths carries on Abhishiktananda's legacy and has expanded it in a number of books, including *Christ in India*.

This approach suggests quite another path than the philosophical route to pluralistic theology. Interiority and personal integration are its watchwords. It seeks not so much to "account" for religious diversity as to participate in the inner, ultimate meaning of faith for believers. We turn now to perhaps the most tireless advocate of this way across the Rubicon.

MANY TRADITIONS, ONE FAITH

Wilfred Cantwell Smith, professor emeritus of Comparative History of Religion at Harvard University, has been one of the most consistently stimulating advocates of new visions of interfaith understanding. Unlike Hick, he is not primarily a philosopher but a historian of religion, a respected Islamicist who brings to the discussion a deep first-hand knowledge of that tradition. Hick's approach to a pluralistic theology seeks to account for religious pluralism by postulating the metaphysical and epistemological conditions that undergird it. He readily takes up the eschatological question, seeing in it the foundation of religion's cognitive content and the verification of its generic validity. Smith by contrast focuses his consideration on humans' ways of being religious. If in Hick's hypothesis the emphasis moves from the various particular ultimates of historical traditions to the Real that lies above them, in Smith's analysis it moves from those ultimates to the human attitudes and experiences that lie beneath them. His famous distaste for the word "religion" itself and his commendation of "faith" as the more apt singular noun is a reflection of this (Smith 1979 and 1964).

The point of departure for Smith's approach is his conviction that a certain unity of the world religions already exists. It is the unity of humankind's religious history, the fact that all manner of influences, borrowings, and relations have intertwined the various religious communities throughout their existence. In *Towards a World Theology* Smith's two delightful illustrations of this are mini-histories of the rosary and of the legend of Barlaam and Josaphat. He traces the latter from its origin as a tale of the Buddha, through widespread versions in Muslim and Jewish piety, to its popularity as a medieval Christian legend and its eventual effect on Tolstoy as the story of a Christian saint. It is impossible to give a full account of one tradition without tracing the threads that lead to and from others. This truth, he says, is "newly discovered" (Smith 1981, 6). It has been revealed by means of the history of religions, Smith's discipline. As discerned by historical study, religions are constantly shifting processes, hence the inappropriateness of the term "religion" itself.

For Smith there are two fundamental and complementary truths. The first is that there is only one history of religion. This has hitherto been obscured by ignorance and parochialism, which led us to look no further than the discrete studies of Buddhism or of Islam. But serious historical inquiry reveals that like the religions that are their ostensible subjects, these studies are but arbitrary portions of a whole. There is no unity within even one "so-called religion." Traditions are so varied, internally and collectively, that the boundaries between them are largely fiction. The only adequate history is one which is global and singular, dealing with the seamless project of human religiousness. Smith tells us that he has long aspired to write such a history of human faith, century by century, as a unitary reality rather than varied systems (Smith 1981, 6). The oneness of the history of religion is a historical fact, given in enlightened methodology.

Religious traditions are quite different and Smith does not minimize this. In his view, no two people are religious in the same way, let alone two religions (Smith 1981, 50). It is "only the historian who can hold all the evolving diversities of any one religious community's developments in interrelated intelligibility; and, a fortiori, all the evolving diversities of all religious communities" (Smith 1981, 4). The unity of religions stems from participation in a single historical continuum. For this reason each devotee of one tradition is, however distantly or unconsciously, a participant in the others. The task of a pluralistic theology or what Smith calls a world theology is to make this participation explicit.

The complementary truth is that the substance of religion does not have to do with ideas or practices but with faith, "a universal quality of human life" (Smith 1981, 113). We deceive ourselves by reifying religions. This misplaced concreteness leads us to see doctrines, ethics, and rituals as the constitutive elements of the "religions" we have constructed. To the contrary, the study of religion rightly understood has as its subject a personal quality, a "serenity and courage and loyalty and service: a quiet confidence and joy which enables one to feel at home in the universe and to find meaning in the world and in one's own life, a meaning that is profound and ultimate and . . . stable" (Smith 1979, 12). This is the quality Smith calls "faith," although he acknowledges that a world theology may evolve a new vocabulary which would be more tradition-neutral.

These two basic points are summarized in a characteristically aphoristic sentence: "One's faith is given by God, one's beliefs by one's century" (Smith 1977, 96). Beliefs are intellectualizations about faith. They are formed within a seamless historical process such that no individual's complex of convictions is precisely identical to another's and yet all draw upon elements interwoven in others' beliefs. Faith itself however does not vary in its nature, for it is a quality, not an idea. It is the true transforming dimension of religious life, the essence, we may say, of the human response to Truth or transcendence.

In so stressing this quality of human experience, Smith does not intend to view religion in a reductionistic or "non-realist" manner. Faith is not a purely subjective aspect of experience but a mode of knowing which puts us in touch with a real aspect of our world. A secularistic objectivism which rules out everyday human commerce with the "more than mundane" is in Smith's view aberrant, a form of tone-deafness. Seen as a unitary reality, religious history is one monumental fact testifying to the reality of transcendence as the true horizon of human life.

On this count, the groping toward a world theology is part and parcel of a reconsideration of enlightenment rationality. Objectivity is a fine thing and usefully applied when studying the artifacts of religion, whether rituals, texts, or ideas. But Smith argues that we are increasingly aware that such a behavioristic method is inadequate when our subject is another person. When we further realize that the heart of religion is an intensely personal (by this he does not mean purely private or intrapsychic) dimension of life, we see that a full appreciation of religion and a fully humane science will go hand in hand.

In the areas of the "humane sciences," those that involve knowing other human beings, Smith proposes to move beyond the alternatives of scientistic objectivity and sectarian subjectivity to another ideal: "corporate critical self-consciousness." In such consciousness a community—ideally the whole human race—"is aware of any given particular human condition or action as a condition or action of itself as a community, yet of one part but not of the whole of itself," an awareness at once existential and critical. Smith notes that we increasingly recognize our own participation in the supposed "objects" of our study: the influence of the physicist's observation on the events observed, the implication of the white researcher in the very constitution of the racial relations she investigates.

He contends provocatively that in the realm of the humane sciences any inquiry into the life of some persons whose results are sought primarily in the interests of another group (say an audience of colleagues in one's discipline "back home") is intrinsically immoral (Smith 1981, 73). The immorality consists in failing to give a central place to the questions and the perspectives of those who are the subjects of study. The sociologist of religion, of whatever personal spirit, who sojourns in East Africa with the principal purpose of testing theories and reporting findings to professional peers in North America is kin in Smith's mind to the Christian missionary who sent careful observations of "the natives" home to church sponsors. He holds the entire system of academic disciplines and the modern universities which foster it are epistemologically distorted when it comes to understanding human life, however well they may serve to know things. In this sense, Western modernity and particularly the attempt to extend scientific methods into the social sciences receive regular and caustic rebukes from Smith. True comprehension of anything human involves both the critical understanding of its conditions *and* existential participation in its self-consciousness.

Smith instances the study of a Hindu temple (Smith 1981, 62-63). In the course of Western contact with India, knowledge of such a temple has passed from complete ignorance of its existence, to construal of scattered impressions of it through entirely Western categories (e.g., "idolatry"), to systematic "objective" study of the facts about the temple—its art, rituals, priests, myths and functions—to recent appreciation that the real meaning of the temple rests in the consciousness and lives of those who frequent it. In this last stage, religious studies has reached a point where interpretation cannot ignore the conscious participation of those whose experience is being interpreted. If an account of the temple does not square with that of those whose temple practice and perception constitute it as a temple in the first place, that account is neither objectively nor subjectively accurate.

This leads Smith to a simple, but far-reaching principle. "No observer's statement about a group of persons is valid that cannot be appropriated by those persons" (Smith 1981, 97). And this may be given a reciprocal form also: no group may make a statement internally which cannot be accepted by those outside. As no statement about Islamic faith is true that Muslims cannot accept, so no statement *of* that faith by Muslims is true that non-Muslims cannot accept.

This is a dramatic thesis, though Smith is often somewhat ambiguous about its specific application. The apparent difficulties in getting, for instance, all Muslims to agree that a given account is acceptable melt away, since Smith has already denied the existence of a single inclusive entity "Islam" (whether this judgment passes the test Smith himself has just laid down is another matter). In his view the only appropriate statements are very concrete ones: "most Muslims will agree," or "this group of Vaisnavite Hindus accept," rather than "Islam teaches." He believes his rules can be very directly applied to such concrete statements.

An even more substantive qualification is Smith's observation that his principle "applies to faith, if not to tradition (which latter can be known objectively)" (Smith 1981, 97). It is any statement "about personal faith" that should be intellectually persuasive to believer and outsider alike (Smith 1981, 101). Given Smith's sharp dichotomy between faith and belief, this amounts to a massive exception to his apparent insistence that *no* statement can be valid which outsiders and insiders cannot both appropriate. Only descriptions of an existential sort qualify for this dramatic aphorism: an observer's account of the Qur'an need not tally with that of believers, but the observer's account of what the Qur'an means to believers must tally with the believers' accounts. He clearly does not mean that outsiders cannot make critical judgments which believers reject; "tradition"—which Smith is confident can be known objectively—is fair game for such judgments.

For instance, the historian of religion can appropriately conclude that Christians who claim that the rosary is a unique Catholic development are wrong. So too, the historian can judge that the profession by a Muslim that the Qur'an is the final and supreme direct revelation of God's will for all people is in error. This is a matter of tradition. That is, it has to do with propositions, something to be believed. As such, in Smith's eyes it is quite distinct from Islamic faith and as open to investigation and judgment from without as within. In fact, the historian is the only one who can properly judge such statements, which believers mistakenly take to be the substance of their religious life. The existential significance of belief in the Qur'an as final revelation is something only the believer can judge, and those judgments must be honored by the historian. The drama of Smith's principle then hangs entirely on where the dividing line falls between faith and tradition.

The broad context for Smith's pluralistic thesis is a new human situation. We are today reaching a stage in human history and religious evolution, he says, "where consciousness must be a universal self-consciousness: corporate; critical; both analytic and synthesizing" (Smith 1981, 97). The goal of any student of human affairs is to be able to reconstruct a past or alien situation with such accuracy that "we can know how it felt to be a human being in that situation" (Smith 1981, 68). This is always possible because we are all persons and two fundamental qualities of humanity are the capacity to understand and to be understood.

There is no reason why all people who direct their attention to that Hindu temple should "not ideally converge in synthesizing all this truth into one conceptual apprehension" (Smith 1981, 66). The comparative study of religion, in dealing with its own problems, has stumbled upon the only way forward for all human knowing. This is the advance to a state of global self-consciousness where our discourse becomes always "a 'we all' talking together about 'us'" (Smith 1981, 101). In this, the only epistemologically sound position, we will all know what we are doing in being religious and "rationally approve (or at the very least rationally understand)" our various ways of doing it.

At this point Smith's argument has a great deal in common with several other approaches to pluralistic theology that focus on ideal conditions of discourse. In his view, the primary need is to realize what is the fact: that we are all participants in the one religious history of humanity, that faith is found identically in all of us, and that only in global self-consciousness can we know any particular religious tradition as it actually is, namely as a part of the whole, one of "our" ways of being religious. In order to realize this, we need to become active participants in each other's religious discourse.

Smith acknowledges that his vision of a time when Muslims, for instance, would not wish to believe anything but what is intelligible and acceptable to all others may be a dream at present. But it is a dream that is inevitably coming true. We all must see ourselves as primary participants in one community: the human. It is the form of life of this community that should shape the lenses through which we view all other communities. A theology of religions that is Christian or Muslim is fundamentally misconceived, whether critical or charitable, since it looks out from within one tradition upon others. Instead, Smith says, the point is to look always from the corporate human perspective of "us" upon all the specific faiths, including our own, as a portion of our collective self-knowledge.

"Our solidarity precedes our particularity" (Smith 1981, 103). True knowledge is that knowledge that all intelligent men and women "can share and can jointly verify" (Smith 1981, 102). Those who would question this vision of religious diversity, Smith says, must either disdain all religion, at least all other than their own, or else disdain reason, which so clearly leads to the epistemological conclusions he suggests. He rejects the "theology of religions" project as the different faiths have practiced it. As a Christian his aspiration is a collaborative one, to "participate Christianly in the total life of mankind" religiously, as already today those of various faiths participate together in a single shared life economically and politically (Smith 1981, 129).

A "Christian theology of religions" is problematic on two counts. First, if Christian (or Jewish or Hindu) it can only imperfectly be theology at all, since it has limited itself only to a narrow slice of the relevant data on transcendence. "Christian" is descriptively honest—indicating the inevitable particularity of our situation as one among many—but objectively contradictory, since by subordinating other forms of faiths to its own categories it necessarily misunderstands them in their own right. Second, a theology "of religions" is a category mistake. It can at best be a theology of *traditions*, of beliefs and practices grasped without an existential participation in them. But faith is the organizing principle, the instrument and lens through which all else is done. As such, one community's faith is outside the range of another's theology. From our perspective, we have a way of seeing the stuff that makes up another tradition. What we cannot see is the way of seeing that looks out *through* that form of life.

A world theology then should not be confessional. But Smith interestingly also argues that it must be formed by addition rather than subtraction. It cannot be only Islamic, but it must be substantially and cumulatively Islamic, Hindu, Christian, Jewish, Buddhist, with none surrendering any part of their truth. At present, he allows that this looks like an impasse. However, it can be expected to change by a certain process of convergence in which what is distinctively Muslim or Jewish will increasingly be held by Muslims and Jews in a form which can be understood and accepted by all others, and for the same reasons.

One key to this convergence can be found by looking back. Smith argues extensively that the formulations "Christian faith" and "Christian theology" are relatively recent developments. Faith is a powerful theme of the Christian scriptures, but he claims that the notion of "Christian faith" is absent. Classically, Christians conceived the divine gift to humanity in absolute and not particularist terms. "Until Schleiermacher, the faith of Christians was thought of simply as faith; not as one kind of faith, out of many alternatives" (Smith 1981, 117). There was a primordial wisdom in this, and Smith bemoans the development of the view of Christianity as a religion among other alternatives. This was only one more unfortunate effect of the rise of the fictitious idea of "religions." Theology and faith are properly singulars and there are, in the true sense, no alternatives.

THE WORLD'S ONE THEOLOGY

Today the task for Christians and others is to revive and reform that "endeavor to understand faith as a universal human quality" (Smith 1981, 122). We can construct a single appropriate theology on the basis of this universal reality, not varied theologies built around the diverse religions (the variety in both cases being mistaken). Instead there will be a theology of faith done by the religions and for the religions: the single world community reflecting on itself. This can best be called "a theology of the religious history of humankind," which recognizes there is but one theology and one religious history (Smith 1981, 125).

This world theology will give intellectual expression to our faith, "the faith of all of us, and to our modern perception of the world" (Smith 1981, 125). An ecumenical Christian theology, Smith suggests, is neither a Presbyterian theology of ecumenism nor a Catholic theology of ecumenism and yet it is not truly ecumenical unless it is in some authentic sense Presbyterian and Catholic, though not merely these. So too, a world theology will be "Islamic plus; Jewish plus; and so on" (Smith 1981, 125). The formulation of this is a long way off. But if we are truly concerned about God, there is a "touch of blasphemy" in speaking of God on any narrower basis.

Those who talk about God usually do so only from one tradition. Those who talk of comparative religions usually do not talk of God. It is time for convergence. Smith commends theology that is "literally, talk about God; or more generically, about the transcendent dimension of human life and of the universe." But such talk can only now proceed on the basis of the entire history of God's revelation, which is the history of every human community. The data of theology is the data the study of the history of religion provides. Any interpretation of humanity, God, and salvation must draw upon the full sum of this data. All revelation that has taken place has taken place in history: the history of religion is thus the full repository of revelation and the only basis for an understanding of "God and His diverse involvements with humankind" (Smith 1981, 126). The historian of religion, then, is the true exegete of the divine word, prophet and priest of the world theology.

If confessional believers have to overcome parochial loyalties to reach this wider view, many historians and academics must overcome an equally disabling prejudice. This is their insistence on excluding a transcendent reference from the understanding of history. This parochialism too must go. Historical study reveals that the secular West is anomalous and, Smith suggests, pathological in not recognizing the massive fact that history is an open system where humanity lives in touch with the infinite. The history of religion is one of humanity's "continuing involvement, within history, in transcendence" (Smith 1981, 127). No understanding is adequate which stops with human response and does not include "that to which the history of religion has at its best been a response" (Smith 1981, 186).

Knowing this history, Smith says we should not be intimidated by aberrant Western trends that see God as a question. Rather than defend the awareness "of what some of us call the divine" before the bar of skeptical reason, he would rather summon these modern skeptics "before the bar of world history to defend their curious insensitivity to this dimension of human life." Such a group is a minority in time and space and we should have only compassion for "its incapacity to see" (Smith 1981, 189).

Smith argues at length against what he sees as a confluence of misunderstandings of both revelation and history. A "big bang" view of revelation as occurring only at privileged times and places has mixed with a historical fixation on origins to set us thinking of religions as defined by their beginnings. We look to the first Christian centuries, the first Muslim centuries, expecting to find there a verdict on whether these faiths are divinely derived. He regards this as a historical superstition. What the Qur'an means "in itself" by reference to the circumstances of its origin is hardly a relevant question. Far more important is what it has meant to millions of Muslims over each succeeding century and today. This is the historians' proper realm.

As a historian Smith believes he can demonstrate that God has spoken to humans through the Qur'an and the Buddha, even more that people have been saved through them. By "saved" he means empirically liberated from despair, bondage to self, social chaos. "Faith differs in form, but not in kind . . . in so far as she or he has been saved, the Muslim has been saved by Islamic faith (faith of an Islamic form, through Islamic patterns; faith mediated by an Islamic context); the Buddhist by Buddhist faith; the Jew by Jewish" (Smith 1981, 168). God saves us any way God can, he says, but primarily through the religions.

If Smith knows unequivocally as a historian that all religions save in a mundane sense, he says that he knows equally that "cosmic salvation too is the same for an African tribesman and for a Taoist and for a Muslim as it is for me, or for any Christian" (Smith 1981, 170). This additional and extraordinary fact he knows because of what he knows "of God through Christ." This God is one who delights to save, and familiarity with other traditions joyfully confirms such a revelation. That God acts so through all faith confirms the Christian understanding of God; any other result would severely threaten claims for that God's justice and mercy.

There is no reason, in Smith's view, to speak of degrees of fullness of revelation. Whether God was revealed fully in Christ or not, "God is not revealed fully in Jesus Christ to me, nor indeed to anyone that I have met; or that my historical studies have uncovered" (Smith 1981, 175). Whatever the dimensions of the revelation given to us, we vary widely in our capacities to receive it and this more than swamps the significance of variations on the sending end, if such exist. Far from contending that all religion is equally true or that all religious statements are so, Smith holds that "not even one 'religion' is *equally* true, abstractly, in all its instances through history" (Smith 1981, 187). It becomes more or less true for particular persons at particular times as it nurtures or does not nurture faith for them. Truth, like faith, is a personal reality. It does not lie in propositions and should not be attributed to them. Truth is a quality of meaning for persons and it is sought through, not in, the traditions of all religions.

The important thing is not what God did in Christ in the first century, but that God can do something for us today. "The channel of that revelation in the Christian case is Christ, a historical figure" (Smith 1981, 175). Saying that God came into the world in human form at the coming of Christ has been the way in which "most of the West articulated symbolically the fact (it is a historian speaking) that every year, every day, transcendence entered its life anew" (Smith 1981, 176).

To the objection that Christ is insufficiently central to this vision, Smith replies that his proposal is theocentric, not Christocentric. He chides the churches for losing sight of the God beyond Christ and losing touch with a fully trinitarian approach. He regards his proposals as radical, but not out of continuity with major aspects of the Christian tradition. In his view the cosmic scope, the universal intent, of Christian faith is fundamentally correct. The only way to make good its own intimations of universality is to realize that Christ is a means, not an end.

THERE ARE NO OTHERS: A PLURALISTIC ASSUMPTION?

Smith's many works breathe a different air than John Hick's, however many points they may share. Though lacking Hick's rigor and clarity, Smith's writing is rich in the detail and texture of religious history, particularly of Islam. Where Hick has the philosopher's readiness to formulate and debate opposing views, Smith tends to deflect them with a mixture of humility and imperiousness, treating them not so much as arguments but as historical artifacts whose roots can be remarked and whose destinies can be predicted. Though critical self-consciousness is perhaps the heart of Smith's creed, he applies this genetic analysis to his own ideas primarily only to attribute them to the dawning consciousness of a new stage of human history. Hence the mixture of humility and hauteur; one who is both intelligent and modern, he regularly implies, can scarcely think otherwise than he does. This attitude frees Smith for wide-ranging reflections that would be superficial in a lesser talent but which rarely fail to stimulate fresh inquiry. His tastes are catholic and his particular judgments fit no simple model.

Smith's work revolves around the understanding of faith. His hallmark insistence that faith is a noun that takes no plural form and his exhaustive arguments against confusing faith with belief are both well known. He begins the conclusion of his major work on the latter topic (*Faith and Belief*) by asking "If faith is not belief, what is it?" and responding that his aim is to illuminate the profundity and universality of that question, not yet to answer it (Smith 1979, 128). It is not that he does not have a great deal to say on the matter, but that he resists giving a propositional statement of the faith whose non-propositional nature he has so strongly argued.

The temptation to define faith is very strong. Smith is tempted to say that it differs from unfaith in seeing "that life and the universe do, indeed, have a point—a cosmic point," while particular faiths differ in seeing that point and the world in differing fashion (Smith 1979, 133). But this temptation must be resisted: "Faith can never be expressed in words." Whatever idea of faith one forms, Smith insists, must be one adequate to faith as a universal human quality. So does faith vary or is it the same? No two people have the same faith, Smith is fond of saying. But he says equally that all faith is of the same kind. Peoples' faith differs, but faith is a single reality.

It is to this nexus that any evaluation of Smith's views must turn. Much of his writing and lecturing is exploratory in form. But it proceeds on the basis of an unshakable postulation about the ostensibly undefined nature of faith. We can turn for instance to his treatment of epistemology. He argues that knowledge is corporate critical self-consciousness. True or full knowledge, it follows, demands a "stage where consciousness must be a universal self-consciousness" (Smith 1981, 97). Happily, this is just the stage we are reaching today. For human beings to know each other they must be part of one community: only as we have begun to become a single community could we recognize that we might *all* know each other. But even more, "to study man is to study oneself" (Smith 1981, 79). As all knowledge is self-knowledge, it follows that in learning about others we are in fact discovering ourselves. It is an important step to recognize the faith of other people. The next crucial step is to recognize there are no *other* people (Smith 1981, 103).

Faith is "the human potentiality for being human," a quality in all of us "that lifts one above the merely mundane and the immediate, and means that one may be always in part but is never totally simply a product or a victim of circumstance" (Smith 1979, 142, 129). The unitary nature of faith and the unitary nature of humanity are two sides of the same coin, both reflected in the existence of a single, seamless human story that is revealed to the serious historian. Smith maintains that the unity of humanity is a historical conclusion and not a religious insight. For one thing, if knowledge of the unity of humanity came to us as a religious insight, it would seem very close to a substantive element in faith. But Smith emphatically maintains that faith itself has no uniform cognitive content but instead consists in an existential disposition. So, interestingly, the unity of humanity and the singular nature of faith are two items that Smith does not believe are revealed through faith itself; they remain conclusions of the objective knowledge whose limits Smith often critiques. It seems highly questionable whether either is in fact simply a conclusion of historical study, or whether one must import a good deal more than historical data to "know" them as Smith does.

At any rate, he is quite right to note the continuity between his approach and that of the classical rationalist and humanist traditions (Smith 1981, 51). The bedrock of his view is the conviction that universal knowledge is possible because of our identical natures. To a universal common rationality he has added a universal quality of faith. But the principle remains: I will find nothing human in another that I do not find in myself. Of course I will find *things* in others that are not mine: ideas, practices, stories—all of which can be studied objectively. This is what Smith calls "tradition." But in the realm of what can be known humanely there are, literally, no others. Only a "we" that is also an "I."

Smith says that one of the most telling questions we can ask is what we mean when we say "we." He contends the only truly proper use of the word is when one intends to speak literally for all of us. Smith emphasizes this again and again in describing the coming situation where he would expect no one in a different tradition to believe anything, "if he were intelligent, that I would not find both intelligible and intelligent. (What reason could he have for believing anything that I would not?)" (Smith 1981, 101-102). For all his critique of secular modernity and appeal to a new wave of human consciousness, this conviction seems a pure throwback to the eighteenth-century enlightenment. That any "intelligent person" (a regular qualifier in Smith's formulations) would have reasons not equally cogent to another could only be due to removable prejudices and ignorance. Looking inward, he sees in himself a rationality and a natural religion strangely unconstituted by the processes of history; in commending them he is confident he represents at the same time the humanity of all of us.

Smith sees no material problem in the intellectual taking the content of all human consciousness as subject. He acknowledges no doubts that the intelligent and critical historian, for instance, qualifies as a neutral judge of what should count as a good reason for believing something inside or outside a religious tradition. He emphasizes the historical conditioning of religious views, but tends to exempt from these same strictures views, like his own, that allegedly arise from considering history itself in its entirety, without limit to only one or a few traditions within it. This totalizing approach really surpasses past exclusivist accounts. Such accounts subsumed various religions within one large system they believed to be true. Although the others existed in subsidiary status or in opposition, they did still truly exist as other. Smith's vision annihilates every other within a supersystem which recognizes no alternatives and can hardly be questioned because it is "ours"—and "ours" is all-inclusive. As Smith puts it, there is no point in trying to speak theologically unless you are trying to speak on behalf of everyone. This liberal, rational confidence in articulating a universal system grounds Smith's whole approach.

Nowhere is he more the modern than in his exaltation of the role of the historian as arbiter of matters of faith. His biting criticism of the discipline and of the sciences generally is in the nature of an internal methodological dispute. The methods of history must be made "faith-friendly" and must recognize the existential, meaning-granting core of religion. But, since this "faith" that Smith so strongly defends is emphatically an inner, contentless disposition—not to be confused with any of the forms through which it is expressed—everything else that has to do with religion is handed over in its entirety to the objective knowledge and judgment of the historian. The academic expert, with his or her methodology and broad data base, is the one who must set the only acceptable categories of understanding. In this respect Smith's work can be viewed as the latest stage in the Western rational project of a single universal system within which each particular will have its place.

Objectifying knowledge cannot grasp the heart of religion, Smith protests. But it can dispose of everything else. And he takes a back seat to no one in dispensing these judgments. Like many modern Christian apologists, Smith sets up a fortress deep in the subjectivity of the individual, insists that secular knowledge concede it cannot enter here and acknowledge that the historical matter of religion which it can treat reductively in fact flows from this secret source.

The striking thing about this approach is not the rather minimal limits Smith tries to set on what he regards as objective historical knowledge, but the utter confidence in it he demonstrates. The question he asks is "How far may it go?" Yet all around him, whether in philosophy of history, philosophy of science, literary or hermeneutical theory, it is this dream of objective, universal knowledge that is sharply contested. Perhaps Smith views such discussion as another instance of aberrant modern thinking. If so, it would be helpful to know how he can so clearly distinguish the modern West's unique "new human consciousness" from its historical deviancy.

Smith consistently employs a dualism which views history on two planes. One is a plane of essences and human subjectivity and the other is a seamless flow of historical forms. "Faith" exists on the first plane, beyond words, defying definition, but powerfully determining human life. Religious beliefs and practices exist on the other plane. Faith passes through them like water through a pipe, its true nature neither sharing their substance nor constituted by them. If it were so constituted one could meaningfully speak of "Muslim faith" and "Jewish faith," of faiths in the plural, and Smith insists we cannot.

Smith does not suppose we can ever encounter faith "naked"; faith and tradition must be distinguished but they are never separated in historical reality. "Traditionless" faith is a contradiction in terms. The historicity of human life can't be scraped off the outside of religion and leave anything that humans can actually practice. Nevertheless, Smith insists we must always segregate conceptually what we cannot separate historically. Fundamental human attitudes take on historical expressions but are not themselves *constituted* by specific historical process so as to differ from those of people in differing contexts. In short, though faith always has an embodied form, these differing embodiments cannot in Smith's view affect faith in any way that would alter its one consistent nature.

This dualism has two serious effects on Smith's approach. It sets his interpretation of the faith traditions at fundamental cross purposes with them, in that the faith/tradition dichotomy he enforces as the point of departure is largely alien to them. Despite his arguments that he can find it mirrored in all religions, the priority Smith gives to the sharp division between the faith I believe with and the faith I believe in would seem to stem directly from his Protestant background. It also oddly immunizes his view against considering seriously its own historical formation. Smith studies the historical manifestations of faith. But what he knows about the distinction itself between faith and these manifestations he knows not through historical study (since faith per se is quite different from its historical forms) but more by intuition or divination, the glimpse into his own soul that stands for all others. No amount of historical evidence or argument will shake him on this point.

Some of the most telling criticism focuses precisely on this issue. Taking up Smith's insistence on a universal "we," Kenneth Surin has written perceptively of a more particular "we" in whose voice he would rather speak, a "we" that includes anyone who sees the need to move beyond the faded and fading modernist intellectuals who define themselves in terms of the large and impressive narratives they provide, narratives which invoke such notions as "the human story," "the truth of 'all of us,'" or the "world community" (Surin 1990a, 209).

In telling such stories circumstantial oppositions are neutralized and all difference is subsumed under a homogenous logic and its comprehensive categories. Smith's "we" supposes conditions that are the exact opposite of what actually obtain for the mass of humanity. It supposes conditions of exchange and conversation which are not themselves through and through shaped by inequalities and historical particularities. For this reason Surin sees Smith's vision not as an idealistic anticipation of a new world yet to come but rather a convenient dominant ideology for the present one, where nations and cultures "are obsolete if they are maintained in their old forms as fixed and intractable particularities" (Surin 1990a, 201). Insistence that religions are all simply "forms of faith" is the perfect correlative of a global consumer culture, which subverts any alternative structures but welcomes the "franchise" mentality. Religious faith, like brands of detergent, becomes a choice with no structural implications but only personal, expressive ones.

The notion of a common history, which is the very foundation of Smith's work, is ineluctably ideological. It overrides the particularity of the world's majority poor, affirming their voices as just another "form" of a shared reality, when in fact they witness to the truth of divided histories: one for the wealthy, quite another for the rest. Despite Smith's claim to transcend nineteenth-century liberal theology, Surin maintains he is its quintessential extension (Surin 1990b, 126-127).

But the criticism need not be limited to the instance Surin offers. Another concrete example of the dynamics involved appears in a recent exchange between Seyyed Hossein Nasr and Hans Küng. Responding to a presentation on Christian dialogue with Islam in which Küng had said that "it is important that the Koran as the word of God be regarded at the same time as the word of the human prophet," Nasr made the observation that very few Muslims indeed would view the Qur'an as other than the actual word of God received directly by Muhammad. "To assume such a view as a possibility to facilitate dialogue with the Christian world or with the Western world in general does not respond to the reality of the situation" (Küng 1987, 87; Nasr 1987, 98-99).

Küng rejoined that this was as if a Christian were to say to a Muslim, of the Trinity, that all Christians believe it: if you don't, there can be no dialogue. Should the Muslim object that at least some Christians themselves seem to have reservations about the Trinity, the Christian would say, perhaps so, but they are wrong. Küng goes on, in regard to the critical historical consciousness he commends to Muslims: "This is not specifically an Islamic problem, because for a long time in Christianity we had exactly the same thing. And this question was just not allowed to be asked; it was deadly. The story is more or less the same in all religions" (Küng 1987, 120). With so many bright Muslim students all over the world, he added, it will be impossible in the long run for Islam to avoid these questions. Küng is convinced that "to take a more historical approach to the Qur'an would not damage Muslim faith in the one God and in Muhammad his Prophet, but could strengthen this faith" (Küng 1987, 121).

Nasr in return makes several points. One is that he has not said the Christian must accept the Muslim belief in order to dialogue, only that Christians have to recognize the actual beliefs of the Muslims they may be talking with. To talk meaningfully with others you must see what they are, right now, in themselves, and not what you would like them to be in order for you to talk to them. He also rejects Küng's assumption that the categories of Western modernity are universal and obligatory for all. "Let us imagine for a moment that we are all in Cairo carrying out this dialogue and a Muslim scholar speaks and Professor Küng answers for the Christian side. The Muslim may say that since the Islamic world has followed a certain path and carried out such and such actions, if the West begins to follow the same course, which in all likelihood it will, we will all be able to speak together. Returning to this hemisphere, we see that here there is a presumption that the history of Islam in the future will follow the same path as that of Western civilization from Spinoza to the present. I am very doubtful about that" (Nasr 1987, 123).

Aside from the shaky analogy Küng seems to assume between the role of the Bible and its historical-critical interpretation within Christianity and the role of the Qur'an within Islam, we can see the main issue here. Küng would not think of saying that in the long run Muslims—especially bright, young ones—will be unable to avoid a doctrine similar to the Trinity, or of saying that on the grounds of his Christian faith he rejects certain Muslim tenets as impossible. That would in his view be particularism of the worst sort.

However he does say that to contemplate preferring the Muslim version of the crucifixion to the gospels' version, when it is the case of a seventh-century source over against those six hundred years earlier, is "for a historically thinking man, I think, personally impossible" (Küng 1987, 121). Nasr inconveniently fails to agree that this is simply a neutral statement of universal principles that apply equally to people in all cultures and religions, the application of these principles being an area where Muslims have just not yet caught up. Küng's assurance that adopting the categories of historical consciousness developed in the West need not be feared because Christians have developed ways to cope with them—ways Muslims presumably would adopt—seems not to envision the possibility that those ways might be anything less than enviable to others. Nasr gently chides Küng's confidence that the modern problems, if not the traditional answers, of Christianity constitute the necessary crown of other traditions' development.

Smith gives an example which illustrates the same point. He points with justifiable pride to his McGill University program, which mandated an equal proportion between Christian and Muslim students and faculty. Here, he suggests, there is an instance of ideal conditions for developing the "theology of faith" he commends. Clearly, part of the ideal is that the voices meet on the ground of Western academic principles which Smith assumes are universal, once purged of their secular excesses. But the voices of most Muslims, as of most Christians, are strained out of this situation, not least of all by the assumption that they are not "intelligent" or "informed."

The "we" of a world theology will be a "we" of liberal intellectuals. Smith views this monopoly as their particular vocation and burden, not as a privilege for their faith over that of others. He says, "I myself am more at ease with, feel more at home with, several of my Muslim friends (liberal intellectuals, like me) as we consider together the meaning of scripture in the modern world . . . than I do with certain fellow Christians, as we speak together about the Bible" (Smith 1992, 57). This honest sentiment would be less telling if Smith had not so clearly made it absolute as a norm for all others who wish to participate in the interfaith process.

Smith is quite clear that there is no future for particularist reflection. From now on only theologians who take the thinkers and texts of all other traditions as prime elements in their work can claim to be critical or to approximate the truth (Smith 1981, 190-191). Smith says that he does not "affirm that no one may legitimately think, any more, within a limited framework" (Smith 1979, 152). Ordinary people presumably may do so. But those who venture into philosophy or theology are forbidden this failing. In principle there should be no more theological works done, say, by a devout Orthodox Jew revealing the world through the eyes of one steeped in study of that tradition, or by a Buddhist monk isolated in meditation and study among Mahayanist sources.

At best these might be purely private, devotional matters. But in Smith's view they should not darken the halls of our future theological discourse with any universal claims. His world theological enterprise aims for a blandness apparently at odds with the pleasure he himself takes in the particularities of religious traditions or relegates such pleasures to antiquarian studies. From Smith's viewpoint his global transreligious perspective provides the only legitimate ground for affirmation of religious particularities. Construed within such a global scheme he believes these specifics can be savored as flavorful variety. But if particular religions assert their own global scope in such a way as to resist assimilation to a scheme of Smith's type, he sees that particularity as venomous. There is no doubt Smith delights in religious specificity, but the delight hinges on a certain domestication of diversity. It is hardly clear that he regards these specifics in anything like the same light as devotees within the traditions. Yet he makes every effort to enlist their devotion as support for his theory.

The fundamental division of faith and belief is probably the single item on which Smith lavishes the greatest scholarly effort. Indeed, he expends a great deal of energy proving the unexceptionable contention that great Christian theologians meant by "faith" more than a notional consent to propositions. They stressed faith as an engagement, a giving of one's self to God, a venturing and trusting. Indeed, Smith piles up incidences of such emphasis and seems to believe that he has thus proved something quite different: that the essence of "faith" as such people understood and experienced it *excluded* the particulars of *what* it gave itself to.

Thus Smith puts great weight on references to faith by Jesus in the gospels in which the word figures unqualified in a sentence; for instance, "Nowhere in Israel have I found such faith." Here he suggests we can see that both Jesus and his followers, like Smith, recognized that faith was a unitary and fundamental human attitude—the religious point being to strengthen it and purify it. In response to a book by Oscar Cullmann which argues that "faith" in the early church means faith in Christ, Smith notes that it may be the case that *insofar* as believers' faith was "in" anything, it was in Christ (Smith 1977, 91-92). "But to *our* question"— what is faith alone in itself—Cullmann "does not attend" (Smith 1977, 92). This leaves unruffled Smith's contention that what faith essentially is has nothing to do with specific objects.[2]

The serenity of Smith's viewpoint is understandable. On his terms there can be no counter-evidence. Any reports of faith which note or emphasize particularistic features are telling us about the objects and not about faith. Only if the texts address the question of what faith is in itself, apart from its objects or conditioning factors, would they be addressing Smith's question and thus provide evidence he would recognize. But of course the texts would not treat the question that way un-

---

[2] It is instructive to consider what an understanding of "love" analogous to Smith's treatment of "faith" might look like. While recognizing that love takes different forms—love of country, love of child or spouse, love of work, love of art, love of this particular person as opposed to that—such an approach would insist on stressing a constant quality of love alone and in itself, without distraction by its objects. Emphasis would rest on a supposed universal quality and effect of "love," which works itself out in these various ways. What this approach rules out is any deeply relational view of love, any that might consider the character of love always in its very texture and nature crucially constituted by who or what is loved and by interaction with them in their particularity.

less their writers and communities already agreed with Smith on the nature of faith. Some students of religion maintain that the reports of mystics about qualityless, contentless consciousness should be taken as evidence for such prethematic experience. Smith is hardly so cautious. For him, all accounts of thematized religious experience testify to the unthematized reality of faith. To find such evidence, one simply sub-tracts the content.

Smith contends there has been a momentous historical transition. At one time "I believe" meant that a person, assuming God's existence, pledged God personal love and loyalty. In the modern situation a per-son, in light of the intellectual uncertainty surrounding the whole idea of God, uses the same phrase to report that nevertheless he or she thinks the existence of such an entity more probable than not (Smith 1979, 118). A shift like this, though not so absolute as Smith paints it, did take place and his account of it has many instructive features. His diagnosis can be summarized by saying that the world-views (including religions) *through* which faith had been exercised became increasingly themselves *objects* of faith. Rather than expressing one's personal loyalty to the transcendent by means of confessing faith in the God and God's word assumed in one's world-view, one increasingly had to focus effort on "believing" the elements of this world-view itself as they became ques-tionable. Thus arose the whole misguided notion of "believing" in "re-ligions."

It appears that Smith's further prescription is that for true faith to flourish and for our focus to return to faith, it is necessary again to have a noncontroversial vehicle for it. If my faith is expressed via an exclu-sive claim for the dharma, for instance, then I and others will be side-tracked into fruitless argument over the propositional validity of state-ments about the dharma. What would have worked perfectly well in a historical environment where the dharma's universality was not doubted, no longer does. Hence Smith's insistence that no person should now believe (i.e., hold intellectually) anything religiously that those in all other traditions could not hold also. Such a situation would allow us to *recognize* what Smith argues is always actually the case: that whenever any of us "believes," it is the same faith we believe with. If we had no propositional differences in interpreting each other's religious ideas, our gaze would shift from the forms that vary to the commitment which unites them.

I have already noted the way in which this entire approach itself as-sumes a radical dualism. In the field of religion, Smith says that histori-cal study indicates "the empirical symbol does not itself participate in . . . transcendence" (Smith 1981, 87). One must say instead that there are persons to whom certain symbols appear to participate in transcen-dence. Though his own analysis indicates that empirical elements were integral aspects of faith in earlier centuries—that convictions about the

Qur'an, for instance, were integral aspects of Muslim faith—he contends these elements themselves have no participation in what they represent. Faith, our attitude to the transcendent, must go through something. But these historical somethings are used by human beings to express an attitude: their attitudes are not decisively shaped and elicited by distinct revelations. So for Smith there is a radical detachability between the historical elements in faith and faith itself.

We can see this for instance in Smith's treatment of a specific question: Is the Qur'an the Word of God? (Smith 1982, 22-40). Eventually, he suggests, there must be an answer to this question equally acceptable to Muslim and Christian, as well as all others. Those who answer no can account for the Qur'an but not its effect on those who answer yes. Those who answer yes can also account for the Qur'an but not for the manifest reality of those who answer no. Smith strongly implies that resolution can only come by turning away from questions about the Qur'an itself and toward the attitudes of those on either side. It *is* the word of God for those who respond to it so; that is, through it their faith is expressed. It is *not* the word of God for those whose faith is also expressed, but through another medium.

Smith prefers this formulation: Has the Qur'an "served God as a channel for His Word" among Muslims? And his answer is "in some cases yes, to varying degrees, in some cases no" (Smith 1992, 59). The striking thing is how closely Smith recapitulates the nineteenth-century liberal Protestant approach to religious pluralism, grading the degree of human response to the divine. Like that approach, Smith's too seems to have a strong evolutionary element. He regularly refers to the new stage of humanity and the new stage of consciousness that makes his perspective possible. Whereas nineteenth-century liberalism tended to operate wholesale in its judgments, religion by religion, Smith is confident he can make much finer evaluations—person by person in some cases. Of course earlier liberalism assumed the highest degree of revelation to be found in Christianity, a view Smith renounces. But the format remains the same.

Earlier liberals often stated an explicit moral basis for their judgments of the degree to which a religious tradition was serving as a channel for divine revelation. Hick follows in this tradition to some extent with his specific ethical criterion. Smith is much less clear about the ground for his judgments. Yet he is rarely bashful about telling us to what extent God is succeeding in communicating with one group or another. Most often he simply says something like "no one who is familiar with Islamic history can deny that it has been a channel of divine grace." Leaving aside the questions which arise from claiming this, as he does, as a simple historical judgment, the sharper question is how Smith distinguishes those moments when it has been from those when it has not, and even the degrees in between. This seems to imply a grasp of the essence of religion such that any specific instance can be checked against it.

Smith maintains that coming to some common understanding of the Qur'an would not mean that Muslims and Christians would cease to be different. Reactions to the universe, "the existential religious response," will continue to be communal—that is, exercised through some symbols. "Theory, on the other hand, it is the business of those of us who are intellectuals to universalize" (Smith 1982, 39). Smith plainly believes there is but one fundamental existential religious response, expressed in various symbols. In his view intellectuals should know there is no intrinsic connection between peoples' faith and the symbols through which they receive and confess it. There is an inevitable *historical* connection, but it is not substantive enough to give rise to a distinct variety of faiths that might belie Smith's insistence on a univocal "faith."

The confidence with which Smith deploys this dualism is striking. It accounts for the antiquarian joy he takes in the historical diversity of traditions and the absolute certainty he simultaneously expresses that true religious experience anywhere is identical with his own. No matter how strange or distant some tradition may appear to be, Smith's own experience is the key to understanding its heart. The distorting potential in such an approach is, in his mind, defused by the knowledge that his own religious experience, insofar as it is actually faith—a judgment he is also confident to make—is not intrinsically Christian or Western but human. To question the application of his interpretive scheme to other religious traditions arouses Smith's great indignation since in his view it amounts to denying the *humanity* of those in the varied traditions. Are they not every bit as human as he is?

Such an approach is markedly at odds with much of recent scholarship in the study of religion which stresses the inseparability of content and form and is suspicious of essentialist theories. If faith is a human experience—and it is precisely as a historical phenomenon that Smith claims to treat it—many would object that there is no such raw experience "logically prior to any sort of conceptual articulation" (Wainwright 1984, 357). Despite his extensive writings, it is not clear how Smith responds to this. He denies that he means faith is the same everywhere, since it is not even the same from one day to the next in the same person. But for Smith this would seem to mean only that faith varies in its intensity or purity, for any other alteration would involve faith's content or object and would, on Smith's terms, not have to do with faith at all. So, for instance, an individual's conversion from Islam to Buddhism might involve day-to-day changes in which historical elements of the two traditions served as instruments of the person's faith and might also involve some oscillation in the intensity of faith itself during the turmoil of transition, of the same sort that might occur to a person within one tradition for other reasons. Neither of these variations changes

Smith's contention that faith is a single human quality. So the criticism that he is positing a non-thematic type of experience still seems entirely on target.

Smith says that "what matters in religious life is not the external visible forms through which the spiritual is mediated, so much as the role that these play—that these enable the Spirit to play—in the personalities, and the living of those affected" (Smith 1992, 56-57). Faith then can be seen as a function, a pattern. To say that the Qur'an or the Bible has been the word of God is to say that it has been part of such a pattern in some peoples' lives. What matters is not the elements in the pattern, but what the pattern *does* in the person's life. Smith acknowledges there is no generic way to be human, only particular ways. So one can have faith only in a contingent form, but "to have faith is to be human, in the highest, truest sense" (Smith 1979, 138). Why not say "to have *a* faith is to be human"? The only consistent reasons Smith provides for making faith a universal singular are the observation of certain similar general effects (serenity, purpose) in persons in various religions and the argument that having *a* faith is characteristic of human beings.

To take an analogy, language is a characteristic of humans: all have one. We can say then that "linguisticality"—our capacity for language—is a single generic human attitude toward the universe. No one exhibits this attitude except through a particular speech tradition. Like Smith, we could argue that it is misguided to talk of languages in the plural and that instead we should recognize simply different forms of language: the French form, the Arabic form. Like him we could further claim that each particular tradition of words is a vehicle through which human language expresses our alignment with the world, but that these words themselves do not significantly constitute the world they represent. In fact, Smith seems to be committed to just such an argument. But it is hard to see how it can be supported, short of arguing total agnosticism about the referents of words and faiths or claiming a "God's-eye view" of objective reality and our many approximations to it. Smith inclines in the second direction, taking history as understood by the modern historian to be an approximation to that definitive revelation: "Evidently the new way that we are beginning to be able to see the global history of human kind is presumably the way that God has seen it all along" (Smith 1981, 18).

For someone who puts such weight on the revelatory quality of modern critical scholarship, Smith takes strangely little note of major streams within it that run counter to his assumptions. Religious studies today are methodologically skeptical of claims like his for a "God's-eye view" and take more seriously than he does the possibility that religious language and culture are fundamentally constitutive of the experience of believers. Many who are no less "liberal intellectuals" than he argue that the "faith" Smith describes is not the foundational substrate in all religious traditions, which his historical acuity has allowed him to discover, but itself a conditioned notion in whose terms each tradition can be construed, and by the construal changed (see Surin 1990a and 1990b). Such postmodern convictions may be in error. What is striking is not that Smith disagrees with them, but that he provides so little in the way of argument to confront their challenge.

Even abstracting from these crucial philosophical questions, much contemporary study of the religious traditions sees benefit in what is different and even incommensurable in other faiths: the ways in which those traditions may constitute meaning fields that challenge culturally conditioned dogmas like that which views faith as an "existential attitude." The special value of the religions is not their pre-known generic humanness (coming to expression in a profusion of outward forms), but precisely their capacity to specify alternative human visions, putting our categories in question. In turning to the religions, Smith expects to find in all of them instances reflecting his own religious experience. He does not even consider finding in them an account or framework for interpreting that experience which would be alternative to his modern-historical-rational world-view. He doesn't consider this, since according to his account religion is not truly about such things at all! World-views are contingent and adventitious to faith. Therefore all the particular religious world-views are relativized and Smith's liberal global world-view is effectively absolutized. A more complete insulation would be hard to imagine.

At an ecumenical conference we both attended a few years ago, Smith made a characteristically vivid reproach to the assembly for the scandal that Christianity had still not recognized the teachings of the Buddha as a revelation from God. This condemnation quite caught my imagination. Few Buddhists I know are covetous of this characterization for the Buddha's teachings. It appears a classically inclusivist claim, an example of the supposed subordination of others to our categories that Smith frequently deplores. It would be more to the point to recognize that from a Buddhist perspective the gods, if such there be, have themselves no path to liberation but the teachings of the Buddha. Why would Smith speak in such inclusivist terms, commending the assimilation of Buddhists as "anonymous theists"?

As best I can gather, the assertion that "the Buddha's teachings are a revelation from God" is shorthand for Smith for the more complex claim that what a "revelation from God" is for Christians as a symbol of transcendence, the teaching of the Buddha is for those who use that symbol of transcendence. In other words, such a confession by Christians would not be a recognition of any determinate content in the dharma, but an acknowledgment of something about the subjectivity of Buddhists. That something is the human quality of faith. Since Christians have faith also, and have it in the *form* of belief in God, then so long as they speak their own particularist language they can—they must—affirm that it comes from God in the case of the Buddhists as well. However, Smith's Christian intellectual knows this is only particularistic code, which outside the family would better be translated further to make clear that since the faith is the same, that to which it is authentic response—the transcendent—is also the same. The problems with this formulation have already been raised in discussing Hick's hypothesis.

It is in this vein that we can understand Smith's confession that he knows all faiths save cosmically because "of what I know of God; by what I find revealed to me of God in Christ. The God whom Christ reveals is a God of mercy and love, who reaches out after all men and women everywhere in compassion and yearning; who delights in a sinner's repentance, who delights to save" (Smith 1981, 170-171). This too would appear to be a thoroughly inclusivist statement, judging different faiths on the basis of the "big bang" revelation of one's own tradition. That such inclusivist judgments may sometimes, as here, be positive ones in no way mitigates their imperialism in Smith's view. What then does he mean in speaking this way?

Elsewhere in *Towards a World Theology* Smith provides a key to his pluralistic interpretation of such comments. He points out that the word "God" might be taken by an unwary reader as indicating a transcendent personal being who actually has certain qualities such as love and mercy. Smith himself certainly appears to attribute these qualities to such an active divine being as the warrant for concluding that this God would necessarily save through all traditions. In reality, he tells us, the word "God" is a symbol with both virtues and liabilities, and "intellectuals sensitive to the transcendent dimension within and around humankind have to decide whether or not to opt for this particular way to think the matter and talk it" (Smith 1981, 183). It would be more adequate to define "it" as a "truth-reality which explicitly transcends conception but in so far as conceivable is that to which man's religious history has at its best been a response" (Smith 1981, 185). So, for instance, he notes some might reject his contention that the Qur'an has served God as a channel of grace because they speak of transcendence in other symbols and "yet are unwilling or unable to translate into that framework my theistic vocabulary" (Smith 1992, 60). Theism amounts to a vocabulary for transcendence, then. But this vocabulary provides no valid basis for any religious conclusions that cannot be translated into other frameworks. This casts a somewhat ironic light on Smith's contention that his theology is "theocentric," since this word for him does not actually designate a reality with any concrete qualities of *theos*. The word "theocentric" itself, on Smith's explanation, stems only from one dialect for speaking of a reality whose nature could be more accurately described by "sensitive intellectuals" as "the transcendent dimension within and around humankind." It is up to such intellectuals, in Smith's view, to decide which vocabulary is best for a particular need.

Thus exegeted, we can understand why Smith's apparently particularistic claims about God's revelation in the Buddha or about Christ-based knowledge of other religions' saving power carry no distinctive content. The focus in Smith's statements is personal. Cosmic salvation of human beings is not grounded in Christ or in God; to claim so would be exclusivistic in his view. No. Smith, as someone who happens to be in a Christian tradition, will receive and express knowledge of the transhistorical universality of salvation "by what I find revealed to me of God in Christ." There is no authority here that can be claimed in distinction from any other tradition's symbols.

To speak of what he "knows of God through Christ" is analogous to speaking of what a Parisien "knows of 'le monde' through French." "Le monde" is not properly descriptive of our total environment any more than "the world" is, nor is the French language the sole avenue to true knowledge of it. Our relation to the world is fundamentally independent of the language or culture through which we express it. So the statement amounts only to describing a medium, not providing a ground for the knowledge claimed. Smith himself emphatically insists that no reasonable claim to theological knowledge can be made on the basis of one religious tradition alone. Therefore, when he says that all cosmic salvation is one and the same, and that "as a Christian" he knows this on the basis of Christ, he is begging an enormous question. On what ground does one know this as more than or other than a Christian conviction?

His failure to provide a clear treatment of this issue is telling. He might argue that others know ultimately there is one and the same cosmic salvation, but they know it "as Muslims," "as Buddhists," and so on. But of course, Buddhists believe that there is but one true "salvation" and it is the one the Buddha achieved; Muslims believe there is but one, and it is the one the Qur'an describes. Smith moves facilely from the suggestion that each religion envisions a religious fulfillment, to the claim that his tradition's vision is but one way of expressing the single religious fulfillment of all the faiths' expectations. Smith's logic demands some sustained argument that all "cosmic salvation" is the same, but he provides nothing comparable to Hick's extensive effort in this area.

That he treads lightly in this area is perhaps understandable. Since it is crucial in Smith's perspective for faith to remain an existential orientation without any intrinsic object or confessional elements, it is equally important to maintain an agnosticism about the nature of ultimate religious fulfillment. The "mundane" forms of salvation in Smith's view are functionally equivalent, because generically or negatively defined: finding meaning or overcoming despair. It is important to him that "cosmic salvation" be one and only one, but just as important that it have no concrete features. Otherwise, that salvation would threaten to provide faith also with some determinate character and so undo all his efforts to remove it from the realm of historical contention. In the end the vast and diverse sweep of religious history which Smith claims as his special field takes on a surprisingly homogenous significance. All its rich variety serves the simple and transient function of linking the one ineffable human quality of faith with its sole ineffable fulfillment, mystery with mystery.

The great strength of Smith's work is his emphasis on the concrete function of religious beliefs and practices in human life. His inquiries into what the Qur'an has meant to believing Muslims through the centuries, or what the great Menakshi Temple in South India means to the devotees who frequent it are welcome reminders that the perspective of believers must find a place in accounts of their faiths. He refuses to limit religious issues to problems of logic but constantly sends us to history, to actual people and actual communities, to test our theories.

But Smith's twin emphases on concrete history on one hand and on faith as an existential, contentless orientation are in tension. The more strongly he insists upon the distinction between the two—faith's essential insulation from the vehicles that express it—the less plausible his claims to make the historian the arbiter of religious questions. Whatever may happen in the "cave of the heart," we enter it from the stream of history and return from it to the stream of history. Within that stream, faith does not just "have" transient forms, any more than human beings "have" bodies. Unless we make of faith a completely non-historical postulate, as noumenal as Hick's Real, we must acknowledge that particular faiths partake of the concrete substance they express, whatever else might be claimed of them as well.

John Hick stresses the inherent human diversity of historical location and perception to explain why, if we postulate a single ultimate Real, that Real has been apprehended so variously. Smith, by contrast, stresses the unity of human religious history itself as the monumental fact which leads to acknowledging the transcendent, a "truth reality." For Hick, human religious experience—including what Smith calls faith—is irreducibly particular in all its manifestations. It is precisely this pluralism that pluralistic theology must account for. For Smith the primary datum is the single historical phenomenon of faith, and the primary task of a world theology is to find vocabulary and concepts consistent with that presumed unity. The two authors' conclusions can easily converge, but their premises seem deeply in tension.

What they do share is a sharp dualism. In Hick's case this is applied primarily to the beyond, "the Real," which cannot be conceived in any meaningful way except though myths which, having no purchase on the nature of the Real, yet induce in *us* dispositions which are appropriate ones to orient us to that absolute. In Smith's case the dualism is applied primarily internally rather than externally. Faith is an existential, generic human attitude locked deep in human subjectivity which, again, is beyond and separate from any forms used to express it. To give it any content would be to make it particular, when he claims its nature is universally human. Hick's ultimate, the Real, is without features so as to save it from identification with one human tradition more than another. Smith's focus, faith, is contentless for the same reason. The last thing that either an undefinable faith or an empty ultimate has to fear is unbelief.

Smith has rightly pointed us toward history. An adequate understanding of religious diversity will have to take history seriously. I would argue that such understanding requires reasons to take the historical specificity of various faith traditions seriously, as more than just the expressive forms of a deeper reality or quality we already know. Smith is fond of noting that among the religions "the claim to uniqueness is not unique." Although this quip suggests something humorous and naive about a religion's sense of its own distinctness, the humor does not amount to an effective argument. Perhaps the historical fact that most if not all religious traditions make this claim represents the kind of consistent data that should alert us to something deeply significant about the faiths. Perhaps our interpretation will be more comprehensive if rather than disparaging this testimony we discover good reason for each tradition to offer it.

3

Practicing Dialogue, Practicing Justice

Paul Knitter and the Liberation Theology of Religions

Driving south of Delhi, we passed the massive ruins of a fortress from the age of the Mughals and then stopped for lunch at a new resort catering to the urban middle class on holiday. From there it was an uncomfortably short trip to our destination: a haphazard expanse of stone quarries spread over a wide and treeless landscape. In the nearest pit a man stood barefoot, swinging his sledge hammer against the rock face. Two women in saris collected the rough gravel in shallow pans which they settled on their heads and carried up the steep incline with grave dignity. Huge trucks bounced by in clouds of dust on the narrow tracks between the pits.

Our host led us on up a small incline to the workers' village. It was a honeycomb of huts laid out in rows, each sharing a wall on two sides with its neighbors. They stood not much more than waist high, and when we bent to enter from the bright sunlight the interior was an unbroken dark except where a child's eyes leaped out. The narrow walkway between the homes was beaten earth, swept smooth. Before some entrances the ground was marked with a delicate pattern painstakingly laid out in chalk dust. A small school building stood free at the village edge.

The quarry workers were indentured laborers. Most had migrated from their farms during times of famine and ended in virtual bondage. They paid rent to their employers for the ground under their huts, paid likewise at a premium for their food and water. Most fell steadily deeper in debt, in ledger books whose arithmetic they had neither the education nor the power to question.

71

The villagers were overwhelmingly Hindu, but Muslims and Christians were sprinkled among them as well. The same could be said of the quarry supervisors, the directors of the companies that owned the quarries, and the contractors building the Delhi apartment houses with their stone. Our visit was the result of a campaign waged for the workers' economic and political rights. The proud whitewashed school was a small step the village had taken with this support. The movement was led by a Hindu reformer, Swami Agnivesh, and its modest ranks too were a cross section of India's diverse faiths.

A day earlier I had questioned him about interreligious dialogue. He had paused a moment and replied, "I desire a dialogue in accord with nature, the basic needs of nature." By that, he said, he meant a dialogue whose goal was development: the development of the simplest means of life for the poorest of the poor. Of course, he shrugged, he was a minority. There must be several million swamis in India, he said, parasites who eat well and cover the sins of the rich. To which one Christian member of our group nodded. Yes, she said, our traditions are so much alike.

There is nothing unique about this story. But it introduces yet a third path toward pluralistic theology, the path of justice. This route is grounded not in philosophical reason or the silence of existential faith, but in the struggle against hunger, exploitation, and persecution. In contrast to the philosophical focus on "the Real," this approach holds that "theology as God-talk or God's talk is not necessarily the universally valid starting point, or the direct object, or the only basis, of interreligious collaboration in the Third World. But liberation is. Soteriology is the foundation of theology" (Pieris 1988, 107). In contrast to a focus on faith as an existential, interior orientation, this approach is suspicious of a stress on a unity of ineffable spiritualities. "And what of the horror of caste and sexist discrimination that thrives on religious sanction? How many prayer centers have cared or dared to go against the grain? The Ashramic Christ seemed no more sensitive to the demands of justice than did the neocolonialist Christ" (Pieris 1988, 95).

The pluralist's Copernican revolution begins with revulsion at the crimes of religious pride. Holy war, intolerance, inquisition, and pogrom are brutal facts, their victims achingly real. It is a misunderstanding to treat pluralistic theories only as philosophical or historical propositions. Those propositions deserve careful criticism in their own right. But we are willfully deaf not to appreciate the consistent ethical passion undergirding the constructive positions I have reviewed in the first two chapters. Before it is any kind of theory, pluralism is a commitment to exorcise the religious sources of human oppression.

From this perspective belief in the superiority or unique truth of one faith is itself an intrinsic evil. It provides an inevitable motive for dehumanizing one's neighbors and so multiplying other oppressions. This toxic particularity is a demonizing disease that poisons the life of any tradition that it touches. To this much all pluralistic thinkers tend to agree.

But some explicitly shape their entire approach to religious diversity around this concern. This adds another level to the equation. Religious exclusivity is only one feature in a more extensive matrix of evils. It may be regarded as a root of the other evils or primarily as an obstacle that prevents religions from addressing them. In any case the discussion of religious diversity is drawn firmly into the context of ethical concerns.

The Sri Lankan theologian Tissa Balasuriya asks, "Can the self-understanding of churches that legitimated sexist, racist, classist and religious oppression be theologically true?" (Balasuriya 1985, 202). Here is a proposal to test all religious conviction and practice by an ethical norm: what yields socially destructive fruit cannot be held to be true. It is also a program for the renovation of all traditions. Whatever has served cultural imperialism, whatever might be enlisted to encourage war or persecution, must be rooted out. Soteriological distinctiveness is a cancer; even a single cell is deadly. We must cut deep for the cure. These pluralists question the moral seriousness of those who prescribe anything but major surgery.

Here we encounter the heart of pluralistic theology and the source of its authentic power. Though these concerns lie at the origin of the movement, their fullest expressions have lagged behind those we have examined already. For a considerable time, those who placed liberation at the center of the religious agenda and those who placed interreligious dialogue there had little or difficult interaction. This was partly because liberation theology grew in Latin America—ostensibly an area of Christian predominance—and the focus of interreligious dialogue lay in South and East Asia (see Pieris 1988, 87-88; Fabella 1980). With increasing contact between theologians from these different contexts, the two approaches came into more intense interaction. In North America as well these issues converged in the work of some theologians such as Rosemary Ruether, who has dealt in depth with both anti-Semitism and sexism (see Ruether 1974; Ruether and Ruether 1989; and Ruether's many works on feminist and liberation themes). Today there is a rich cross-fertilization of liberation theology and the theology of religions.

FROM THEOCENTRISM TO SOTERIOCENTRISM

Each of these disciplines puts great stress on *praxis*, though of different kinds.[1] Liberation theology called for social engagement on the

---

[1] For a discussion of various forms of this praxis emphasis see chapter 6, "Praxis and Solidarity," in Max Stackhouse, *Apologia*.

side of the poor as a condition of authentic knowledge. Religious pluralists called for active conversation and interaction with adherents of various faith traditions as a condition of any meaningful religious judgments. Despite continuing tensions, there is a convergence of sorts in the two perspectives. The advocates of interreligious dialogue increasingly recognize certain fundamental economic and political freedoms as necessary conditions for that dialogue to be truly authentic. And liberation theologians increasingly acknowledge that decisive social action for justice itself runs perilous risks of evil if its participants do not engage in the broadest possible dialogue to reform their operative understanding of justice itself.

Paul Knitter is one distinguished advocate of pluralistic theology whose work reflects this convergence most dramatically. A Roman Catholic and former Divine Word missionary, his theological writings on religious diversity are notable both for the breadth of his sympathies and the seriousness with which he melds ecclesial and academic concerns. In his earlier work, Knitter proposed to make the conditions of interreligious dialogue themselves serve as substantive theological norms. He suggested several "conditions for the possibility of interreligious dialogue" as commitments that should be shared by all participants. These included 1) grounding dialogue in personal religious experience and firm truth claims, 2) acceptance of the hypothesis of a common ground and goal for all religion, and 3) openness to genuine change or conversion (Knitter 1985, 207-211).

Knitter's position was quite nuanced. He held, for instance, that a tradition's claim of unique religious value should be *provisionally* suspended, since interreligious engagement is the only context in which such a claim could be validated. Until that interreligious conversation has reached its ideal fulfillment, all parties must recognize that such claims are, literally, baseless. Christians, for instance, have not learned and worked with other believers extensively enough to conclude plausibly that Christ surpasses and is normative for other faiths (Knitter 1987c, 192). We don't know this claim is either right or wrong. It is just methodologically impossible as yet.

The conditions for dialogue that Knitter proposed to enforce were instrumentally absolute. Dialogue could not proceed effectively without them. Dialogue was the only path to true religious insight. Therefore the requirements of dialogue were in practice the primary theological norms. What insight would be forthcoming, no tradition or participant could know in advance. It might even be the verification that Jesus Christ "surprisingly surpasses all other events" (Knitter 1985, 230).

Christians may maintain their personal commitment to Christ, as devotees of Krishna maintain their attachment. Commitment to Christ as the universal savior is not definitively ruled out as a possibility—that would also be to reach conclusions ahead of the dialogue. But the assertion or advocacy of such a commitment in regard to others must be suspended for the foreseeable future. And since religions presumably function perfectly well in the interim without such universal claims, it would appear a necessary axiom that, true or not, these claims cannot be essential to the faiths.

Knitter endorsed "doing before knowing" as a religious imperative. Dialogue is the only practice out of which truth can arise. Therefore the conditions that make dialogue itself possible provide a thin interim norm for the faiths, one which is itself presumably universal and impartial. Modest though its implications may appear, the emphasis on the practice of dialogue provides an ethical foundation to this "theocentric" phase in Knitter's thought. Theocentrism implies a shift from defining the divine in terms of one particularistic pointer (whether Christ or Krishna) toward emphasizing the limits of those pointers in terms of their object. Religious norms are instrumental; Christ has value only insofar as Christ points us to God. If we lift our eyes to the divine we meet through Christ, and learn more of this divine through other channels, we are in a position to relativize this pointer as one among others.

Consistent with his principles, Knitter practiced dialogue inside and outside the Christian community. He changed his position as a result.[2] In particular he acknowledged the difficulties in giving content to theocentrism apart from some particular standard and the inadequacy of *theos* as a description for a common focus among the faiths. The conditions for dialogue—especially the presumption of a common religious goal—had served as a provisional norm for the theocentric vision. Now Knitter looked to a further stage. "If Christian attitudes have evolved from ecclesiocentrism to christocentrism to theocentrism, they must now move on to what in Christian symbols might be called 'kingdom-centrism' or more universally 'soteriocentrism'" (Knitter 1987c, 187).

The internal dynamic of this development is not hard to follow. If dialogue demanded conditions where each could authentically speak and be heard, liberation theologians pressed home the impossibility of meeting such conditions so long as poverty and oppression remained. The practice of dialogue as Knitter had earlier defined it now seemed an abstract ideal that ignored the actual circumstances of most adherents of all religions. Therefore he proposed to make liberation itself the basis for interreligious relation. "If the religions of the world . . . can recognize poverty and oppression as a common problem, if they can share a common commitment (expressed in different forms) to remove such evils, they will have the basis for reaching across their incommensura-

---

[2] For a sample of the discussion see S. Mark Heim, "Thinking about Theocentric Christology," 1-16, as well as the responses from various writers and Knitter in the same issue.

bilities and differences in order to hear and understand each other and be transformed in the process" (Knitter 1987c, 186). Where once injustice figured only as an impediment to dialogue, now dialogue is fundamentally an instrument of liberation.

Theocentrism assumed common ground in the religious "object" and oriented dialogue on that basis. Soteriocentrism seeks common ground in human need—the religious subjects—and orients dialogue on that basis. In making this shift, Knitter and others move courageously from an area where assertions of commonality are notoriously easy to make and hard to test, to an area where they are much more costly. It is almost banal to say that "transcendence is grasped in all religions." It is hardly so to say "no religion can be valid that does not foster the economic independence of women." What constitutes injustice, what counts as removing it, and what will actually effect the removal are all matters over which we know there are the most vehement disagreements.

In Knitter's revised view, religion that does not make a primary effort to address poverty and oppression "is not authentic religion" (Knitter 1987c, 180). Only "First World mystics or scholars" can afford the luxury of dialogue with or between such religions. Therefore—contrary to Knitter's own earlier hypothesis—dialogue and pluralism should not be one's first concern. It is now the "methodology of liberation thought" that provides the context and standards for dialogue and theological reconstruction, not the methodology of dialogue that provides a thin content of ethics.

Knitter is sensitive to the criticism that in moving to this next stage he has reintroduced a distinction between true and false religion. Having set out at first to question this distinction, has he reinvented it in the categories of inauthentic and liberating faith? John Cobb objects that Knitter will dialogue only with those that share his view of salvation, replicating the behavior of exclusivists. Cobb suggests that Hindus and Buddhists have something other than social change in mind when they speak of liberation, and that Knitter seems to prejudge them as misguided (Cobb, quoted in Knitter 1987c, 187, 190). Knitter allows that Christians should indeed hear out the case for a "preferential option for personal enlightenment." But he trusts Buddhists and Hindus recognize that "in the world of today" enlightenment must bring about positive social effects to be a valid religious aim, whatever other virtues may attach to it.

Knitter does not advocate extension of the same openness and respect to all religions. Those that "deny any relationship between the transformation of this world and personal salvation or enlightenment, that call upon their followers to abandon all concern for this world and concentrate only on the next" go beyond the limits of tolerance. Given the pressing needs of the world, Knitter suggests we choose "not to dialogue with such other-worldly religions" (Knitter 1987c, 199). At some later time, under different social conditions, there might be leisure for such conversation.

Knitter thus proposes two fundamental principles for his soteriocentric approach to religious diversity (Knitter 1987c, 207). The first is the primacy of orthopraxis. For Christians, and by extension others as well, the primary touchstone of fidelity to tradition should be advancement of the "kingdom" of earthly peace and justice. A belief, practice, or understanding which serves this end is by definition "still Christian," since it helps realize Jesus' vision. The second premise is a soteriocentric *starting point* for interreligious relation. Knitter shifts away from his earlier hypothesis of a common ground and goal in all religion and instead suggests that "if there is nothing *within* the different traditions shared by all, there may be something *outside* confronting them all" (Knitter 1989, 207).

Some shared norms for truth can evolve from struggles with shared problems of human suffering and the constraints of a single natural world. Religions have more in common in their soteriological starting points than in their doctrinal schemes. The criteria of liberative praxis would not allow us to rank whole religions, but could support judgments about the truth of a particular Hindu belief or a specific Christian ritual by determining whether it "promotes human welfare and leads to the removal of poverty and to the promotion of liberation" (Knitter 1987c, 190). One of the strong notes of soteriocentric views is this insistence that religions cannot only understand each other but must judge each other.

Each assertion of a universal criterion is liable to become a new vehicle for invidious comparison and oppression. Knitter is well aware of this perennial problem. He does not deny that soteriocentrism is still formally liable to the criticism. But it has been formulated precisely to cancel out the substance of the criticism. By elevating concern for the social well-being of the poor and the oppressed to the privileged position of the starting point for all dialogue, he tries to assure that the risk of exclusivism can be run only on behalf of the victims of exclusion.

Knitter argues that an emphasis on orthopraxis over orthodoxy is faithful to Christian sources. The primary purpose of Christian confession is to call forth a pattern of life, not a body of belief (Knitter 1987c, 196). Working for Jesus' kingdom is "more important for Christian identity than is the right knowledge concerning the nature of God or of Jesus himself" (Knitter 1987c, 195). In Knitter's earlier dialogical imperative, he had stressed that Christian "one and only" language about Christ was "love language" (Knitter 1985, 185). Like a woman's statement to her husband that he is "the best man in the world," this confessional language is not meant literally but expresses a real and relational truth: you are the one *for me*. Now Knitter argues that it is better to view this as "action language," intended to urge total commitment to a path of practice (Knitter 1987c, 196). If contemporary Christians retain an un-equivocal—exclusive—adherence to liberating action, while dropping their "one and only" views of Jesus, they will in fact maintain the core content of the original message.

Significant in both the earlier and later versions of this argument is Knitter's emphasis on a "processive-relational" view of truth as opposed to a "classicist" one (Knitter 1985, 7-9 and 182-186). Truth is neither a proposition nor a correspondence but a relation; religious truth is a dis-position that one enters into *by means of* religious statements and prac-tices.

In this view, the factuality of beliefs is secondary to the effects they have on those who hold them, the behavior of the communities that form around them, and the impact of these persons and communities in the larger world. In Knitter's earlier phase, he would say that the ab-stract "correspondence truth" of the doctrine of the Trinity is of purely academic interest; it is the personal meaning it enables in an individual or community that is crucial. In his later phase he would say that if Christianity as constituted by its commitment to incarnational doctrine proves a feeble force against social evil, then the factual truth of its doctrines is of little interest. According to "soteriocentric liberation the-ology of religions, whether . . . discernments about uniqueness and fi-nality are eventually made or not is, in the final analysis, not that impor-tant—as long as we, with all peoples and religions, are seeking first the kingdom and its justice" (Knitter 1987c, 194).

Truth, as properly understood, is precisely about bringing people into right relation. To view Christian "one and only" statements as ei-ther "love" or "action" language is to recover their deepest dimensions of truth. That such statements were ever interpreted substantively by early Christian communities, in Knitter's view, may have been only because they were culturally captive to the classicist view of truth. He is convinced that to shift our view of truth in this way defines away the ground for exclusivism. Relational truth cannot be exclusive, for it al-ways expresses a personal perspective, rather than revealing universal realities or meaning.

Knitter realizes that making justice—right relation—the norm for religion does not overcome diversity. Each religion or tradition will have its own understanding of what liberation entails. But "what makes the soteriocentric approach different from christocentrism or theocentrism is its explicit recognition that before the mystery of *Soteria*, no media-tor or symbol system is absolute" (Knitter 1987c, 190). Yet at the same time, Knitter claims the justice standard will provide a concrete basis by which religions can both validate their own claims and judge others: "From their ethical, soteriological fruits we shall know them—we shall be able to judge whether and how much other religious paths *and* their mediators are salvific" (Knitter 1987c, 193). Whereas doctrinal criteria

"prove too controversial and prone to ideology" to allow such evaluations, an ethical standard may escape this difficulty (Knitter 1987c, 189).

The theology of liberation and the theology of religions need each
other. The unitive focus for interreligious relations, which could not be
found in some common content of all faiths, is provided by the identical
challenge the traditions face to transform life for the poor. The breadth
of perspective and the sheer global clout which liberation theology lacks
so long as it remains a merely Christian movement are both provided by
the religions collectively. "Economic, political and especially nuclear
liberation is too big a job for any one nation, or culture, *or* religion"
(Knitter 1987c, 179).

Having reviewed Knitter's case for the convergence of justice and
dialogue, we can look more closely at two other authors who move toward this same intersection, one from the side of interfaith conversation
and the other from the side of liberation theology.

FROM DIALOGUE TO JUSTICE

David Krieger's *The New Universalism* is one of the most rigorous
and impressive contemporary discussions of the epistemology of interfaith dialogue (Krieger 1991). Knitter argues that the theology of religions and liberation theology need each other. Krieger's thought illustrates half of this thesis by arguing that the conditions for interfaith
conversation require very concrete types of social change.

Past director of the theology of religions program in Zurich, and a
former student of W. C. Smith, Krieger focuses on the conditions of the
very possibility of communication across meaning systems. Building
upon Wittgenstein's thought, he stresses the pragmatic conditions of
meaning, an emphasis similar to Knitter's on relational truth. From this
perspective various faith traditions or "language games" are in order
according to their own immanent set of rules. They are generated by a
communal life and are of one nature with that form of life. The religions
do not only commend practices or make assertions. They provide a self-
referential system within which the practice or the terms of the assertion receive their meaning. These systems construct the categories of
evidence that test their own propositions.

All statements that claim to be universal, to apply across all meaning systems, will on investigation prove to be the imposition of one
game on others. To the proposal that reason or shared ethical concerns
might serve as a basis for dialogue, the questions will arise "whose rationality?" and "whose justice?" Honest answers will acknowledge that
each culture/religion/language game corresponds to its own form of life.
There is no neutral standpoint among them because there is no universal form of life, only specific ones. Communication can take place where

there is overlap in the meaning systems. But where they differ, the very attempt to dialogue is itself necessarily conflictual; each side has no choice but to attempt to fit the other into its own terms of expression. If this is so, participants in interreligious dialogue would inevitably seem to be pursuing particularistic ends by more sophisticated means.

Krieger suggests that the only way toward a truly universal frame of reference would be through a universal *praxis*. If there were some game that all of us played—not instead of but in addition to our particular ones—this would provide the pragmatic basis for common meaning. In our modern world, Krieger argues, such a practice is developing: a "global form of life." We are historically impelled into increasingly multicultural contexts. We live increasingly in a political and economic environment where others' meaning systems are a part of our experience. "Communicative action suddenly receives an epistemological priority and a foundational significance heretofore reserved for subjective experiences of insight, revelatory events and monological procedures of reality testing" (Krieger 1991, 125).

There is a global form of life evolving, with its own inherent grammar of meaning. This multicultural, dialogical practice is the seedbed of true universalism. In the past a monocultural group received or discovered religious truth and *transmitted* it across boundaries, a process Krieger thinks fatally compromised from the beginning by its "in/out" structure. Now, Krieger claims, we can derive some true universals from a practice that is both everyone's and no one's in particular: the practice of universal communication across lifeworlds.

Krieger identifies three levels of discourse. The first he calls *argumentation*. It takes place within a given religion or lifeworld and seeks to establish facts and conclusions by reference to a given set of rules. The second level is *boundary discourse*. Like any boundary, it faces in two directions. Internally, it states the grammar, the regulative practice that constitutes a lifeworld for the community. Externally, it distinguishes this lifeworld from others, and either excludes them or seeks to assimilate them to its own symbols and doctrines.[3] The third level is *disclosive discourse*. It takes place in the space between religions/lifeworlds, disclosing to all participants the existence of other grammars and worlds.

At the first level of discourse we argue in a common frame of rationality. At the second, we reflect on the criteria and practices that constitute this rationality. At the third, we cope in some manner with the discovery of "other-rationality," a framework constituted on another basis. With respect to interreligious dialogue, the first level would incline toward apologetics, argument among varying religious perspectives on

---

[3] "Boundary discourse" is thus very similar to the cultural-linguistic model of theological language presented by George Lindbeck in *The Nature of Doctrine*.

the basis of the overlap in their respective forms of rationality. The second would imply a model of proclamation, stressing the holistic unity of a faith and the need to participate in that integral unity to grasp any single part. The third type of discourse suggests a dialogue shaped by focus on its own conditions of possibility. Krieger maintains that if universal discourse is to be possible it must be grounded not in objective reality or in subjective certainties but "in the pragmatic conditions of a global form of life" (Krieger 1991, 126-127). Dialogue across boundaries is itself the practice, the lifeform, that gives meaning to the insights or convictions that arise within it. Insofar as there is a new form of life, a global community, in which people increasingly share by communicating across cultural and religious borders, this experience may eventually lead to reformulated versions of the first two levels of discourse.

The question of universal religious truth is then an intensely practical one: how to realize the conditions of interreligious communication. Rather than asking what universal criteria or essence exists to allow communication, Krieger reverses the perspective and asks what would have to be the case if authentic dialogue were going on between various types of rationality. Those conditions *are* the universals. They are not given, they have to be enacted. Interreligious dialogue has no pre-existing foundation; it is a commitment to enacting the conditions of its own intelligibility.

Is it true that the pragmatic conditions of existing argumentative or boundary discourse cannot themselves be universalized? There are weighty figures who argue that they can; notably Jurgen Habermas and Karl-Otto Apel in the first case and Hans-Georg Gadamer in the second. Krieger considers their claims and rejects them. Argumentative discourse cannot deal in its own terms with argument about the criteria of argument. Boundary discourse has no option but a test of power to deal with the existence of other myths that set different boundaries. That is, mission and proclamation by one faith can call forth only reciprocal mission and proclamation from another.

Krieger draws an illustration from an anthropologist's conversation with a tribal leader who has attributed a house's collapse to witchcraft (Krieger 1991, 130). Argumentation quickly breaks down in the clash between a lifeworld in which sorcery has an integral rationality and one in which it does not. The conversation inevitably shifts into a boundary discourse in which, whatever their intents, the anthropologist and the tribal leader attempt to convert each other. The communicative act of speaking together, each one necessarily in the terms constituted by his or her own lifeworld, is inevitably a zero sum process. Insofar as the practice of communication takes place more within one boundary discourse, it takes place less within the other. There is no neutral meeting point.

Boundary discourse has two great failings, in Krieger's view. It is unable to recognize the existence of other-rationality. For instance, the anthropologist's most sincere efforts to value and affirm the meaning of sorcery in this tribal life will take place in alien categories: appreciation for its psychological or social function perhaps. It is precisely the rationality of sorcery in its "home" lifeworld that is strained out in such a process in favor of a rationality assigned to it in another lifeworld. The anthropologist can give a description of that other-rationality but cannot participate in it fully unless by conversion. Even if conversion is possible, this does not change Krieger's point; the converted anthropologist now experiences the same boundary conflict with the "other-rationality" he or she left behind.

The second failing Krieger suggests is that boundary discourse cannot be self-critical. Since its rules *constitute* the standards for truth, there is no purchase within such discourse to relativize the framework itself. The power exercised by the boundary discourse in relation to another can never truly appear as a problem so long as that power is defined in its own terms. Such critique can only come from a competing *mythos*, which must figure in the boundary discourse itself as a threat and competitor.

The history of interreligious relations is encompassed by the limits of these two modes of discourse. Krieger argues that a good deal of the exclusivism in religion flows from a failure to recognize the nature of boundary discourse, a failure to note that as it sets up standards that define a horizon, it sets itself off from other possibilities as well. In constituting "the whole world" for us, boundary discourse constitutes one possible world among others. Its universality is its limitation. This paradox can only come clear to us if there is a third level of discourse that discloses difference and allows it to remain just that, difference. The language of disclosure would precisely leave other-rationality other.

Is such a third level of discourse possible? Krieger believes that it has already been outlined in Mahatma Gandhi's conception of satyagraha. Gandhi specifies a pragmatic type of communicative *action* which constitutes a distinctive context for truth. Krieger stresses that Gandhi does not deny or eliminate conflict, but presumes it. Conflict is legitimate. Gandhi refuses to thematize opposing possibilities as good and bad, true and false, or rational and irrational. Therefore argumentative conflict and, Krieger claims, boundary conflict are set in the wider context of a common search for truth. It is precisely by their conflict that two sides advance this quest, so long as they struggle nonviolently and self-critically.

This is the crucial point in Krieger's vision. The practice of nonviolence—not in a merely strategic sense but with Gandhi's full emphasis on self-criticism and the search for truth—is the necessary condition for true communication across religions. Openness to other interpretations of reality is commended from many points of view, but the real issue is "*how* we can be open, that is, under what pragmatic conditions of convincement universality may be achieved" (Krieger 1991, 160).

Conflict between lifeworlds becomes a form of communication which recognizes the other-rationality of the partner. Nonviolence is the concrete form of this recognition, the practice that affirms the other's right to be as other. The practice of nonviolence and its corollaries is itself a form of life and conversion to this form of life is required for it to be effective. The tenets of nonviolence thus represent a blueprint for a new second level discourse, a boundary discourse for a global community, specifying the regulative practice that constitutes such a community of communication. It constitutes a "new myth" of global solidarity.[4] However, it claims not to be a competing religion or culture. People need not renounce their existing boundary definition of truth, but they must commit themselves to advance it without violence and with critical openness to correction from outside those boundaries. Conflict *as* communication radically discloses to each faith its own limitation. But it does so methodologically, practically, without judging the outcome of the struggle. "The pragmatics of nonviolence allow us to remain faithful to our own beliefs while at the same time realizing that they are not the absolute truth, but only an interpretation" (Krieger 1991, 160). Krieger says this new universalism, the norm of nonviolence, is "the inner need of thought itself" (Krieger 1991, 162). It is in this sense an objective rationality.

Krieger begins with a concern for dialogue: how is it even possible to communicate across different meaning systems? His relentless search for the necessary conditions of dialogue leads him to a practical ethical imperative: Gandhian nonviolence. Dialogue is frustrated because the interaction between communities inevitably becomes a test of power, a struggle for dominance. Only a form of life liberated from this dynamic of dominance can support authentic communication. An emphasis on interreligious dialogue thus leads to an imperative to create a new form of life in which all participate equally, to struggle against oppression of one community by another. These characteristic liberation themes rise out of commitment to dialogue, indicating that the theology of religions can provide its own distinctive rationale for commitment to social justice.

FROM JUSTICE TO DIALOGUE

We can look now to the other side of Knitter's convergence, the journey from liberation toward the religions. Marjorie Hewitt Suchocki, currently professor and dean at the Claremont School of Theology, is a

---

[4] Krieger here develops W. C. Smith's notion that the only legitimate theological discourse is one that speaks for "all of us" at once, giving it a great deal more rigor and clarity.

theologian whose commitment to liberation mixes strong contributions from process philosophy and feminist analysis. She has provided a particularly perceptive exploration of what is involved in trying to follow the soteriocentric prescription (Suchocki 1987). She approaches issues of religious diversity with a principle gleaned from liberation theologies: when one mode of humanity is made normative for all, exploitation follows for those outside the norm. We can note that Krieger seems to differ at this point, maintaining that the nonviolent mode of human interaction he specifies is normative for all, at least for all who wish to participate in global communication, and is not a form of exploitation.

By extension, Suchocki suggests, universalizing any religion as a norm to judge others leads to oppression and "falls short of the norm that liberationists consider ultimate—the normative justice that creates well-being in the world community" (Suchocki 1987, 149). Suchocki links religious oppression with sexism by identifying oppression as the application of one particular norm universally; whether a Christ-norm applied to Buddhism or a male norm applied to women.

She acknowledges the tension in affirming the liberation principle that any universal norm leads to oppression and at the same time proposing justice as a universal norm for the religions. She affirms that dialogue is inevitably judgmental and that her own feminist-liberation commitment to the universal well-being of women and the poor will be her standard for dialogue (Suchocki 1987, 150). Does this not substitute one putative universal norm for another and continue the oppression? Suchocki says it would appear so, unless there is an "open recognition of the conditioned nature of the norm of justice we bring, and a commitment to critical exploration of the norm in the very dialogue where it is brought to bear" (Suchocki 1987, 150). The attempt to universalize a doctrinal or cultural norm will inevitably lead to oppression. But perhaps there is some fundamental level of human well-being that can serve as a valid standard.

Suchocki outlines three levels of human well-being which provide the substance for a standard of justice (Suchocki 1987, 154). The first level is physical well-being: food, water, shelter, work, and community—standards that might be met in an enlightened prison. The second level involves human dignity, self-naming, and some standing within a social community. The third level brings the possibility of self-development and self-determination. The latter two levels necessarily recognize "multiple modes of being human, with this multiplicity valued positively" (Suchocki 1987, 155). She admits this three-tiered definition of justice is culture bound and would not receive universal assent. However she argues that the two "higher" levels are those where the widest diversity of interpretation exists over what constitutes human well-being, and she prefers to maximize freedom for the expression of these interpretations, to affirm a free market of visions of well-being. The requirements of physical life seem less equivocal, and Suchocki would give them the highest priority as a standard for all religions.

She presses her exploration one fascinating step further. Even physical well-being can be constituted differently in different faiths and cultural contexts. Existing religious constructions of these values—including Suchocki's feminist one—are so permeated by their cultural sources that it would be imperialistic to apply one to all religions (Suchocki 1987, 158). Despite this apparent dead end, she suggests there is still one point of contact among the religions that *will* allow a nonimperialistic criterion of justice.

Here comes a surprising twist in the argument. At the last moment Suchocki proposes that we turn back again to the doctrinal realm "we supposedly left behind in calling for justice rather than doctrine as the basis of dialogue" (Suchocki 1987, 159). Each religion's highest valuation of what physical existence should be may be discovered, she suggests, not in its culturally contaminated concrete ethics, but precisely in its projected ideal. It is at the level of ultimate rather than penultimate visions of justice within each tradition that there might be the closest approximation to a minimal agreement on basic physical well-being, an agreement that would be the closest thing possible to a universal norm. In other words, it is in the religions' "doctrinal" descriptions of ultimate human religious fulfillment that we may find common elements that suggest a minimal ethic. This ethic could then be a standard to evaluate all traditions. Though Suchocki gives no explicit examples, one might be that the Christian heaven and the Buddhist nirvana are both free of suffering, and therefore the absence of suffering can be taken as a basic index of well-being.

She recognizes that even the most fundamental questions of human well-being find varying answers from the religions. It is not necessarily true that these answers converge more at the "practical" than the doctrinal levels. Suchocki suggests that the applied ethics of the traditions are so thoroughly determined by cultural elements that they may diverge more dramatically than the religions' more abstract formulations of ultimate human well-being. As a feminist, she is also keenly aware that even when the traditions may share a broad consensus about a practical matter, this consensus may hardly imply well-being for women. Leaving aside the question of how closely the ideals of various traditions cohere, her observation about applied ethics is supported by the fact that reformers within particular traditions typically appeal precisely to some ideal in that tradition when they attempt to change the operative ethic of their faith. But, as she acutely observes, this attention to ideals brings us full circle back to the doctrinal areas Knitter rejected as too controversial to ground interreligious judgments.

Suchocki brings a priority for justice to the interfaith arena. However, she believes the social and ethical standards which are normative across religions must be defined through the participation of those religions. Otherwise the liberation imperative too easily becomes the vehicle for domination by one cultural group. Suchocki's passion for justice leads her to a healthy respect for those who do not understand it in the same way she does. Accordingly, she closes her essay with a bracingly frank and rare formulation of pluralistic principle. In noting the inherent diversity that will exist in defining justice, she says,

> Paradoxically, the one employing the norm that affirms diversity must expect to encounter—and affirm—systems that, containing no valuation of diversity, reject or devalue one's norm and the system it reflects. An absolutist, by definition, cannot affirm the pluralist, whereas the pluralist is bound, likewise by definition, to affirm the alternative of absolutism so long as it promotes well-being (Suchocki 1987, 160).

Suchocki believes a thin substantive standard of justice can be derived from the various religious ideals. When this standard is applied as a broad-gauge test, it turns out to validate many non-pluralistic religious convictions. A priority for justice does not necessarily validate the pluralistic approach to religions over others and the pluralistic approach to religions cannot reconcile fundamental diversity in approaches to justice.

Those committed to particular social struggles may dismiss Suchocki's modest conclusion as a lack of ethical zeal. But she maintains that what is at stake is the principle of non-exclusion that lies at the root of human liberation, the principle that objects to making one mode of being human—a male mode, a Christian mode, a pluralist mode—normative for all. To disregard the consistent application of this principle to one's own position is to join company again with either the religious exclusivists, who expect all to abide by their truth because their experience and understanding confirm it beyond a doubt, or to join company with the inclusivists, who affirm other traditions to the degree they replicate in some measure the truth most fully revealed in their own.

Suchocki's scrupulous discussion illustrates that there is in fact continual dialectic between orthopraxis based on the "conditions of dialogue," orthopraxis based on justice as a norm and "doctrinal" dialogue among the religions' own substantial categories. If an attempt to specify the conditions for dialogue leads to the conclusion that justice is *the* fundamental condition and therefore it must be the norm for praxis, further reflection or praxis reveals two things. First, there is no agreement about justice. If we are to deal justly with this difference itself we will need dialogue among the various visions of human well-being and failing. Therefore we have circled back to the question of what conditions allow for such dialogue. Second, there is no way to engage the varying views about justice except to deal with their integral embeddedness in distinct religious textures of belief, narrative, and ritual—to come back to the type of "doctrinal" dialogue that an orthopraxis focus on either dialogue or liberation was to displace.

There is a reciprocity in the orthopraxis of liberation and dialogue. The attempt to make justice the trump card of interreligious judgment bids to become a vehicle for the interests only of some, who control its definition, unless there is a highly participatory ongoing dialogue, open to contrasting perspectives. The insistence on authentic dialogue as the context for any apprehension of religious truth risks irrelevance unless justice is an integral aim of the dialogue. Suchocki, moving toward religious pluralism from a liberation perspective, makes the first point. Krieger and Knitter, moving toward liberation theology from an interreligious perspective, make the second. Justice and dialogue need each other to be plausible norms. They lead us dialectically back to the issue of universality.

FACING RELIGION AS A SOURCE OF EVIL

It is perhaps evident that I find soteriocentrism the most compelling of the three cases for pluralistic theology we have considered. Many of its major emphases will be incorporated in my own constructive statement. But I believe that it remains inadequate in several key respects. Our review of the tensions between dialogue and justice has already indicated difficulties that some advocates of a liberation theology of religions themselves recognize. I will briefly summarize my criticisms.

As I indicated at the beginning of the chapter, the soteriocentric approach sees two dimensions of justice at issue in religious diversity: religion as a cause of violent conflict, and religious resources as the means to right wrongs that stem from other causes. The first has to do with the dangers of religious distinctiveness—applying one faith's standards to another. The second has to do with the effectiveness of a tradition's doctrines and practices in combating nonreligious as well as religious sources of oppression. The Muslim profession of the finality of God's revelation in the Qur'an may thus be an intrinsic religious evil, from a soteriocentric view, since such a claim is thought necessarily to express and lead to domination. A Vedantic Hindu perspective on religions would, on this account, be evaluated more positively. On the other hand, it might be argued that Islam has historically shown greater transformative effect in overcoming some racial and economic divisions in society than Vedanta. On that score, Islam would receive higher marks.

Is pluralistic doctrine the one and only basis on which religiously inspired violence can be avoided? This is more often presumed than argued. The exclusivist form of such a presumption—that only those of pluralistic convictions practice tolerance and solidarity across religious lines, or can practice it fully—is not defensible. And an exclusivist claim of this sort is what is required to provide a distinctive warrant for soteriocentric theologies over all other possibilities. Some writers regularly remind the pluralists that past association of acts of intolerance with certain religious beliefs is no logical proof that the intolerance is inevitably caused by those beliefs or that the beliefs themselves are wrong. This is certainly logically true. And it is well to remember the zeal with which Christian exclusivists in the past seized upon the association of views they disliked with offensive practices (*sati*, physical mutilation, slavery) to conclude that the other religion's fundamental convictions themselves must be demonic. Some Christians in the past, convinced that false teaching must lead to moral dissolution, invested heavily in ferreting out or imagining dark sins in even the most virtuous of their pagan neighbors. The theory demanded it.

Can pluralistic perspectives really wish to repeat this dynamic today in a new key, insisting with dogmatic prejudgment that any but pluralist convictions will lead necessarily to religious strife and violence? Are we to believe, for instance, that the individuals represented in a recent collection of essays critical of pluralistic theology are more prone to religious imperialism, less committed to interreligious mutuality, than the comparable group represented in *The Myth of Christian Uniqueness* (D'Costa 1990)? Do pluralists themselves mean to claim this of John Cobb, M. M. Thomas, Monika Hellwig, Gavin D'Costa, Lesslie Newbigin? It is demonstrably not the case that only those holding soteriocentric views effectively overcome religious chauvinism. The overwhelming proportion of the scholarly work, the spiritual explorations and the interreligious exchanges that pluralists draw on today has been the effort of those who were inclusivist or even exclusivist in outlook according to the pluralists' judgment.

However, to claim that the past sins of Christianity, or any tradition, cast no doubt on the substance of its convictions is willfully legalistic (see Griffiths 1993, 79ff., for a sharp and cogent rejoinder to just such a claim). This is doubly so when the tradition in question itself professes to positively transform communal and interpersonal life. Pogroms and religious war may be attributed to the failings of the faithful, not their faith. The question remains, why was their faith so ineffective? It is reasonable to suppose that either the substance of that faith or its form was in error to so readily allow such results. But the pluralists' is not the only alternative to the exclusivism associated with those events. It is by no means clear that one or more of the types of inclusivism that pluralists reject would not meet this need just as effectively, if as widely accepted as exclusivism had been.

This is a point at which the Christian particularism of pluralistic theologians seems very much in evidence. It is historical Christianity (and

Islam, by extension) whose exclusivism they have in view. Most pluralists, while decrying the "myth of Christian uniqueness," incline toward
an exception in this case. They believe an unrivaled brutality and an
unrivaled exclusivity have gone hand in hand in Christian history, the
brutality being the fruit of the exclusivity. If it does not bear a unique
revelation, Christianity bears a unique moral burden. Pluralists believe
that whatever theological change might prevent future inquisitions, intramural wars, or holocausts, or might expiate the guilt of those already
past, is imperative.

There is little point in this context to debate the relative historical
dimensions and nature of Christian sin. There is abundant evil, inexcus-
able even in the context of its time. Christians hardly have reason to
moderate our shame at these facts even if they are at times caricatured
into even more monstrous shape. A resolutely comparative and purely
historical perspective might domesticate the horror against the general
backdrop of human history. But those who hope the church will be constituted by trust in the Christlike goodness and mercy of God hardly can
turn to such calculation for comfort. Repentance is the appropriate Christian response, and pluralistic theologies are good Christian examples of
it.

In their basic aim to correct and chasten Christianity these theologies
prove least comprehensive and most persuasive. Least comprehensive,
because the substance of various faiths is hardly called upon for this
dimension of pluralistic theology: the religious others need figure only
as victims of Christian evil or examples of goodness on Christian terms.
Most persuasive, because the grounds for the claims are implicitly and
often even explicitly confessional ones. There is no attempt to explain
these Christian behaviors away, no mitigating theory about Christian
atrocities as the product of sound faith but simple scientific underdevel-
opment (as for instance in Hick's rather glib treatment of Aztec human
sacrifice) (Hick 1989, 310-311). Autos-da-fé and Western imperialism
are not to be contextualized and so half-excused. The primary context
for interpreting these evils is the Christian one, where they have the
special force of contradiction and betrayal of Christian ideals.

A historian claiming value neutrality might say, "Given the assumptions and conditions of the time, one understands how things happened
as they did." The dismay of much Christian history for Christians is the
deep conviction that, given their faith, these people should have known—
and been—better. The pluralistic theologian takes this dismay a step
further: "They couldn't have known better, *because* of their faith." It
was the beliefs themselves that were wrong: beliefs in the uniqueness
of Christ, in missionary witness.

Wrong by what standard? According to the norms of other religious
traditions? Certainly it is effectively chastening to point out that Christian behaviors have been shocking at times to those guided by different

convictions. But this is rarely pressed too far by pluralistic writers, since it presents a rather ambiguous precedent. Judgment of one tradition according to the standards of another is the formal evil they ostensibly hope to overcome. To hold Christianity wanting by Hindu standards is thus an awkward move to make. Clearly the generative passion against Christian sin stems much more from the ideals contained in the Christian tradition and the Western tradition of which it is a part: the Sermon on the Mount or the universalistic rationalist ethics of the enlightenment. As pluralistic theologians remind us, we could hardly have had access to some absolute or neutral standard.

The wrongness of Christian exclusivism, then, has the special character of heresy for these writers. The consistent tenor and language of Hick, Smith, and Knitter on this point is striking. They argue that pluralism is the authentic interpretation of Christian sources. Hick argues this with regard to Christology, Smith with regard to faith, Knitter with regard to the meaning of confessional language. Alternative views have, as Smith likes to say, "a touch of blasphemy."

The unique quality of Christian evil, although it is often argued by some pluralistic theologians as a purely objective conclusion, derives its great power among Christians from a counter-expectation of Christian good. If Hick, for instance, argues that the great religious traditions are roughly equivalent in their capacity for "saint formation" and moral transformation of persons, he makes no such extensive reciprocal argument as to their equivalence in destructive capacities. This is presumably because he believes individuals can be more unambiguously judged. Social evils are harder to attribute directly to religions since they are so deeply enmeshed with other, uncontrolled factors like the technological or scientific capacities in one society relative to another. Yet it is hard not to gather that pluralistic theologians see certain faiths—notably Christianity and Islam—as particularly dangerous.

This passion for repentance and correction in Christianity is one I share. I am not so clear why it should provide the normative framework for all religious traditions and their relations. If there are traditions which have in the pluralists' view been much less prone to religious destructiveness, and which yet clearly hold to the universal and distinctive truth of their teaching—Buddhism comes to mind—why should an absolute prohibition of such claims be laid upon them? And yet this appears to be precisely what pluralistic theologies of religion do.

The sins of Christian exclusivism must be addressed. As the sins of white racism must ultimately be addressed by whites, this needs to be primarily the work of Christians. But Christians should be hesitant to make their internal prescriptions the measure for all traditions. In any event, pluralistic theologies are not the only, nor do I believe them the best, path for reformation of the Christian tradition at this point.

JUSTICE JUDGING RELIGIONS:
RELIGIONS MAKING JUSTICE

We have seen the case for a convergence of pluralism and liberation; emphasis on the conditions of interreligious dialogue seems to lead toward concern for justice, and emphasis on liberating practice seems to lead toward the need for dialogue. But there is also a contrary, centrifugal dynamic at work. Suchocki, particularly, is well aware of it. Soteriocentrism is convinced that the religions are more alike as social projects than as doctrines. Yet this seems unlikely, particularly given the implausibility of a radical dichotomy between these two elements. Whether at the level of doctrine or at the level of their embodiment as concrete social projects in history, the faiths stubbornly offer distinctive alternatives.

There is a great deal to be said for the argument that religions at least have in common a starting point in human ill-being. But in saying this, does a soteriocentric view offer any insight beyond that offered by the religions themselves? Suffering, ignorance, oppression, and evil are departure points deeply considered within the traditions: so much so that one might even view the faiths as constituted by their acute and differing diagnoses of the root sources of these human ills. What is distinctive about soteriocentrism is not its claim to begin with the painful human condition—a claim the faiths can all plausibly make—but the modern Western social analysis which it presumes provides a normative account of that condition.

Implicit in Knitter and Suchocki's proposals is the confidence that although there may be uncertainty about the causes and remedy for non-physical human misery—and here the diversity of the faiths may rightly have free play—the causative mechanisms of poverty, political violence, and social oppression are known to us. The religions are to be as accountable to such facts as they are to descriptions of the solar system. It is the confidence that this modern social analysis provides a sound and objective account of such phenomena and religion's role in them that leads to the axioms of soteriocentrism: that convictions of distinctive religious truth necessarily cause oppression, that it is a type of violence to apply a norm from one tradition within another, that spiritual practices must be judged by their social tendencies and not social behavior by its spiritual effects. There may be difficulty in working out causal relationships between religious attitudes and social effects in some specific cases, but the general principles are clear. Regardless of whether any given religious tradition judges its own tenets on their supposed societal effects, soteriocentrism proposes to make this the supreme priority in treating all the faiths. That this focus is more congenial to some than others is not viewed as discriminatory but practical: this is the area where religions are capable of working together and where the results are of some interest to all.

This dynamic is illustrated when Knitter argues that it is not primarily beliefs or practices that should constitute Christian identity but action on behalf of Jesus' vision of the kingdom of God. Though this phraseology sounds as if Jesus plays a substantive role in structuring the action of the Christian, this is not at all necessarily the case. In fact, soteriocentrists maintain that if Christians were decisively directed in their action by justice as Jesus and the traditions of Jesus envisioned it, they would be making "beliefs" illegitimately dominant. A more accurate summary of the soteriocentric view would be to say that since Jesus sought justice as he understood it, we are truly following Jesus when we pursue justice as we understand it. We are following Jesus in a formal, not a substantive, way and need not primarily derive our understanding of justice from the Christ tradition. Instead we see that tradition as one limited part of the vision of justice which we grasp much more fully than it could. The contribution of Christ to the Christian's religious life is, in Knitter's view, that of illustration and motivation. Christ is an example of how one loves justice, an example that for personal and cultural reasons is most affecting to me.

When words like "justice" and "liberation" are proposed as the true absolutes, we must say the same thing that pluralists would say of such a proposal for "Christ," "Qur'an," "Dharma," or "God." It is *our definition* of what these words mean that is actually absolute. In the case of the proposed religious absolutes, these definitions at least have the benefit of having been constructed over many centuries, by many people, across a diversity of cultural contexts. If "justice" is the absolute which is to surpass them all, it should at least give us pause that the operative definition of this absolute stems transparently, exclusively from a modern period and a Western context. This approach can be validated only with a strong argument for the unique, perhaps evolutionary, supremacy of our time and culture, an argument pluralists are consistently hesitant to make in any explicit way.

The confidence that definitions of justice are less subject to abuse than religious aims is curious. The same modern colonial history that includes some telling examples of theological exclusivism also provides powerful complementary examples of cultural exclusivism. In the heartlands of Western imperialism, the exclusive truth of Christianity underwent its own severe domestic challenges after the enlightenment. But any breach in the rationale for domination left by these doubts was more than smoothly filled by confidence in the superiority of Western laws, technology, and stage of cultural development. Whether or not the imperial powers were the privileged custodians of divine revelation, their representatives had little doubt they understood ethics and society— justice—better than their subjects. Colonial rulers had fewer scruples about enforcing their liberal principles than their religious convictions. If it is argued that the two are inextricably intertwined, this is only another reason to question the attempt of writers like Knitter to sharply distinguish them. Considerations such as these lead M. M. Thomas to reject the proposed pluralistic criteria precisely because of their narrow cultural particularity. He submits that "Christ is a more transcendent, universal ultimate" than these criteria (Thomas 1990, 58). It is more imperialistic in his view to approach other faith traditions with supreme allegiance to such principles than to do so with primary commitment to Jesus Christ.

As Lesslie Newbigin writes, "We all long for justice, and it is these passionate struggles that tear the world to pieces. There is a tragic irony in Paul Knitter's citation of Aloysius Pieris's definition of true religion as a 'revolutionary urge, a psycho-social impulse to generate a new humanity' while his beloved Sri Lanka is being torn to pieces by rival claims to 'justice' and 'liberation'" (Newbigin 1990, 146). In the real world, the claim that "justice" is absolute must translate into the claim that some definitions of justice are wrong and others are right. To suppose that such claims can prove compelling to significant numbers of people without some grounding in an account of the nature of humanity, the causes of suffering and conflict, a cosmic order, goes against all historical precedent. There is a peculiar irony in the proposal of a universal "justice" norm today, at a moment when even within the intellectual and popular arenas in Western countries themselves it is notoriously problematic whether any consistent ground or definition can be given for such a norm.[5]

There are many widespread recent claims that justice cannot be grounded in any universal structure—natural law, pure reason, conscience—but is culturally constructed. (Such claims are often grouped under the general heading of "anti-foundationalism.") Many soteriocentrists seem to see this as a positive development, supportive of their approach. Knitter takes such a tack in his treatment of "relational truth." But it is hard to understand the confidence with which soteriocentrists accept this principle. If anything it seems such a shift *heightens* the significance of particularistic traditions. Universal and transcendent principles can relativize particulars. But to stress that all truth is relational, involving a web of specific assumptions and historical conditions, is to say that dispositions or behaviors always retain a particularistic character. In moving from a theocentric to a soteriocentric view, Knitter shifts from emphasis on a disposition toward the divine to emphasis on a social relatedness. Regardless of cultural differences, he affirms that one can reach universal judgments about where any par-

---

[5] Soteriocentric pluralists would seem to be committed to defending a kind of Rawlsian liberalism in this debate (see John Rawls, *A Theory of Liberalism*).

ticular religious practice "stands" in relation to social justice. Whereas "doctrinal criteria . . . prove too controversial and prone to ideology" to serve as grounds of judgment, the needs of the oppressed are presumably not liable to these deficiencies in the same measure. But the claim that thoroughly socially conditioned perspectives on thoroughly social conditions will agree with each other more readily than socially conditioned efforts to articulate universals is breathtaking. The opposite seems plainly the case: people within the same religious tradition, people ostensibly applying the same principles, still often disagree violently about what practically constitutes justice.

This point was implicitly clear in the example with which we began this chapter. The interfaith movement on behalf of the quarry workers also encountered an interfaith opposition. The liberation theology of religions is, unlike the other versions of pluralistic theology, an intrinsically conflictual vision. It is the only honestly missionary and exclusivist form of pluralistic theology, if we might put it that way. It is pluralistic in denying that justice is served more by one religion than another. But it draws a line between true and false religion across every tradition and takes its stand resolutely on one side. In that sense, it wants an end to the conflict *between* religions, the better to pursue *religious* conflict on behalf of justice.

Suchocki's earlier comments suggest a telling question. Why does the soteriocentric analysis of religious diversity not apply in the same way to political/social diversity? If a religious norm cannot be made absolute, why can the norm of justice? This question has two sides. The first asks whether any operative vision of justice is not itself actually religious in character. No political or economic system can be instituted without reference to values or commitments that cannot be validated in entirely political or economic terms, just as no mathematical system can prove all of its own premises. In insisting on a *praxis* and justice norm, are soteriocentrists not simply arguing for one kind of religious norm above others?

The second side of the question would be why we should not seek to "disarm" political and social conflict as dramatically as religious conflict. Whatever the ravages of interfaith violence have been, no one could dispute the unparalleled horrors of the twentieth century which have been carried out precisely in the name of social and political ends, in the name of justice: communism, fascism, nationalism. To stretch the definition of religion to include these phenomena is effectively only to admit that soteriocentrism is disguised religious exclusivism, as the first side of the question suggested. But if these disagreements over justice are themselves source for the most virulent and bloody human conflicts, why not advocate a pluralistic solution for them, a realization that it is unjust to suppose one or some visions of justice as superior to others?

Each political and economic tradition is a historically conditioned response to the need to organize human life in our natural environment. They all have a kind of "family resemblance," and many of them have significant areas of overlap. To follow pluralist principles which have been applied to religion, should we not conclude that it is wrong to suppose only one way of organizing human life or some limited group of ways is better than the others? All the same arguments deployed in the religious realm hold at least as well here. Different views on economic justice, justice between the genders, and political structure should flourish, along with the different practices that go with them. Efforts at conversion in these areas should be renounced for mutual understanding and acceptance. A Canadian immigrant in Saudi Arabia would recognize the cultural insensitivity involved in resisting assimilation to the gender relations there and a Pakistani immigrant in the United States would recognize its sexual mores as simply another form of justice-seeking in human relations. Each person or community could be committed to its vision of justice, but recognize that it is relative, shaped by different communities, and that there is no ultimate justification for preferring one over another, certainly no justification for taking this relative difference of perspective on justice to the point of conflict or violence.

Why isn't a "pluralist" prescription for peace and relief of human suffering in the face of varied views of justice such as I have just sketched advocated by soteriocentrists? Clearly they argue that differences over justice are quite a different case than that of religious diversity. But for what reasons? The intolerance, persecution, and violence that accompany disputes over justice are in the soteriocentric perspective regrettable but necessary. It seems this must be so either because political and social matters are more important than religious ones or because they can be known with more certainty.

The claim that the social steps to human peace and happiness can be known with more certainty and universal assent than any other religious truth is a fascinating one. It can certainly be defended—though Knitter, for instance, has not offered to do so at any length. Usually the argument advanced is that we can at least tell with greatest certainty some conditions that are *incompatible* with human well-being: arbitrary torture and execution, engineered starvation, systematic dishonesty. This is certainly true. And, as soteriocentrists point out, one is hard pressed to find religious traditions that commend such things. There is such widespread cross-traditional agreement on these points that if such behaviors are practiced, they are invariably understood in other categories. Dismemberment of criminals is torture to some and justice to others. The policies of the Khmer Rouge were the necessary medicine of social liberation to some and genocide to others. In fact, we might say that the significant agreement across religious traditions about what is *not* conducive to human good (murder, lying, theft) is most diluted in its impact precisely by the religious differences (within and between traditions) over justice. Killing save in self-defense may be nearly universally condemned. But the exceptions always arise precisely through appeals to justice. This may be in one case an argument that the order of society and its protection against disruptions internal and external justify the exercise of state violence. In another case it may be the argument that the evils of current social structures legitimate whatever active violence is required against whatever persons in order to pursue more just arrangements.

Each religious tradition in various ways identifies conditions incompatible with human well-being and claims that its practices and commitments can be utilized to overcome these evils. Since this is so, the preference for soteriocentrism's "justice norm" must come not from its unique ability to notice such conditions but from the greater certainty of its diagnoses and solutions. This is the crucial problem. Soteriocentrism borrows a certain aura of objectivity from the Western forms of social analysis it uses—whether Marxist, Weberian, Durkheimian, or later feminist or liberation developments of these. But even if we were to grant that there were some kind of functional certainty to such descriptions—bypassing for the moment the sharp conflict *among* them— this would be at best an instrumental certainty. Let us suppose, for instance, that some favored school of economists could tell us steps to take that would inevitably lead, over however long a period, to the permanent elimination of malnutrition and starvation in Ethiopia. This knowledge is effectively worthless without any comparable certainty as to how, or even why, we or others might be brought to take these steps. Even if we limit the contribution of the religions to the level of motivation, we are turned back to their contrasting visions as integrally involved in debates about justice.

In fact, the religious traditions are much more than a source of motivation. It will hardly do to say that since all the religions teach their adherents to do good, once soteriocentrists define the good the religions will fall in line to achieve it. The justice norm is a very sophisticated and serious attempt to make the golden rule a standard across the religions. The attempt is all the more plausible because nearly all faith traditions carry some negative or positive version of that rule: do unto others as you would have them do unto you. The problem is not that this principle is alien to most people. But what you want for yourself may not be what others want for themselves. In sincerely exercising the same principle, we may treat each other quite differently, order our societies quite differently. The question is whether we should do unto others as *they* would wish to have done to them, and whether there is any objective standard to judge between our varying wishes. Divergent constitutive visions of human good thus are unavoidably part of the picture.

Whatever special force the faith traditions can add to specific struggles for justice must come from the independent force religion has in human life. But presumably it has that force only because of the believer's conviction that it makes a difference, that in molding a life through the specific elements of this tradition a person is doing something of distinctive worth even should that process run contrary to the appeals of family, country, self-interest. The characteristic aspect of religious social transformation is the integration of the substance of the good sought and the motivation for seeking it. There is a debilitating paradox in the soteriocentric assumption that the religions can be engineered to provide separately, as it were, the private motives for justice-making while accepting the definition of justice provided from some supervening perspective.

It is not that this arrangement is inconceivable. There seem to be periods and places in various traditions where religion basically adopted this self-understanding: every right-minded person knows what duty is, and the role of God or religion is to give us the power to do our duty. This is a recipe for stifling the religions as independent sources of social critique. Soteriocentrists seem far too satisfied with having ruled out the argument "God is on our side alone, therefore we are right." They have left intact a "Gott mit uns" philosophy of another sort, rationalized by the perennial reverse argument: we fight for true justice, *ergo* we are serving the divine.

The liberation path to pluralistic theology is the main road. As I have indicated, there is an internal imperative for change in the face of the sins of Christian exclusivism. Much of this critique needs to be accepted. The focus on concrete efforts to overcome oppression and human suffering is welcome. And there is some very acute insight in the work of Knitter, Krieger, and Suchocki.

But soteriocentric pluralistic theology is untenable in its full form. It condemns all claims to know a universal religious truth or attain a religious end different from others. Instead, the liberation theology of religions claims an absolute validity for the praxis of justice and liberation. The argument that particularistic religious claims lead inevitably to domination, while claims to know what justice requires lead to liberation is incoherent, not least because the second claim is an instance of the first type. The difficulties of this approach are not overcome by the tentative formulations it is sometimes given as a "heuristic device" or a practical imperative. The instructive interaction between a dialogue imperative and a justice imperative indicates that a viable ethical focus for interfaith relation will require two complementary elements. On the one hand it will require a structural acknowledgment that any set of social norms

is chosen from among others and this choice itself is pervasively constituted by religious elements. Therefore we cannot expect from this quar-
ter a supervening agenda that can be enforced upon the religions. On
the other hand it will require a more straightforward willingness to claim
that certain norms are both universal and superior to others, including
others shaped by contrasting religious elements. I will return to these
issues in chapter 7. But before turning to such proposals, I will seek in
the following chapter to summarize some of the features of the pluralistic theologies we have reviewed.

4

No Other Way?

Pluralistic Theology as Apologetics

If pluralistic views represent a radical revolution in Christian thought, and this revolution applies above all to our relation with other faiths, we might reasonably expect that they would point us toward some dramatic new mode of interaction beyond those already existing. The past three chapters opened with brief vignettes drawn from the interreligious context of India. I return to that context to inquire whether pluralistic theologies in fact do provide any distinctive guidance for a concrete pluralistic situation. Even if we limit ourselves to the relations between Christianity and Hinduism, the extraordinarily rich culture of the Indian subcontinent presents a wide range of options. Observers identify at least four major types of dialogue, with many more variations (see Heim 1988, 88-101).

The first type we might call the dialogue of doctrine, corresponding to the Indian path of *jnana* or knowledge. This interaction focuses on the texts, teachings, and interpreters of the Vedic tradition. From this perspective, Hinduism is primarily the great Sanskritic path that runs from the Vedas and Upanishads down through the epics like the *Mahabharata* (which includes the Bhagavad Gita) to the *bhakti* texts. Dialogue with Hinduism requires careful study and appreciation of the many schools, the varied practices, the cosmic and social visions contained in this tradition. Then it calls for a mutual questioning of Christian categories and Hindu ones. From Robert de Nobili to Raimundo Panikkar, this path has had many distinguished Christian participants. It offers the incontestable benefits of encounter with an intellectual tradition of unsurpassed subtlety and depth. But it is also troubled by the fact that this tradition has been exclusively associated with dominant caste groups and is sharply repudiated by many, perhaps even a majority, of India's contemporary citizens.

The second mode of dialogue could be called the dialogue of spiritualities, similar to the Indian path of *bhakti* or devotion. It focuses on spiritual practice and on the transformation of the devotee. Whether the practice is yogic, meditational, or cultic, this dialogue looks to the inner world, the "cave of the heart," where direct experience replaces concepts. Not study, but participation is the avenue of encounter. This is a dialogue of mutual spiritual discipline. In it, Christians and Hindus engage in each other's practice, seeking a common core of mystical experience. The path was pioneered in modern India by the Frenchman Swami Abhishiktananda and is carried on today in many forms. It can appear to bypass interminable discussion in favor of a practical form of unity. But it also runs the risk of disengagement from both the social and intellectual life of people in both communities.

The third mode of dialogue might be considered a dialogue of reformation, analogous to the Indian path of *karma*. It focuses not on the traditional past or the inner spirit but on the contemporary social needs of Indian society. From this perspective, the encounter of Christians and Hindus should take place primarily around the challenges of nation-building, of economic development, of service to the poor. P. D. Devanandan and his successor, M. M. Thomas, have been tireless advocates of this approach. It has the advantage of being most congenial to the modernizing cultural elites who share some Western perspectives on these issues. But this is also a drawback, in that this tack appears to avoid contact with the deep streams of traditional culture and to be identified for many Indians more with secular than religious themes.

A fourth mode of dialogue has been proposed more recently, a "popular dialogue," which seeks serious encounter with village Hinduism, the folk faith of the vast population which has never fully participated in the Sanskritic culture. This is a piety handed on in oral tradition, in custom and festival, image and code. Attention to this context is especially advocated by Christian leaders of *dalit* or outcaste background, who see this as the true indigenous religious culture out of which they have come. This path has the undeniable attraction of focusing distinctly on the religion of the poor. But it has the constraints of being less accessible to academic study. There are also voices, both Hindu and Christian, which question whether this popular Hinduism has sufficient liberating potential to be given primary priority in dialogue.

This sketch reminds us that the most obvious issues in dialogue are whom we shall choose to talk with (and who will choose to talk with us) and what we will talk about. On this point we see that the various forms of pluralistic theology would have decidedly different tendencies. Hick's pluralistic hypothesis looks toward fellow philosophers and the dialogue of doctrine. Smith's emphasis on faith expressed through traditions has strong affinities with the dialogue of spiritualities. Knitter's concern for justice clearly inclines toward an encounter based on social transformation. This same variety of emphasis exists among inclusivists, as well.

I would suggest that the pluralistic doctrines add nothing distinctive to these existing dialogues. There is no specific type or agenda of dialogue that is added to our repertoire by virtue of pluralistic views. Nor are those views a necessary condition or a uniquely effective motivation for engaging in such interactions. All of these dialogues were in fact pioneered and carried on by persons inclusivist if not exclusivist by pluralist reckoning. These people were involved in rethinking Christian views of the religions, and developed a variety of perspectives responsive to the various aspects of Hinduism they engaged. Today those of pluralist conviction participate, but hardly predominate in these dialogues. And they seem subject to the same kinds of internal conflict over the most fruitful paths of encounter as Christians of other views.

Certainly persons of an obdurately exclusivist outlook are unlikely to value some types of dialogue. But it is hard to see a meaningful difference on this score between inclusivists and pluralists, or in terms of the vigor with which their representatives oppose religious persecution or oppression. And it is not apparent that pluralists enter dialogue with any fewer preconceptions than others; certainly the dogmas about religion reflected in the three theories we have considered in the first chapters severely limit the degree of challenge one might expect in interreligious exchange. Pluralistic theologies, in short, offer no distinctive guidance for the concrete conduct of interreligious encounter and no unique motivation for pursuing it. Their differences from inclusivist views are to be sought not so much in the concrete arena of contact with other faiths, but closer to home.

EXCLUSIVISM IN THE MIRROR: MAKING WESTERN CRITIQUES OF CHRISTIANITY THE NORMS FOR ALL RELIGION

In the earlier chapters I offered some precise criticisms of specific pluralistic theologies. In this chapter I wish to highlight some of their common elements and to frame a more general critique. My primary point is that these theologies are in fact thoroughly inclusivist and culturally particular in their character. These features would not be failings, were they not so contrary to the pluralists' own claims. There is something wrong with principles that lead their adherents to so misread their own project. These principles have their primary roots not so much in discoveries made in the substance of the various religious traditions as in the premises of modern Western critiques of religion.

There is a paradoxical feature of pluralistic theologies. Of the vast religious diversity of the world, the pluralists affirm as fully valid only that narrow segment where believers have approximated the authors' approach to their own traditions. According to them, the many faiths of the world—even in their exclusivist versions—may all save in some sense. But they do so only according to a plan the pluralist understands and others do not. It is clearly stated that those without a pluralistic understanding of their faith stand urgently in need of fulfillment and enlightenment. Without such conversion they and their traditions are at least latent threats to world peace and justice, morally dangerous as well as theologically wrong. Oddly enough, these opponents of religious claims to superiority see no hope, not only for the Christian tradition but for all other religions and the world itself, unless their views prevail.

This is ironic. Given the apparent insistence on the validity of many ways, we might expect pluralists to affirm the full and equal value of religious paths that are inclusivist or exclusivist in character. But they seem very hesitant to do so. In fact they themselves adopt a classically inclusivist posture. Unenlightened, sincere devotees of various faiths may be saved both historically and cosmically. But not on the basis they imagine. It is the Real, or faith, or justice as the pluralists know them that redeem. Ignorance and error need not bar others from salvation. Yet only the priests of world theology can lead us to its full realization. To borrow a phrase from the history of Christian theology of religions, pluralistic theology regards itself as the "crown and fulfillment" of every religious tradition.

We have reviewed with some care three primary versions of pluralistic theology. Some, like Hick, base their theory on a claim about the truth behind and beyond the historical forms of particular religions: a single absolute which can as well be characterized as impersonal or personal, to which all humans respond on the path toward a single ultimate fulfillment. Others, like Smith, work from the hypothesis of a common ineffable human orientation within all religious traditions which gives life meaning. Still others, like Knitter, conclude that appropriate judgments about various forms of faith can be made only with some common standard of justice which measures their social effects. These are significantly different approaches.

Yet there are real similarities. One of the most dramatic is the way that each appears to deconstruct the pluralism it seeks to affirm. They insist that despite any apparent indications to the contrary, there is no diversity in the religious object (Hick), in the human religious attitude (Smith), or the primary religious function (Knitter). Thus they agree that the faiths cannot be regarded as serious religious alternatives. Pluralist authors may object to this characterization, saying that in fact they recognize the historical particularity of the traditions and do not expect or desire an end to variety in the cultural forms religion takes. This is not really a direct response. The relevant question is whether these authors are willing to affirm that in any cases different religions may offer alternative religious objects or truly alternative religious ends or fundamentally alternative religious functions or attitudes. This is precisely what they deny. Religions may be variations on a theme, but not distinct themes. Perhaps no intention is more frequently professed by pluralists than to take religions seriously on the religions' own terms. Yet their agreement that they cannot be true alternatives essentially cancels out the possibility of giving fullest play to the religions in their own terms.

One of the common elements in these different formulations of pluralistic theologies is their profound religious motivation. The somewhat patronizing attitude I have described is animated by a desire to protect the plausibility of all faiths. All three of the writers I have surveyed are committed to providing, to use Hick's phrase, a "religious view of religion." They seek to maximize harmony and parity among the religious traditions, but to do this only on grounds that will validate religious faiths as trustworthy in some intrinsic way. It is not acceptable to any of them, or to most other pluralists, that the religions should be equally illusory, or be seen as equally useful on purely naturalistic grounds. Their task is a fundamentally apologetic one, and their apologetics are of a very particular cultural sort.

Pluralist theologies bear throughout their methods and categories the indelible marks of Western Christianity's conflict with modernity. The global applicability of their theories of religion is hostage to the universality of that conflict. Their arguments for religious equivalence in the traditions depart from very particularistic Western assumptions. This is a problematic quality, given pluralists' own counsel to beware claims of universality and superiority when advanced for other particularistic norms.

Pluralistic approaches are noted for their conviction that the various religious traditions may be seen as equally and independently valid. No precedence attaches to the particular beliefs or experience of any particular tradition. This contention attracts the most notice, both negative and positive. The minor and often unstated premise of this conviction, however, is that if all faiths are valid, they can be so only by passing muster at the bar of critical modern Western thought, the same conditions to which Christianity or Judaism have long had to answer.

Many Christians in the past set terms by which other religions must be considered false. Pluralistic theologies now set terms under which religions must be considered true. The more exclusivistic Christian theologies of religion commended conversion to Christian faith, though not necessarily to a single cultural form of it. Pluralistic theologies require conversion of all faiths not to any form of Christianity, but to the cultural structures of plausibility against which modern Western Christianity has been defined. The fullness of religious truth (i.e., a pluralistic outlook on the traditions) is in fact only available to those suffi-

ciently drawn into the modernized international economic and political
system to have access to the revelatory conditions of pluralism and to
their proper interpretation. Whether this represents the overthrow of all
particularistic norms or the exchange of one for another is less obvious
than pluralists assume.

Philip Almond, in *The British Discovery of Buddhism*, states in conclusion:

> What strikes the reader of Victorian accounts of Buddhism is the
> sense of sovereign confidence with which—however they assimi-
> lated or rejected it—they discussed, summarized, analyzed, and
> evaluated it. However ideologically uncertain they were at the level
> of conscious reflection, they saw themselves as possessing the cri-
> teria upon which the judgment of the religious, social and cultural
> value, not only of Buddhism, but of the East as a whole could be
> made. . . . And it was they who determined the framework in which
> Buddhism was imaginatively constructed, not only for themselves,
> but also in the final analysis for the East itself (Almond 1988, 140).

The framework within which Buddhism was "constructed" by Victo-
rians was determined not only by explicit Christian confessional commitments but to an equal extent by the contemporary critical *challenges*
to Christianity. Almond illustrates how a historical Gautama Buddha
was resolutely assembled and purged of mythical elements, on the model
of the search for the historical Jesus. As for intellectuals of that age a
"usable Jesus" had to be one reconstructed in line with the current standards of historical study, so automatically they assumed the same of a
"usable Buddha."

That such a process might not comport with the religious tradition's
own perspective was of little concern. Religious attributions of value to
either Buddha or Christ which could not be grounded in European historical reason were equally suspect. The Buddha of mid- and late-Vic-
torian times "is an object conceptually related to a developing naturalistic view of the universe, to an emergent critical view of the Bible, to
an India under British hegemony, to a world view increasingly determined by a geologically and biologically based chronology and pro-
gressively less by a Biblical chronology and cosmology" (Almond 1988,
56). Almond notes, for instance, how the Victorian discussion of karmic
rebirth was heavily shaped by contemporary perceptions of Darwinism.

There is ample reason to see similarities between Almond's example
and the construction of contemporary pluralistic "meta-theologies." The
following is a typical recommendation of such a meta-theology:

> We must learn, thus, how to discern the basic patterns and frame-
> works of the several great religious and secular traditions of ori-

entation which were created by humankind in its long history—to discern what I have called their fundamental categorial structures—so that we will be able to compare them with each other directly, evaluating the strong points and the weak points of each as frames of orientation for life today. Thus we will come into a better position to construct a frame of orientation (or a group of such frames) which can provide significant guidance for contemporary existence (Kaufman, n.d.).

The agenda outlined, in the terms given here, could be and in fact is adopted by scholars, apologists, and theologians within any number of different traditions. But what the author has in mind, and what constitutes the effort as meta-theology, is not simply the act of study and comparison and judgment. Rather it is the framework of commitment within which one works, the claim not to impose a particular norm as universal. Christian theology, "dharma-ology," and so on are done in the context of commitment to their own principles, in distinction from other possibilities. Meta-theology compares, evaluates, and constructs without being constrained in the same way by prior limitations of tradition, but only by the supposedly common and objective features of, say, "contemporary existence."

But this is largely an optical illusion. There is no "God's-eye view" from which to discern the "fundamental categorial structures" of the religions, no non-particular interpretation of "contemporary existence." A meta-theology claims to offer a view which is not a Christian one or a liberal Western one alongside an orthodox Jewish one or a liberal Muslim one, but rather a view on a different level and in some qualitative way beyond such particularity. It is a claim that cannot be validated. To demonstrate that one, for instance, no longer grants authority to Christian or Muslim norms is no evidence that one does not hew to others just as particular.

Can any practice actually make good on this project in such a way as to constitute a different *order* of religious reflection? I believe not. Nor is it immediately apparent why such a claim should be needed. Advocates of a hermeneutic of suspicion are not hard put to provide an explanation.[1] Black theologians, feminist theologians, liberation theologians, conservative evangelical theologians, all have a place of purchase as it were from which to insist that their theological concerns be taken seriously. It is because this theology is the voice of African-Americans, of women, of oppressed peoples, of the Bible, that we must attend to it. Take these voices seriously or be racist, sexist, imperialist, secularist. There are significant audiences in each instance who find this a com-

---

[1] This paragraph reflects the substance of such a critique directed at me and others by Thomas Dean in "The Conflict of Christologies," pp. 24-31.

pelling case. The audience for theological concerns, predominantly those of white, male, North Atlantic, academe-based, "liberal" scholars, is in this regard a less readily compelling one. If such views are to compete in the first-order conflict of interpretations, they would appear to be at a distinct disadvantage.

The "meta-position" move tries to borrow from the critiques of some of the other groups and to build openness to such critiques into a positive position whose imperatives will be respected in their own right. Take our theological concerns seriously or be intolerant. A cynic who surveyed the ruling North Atlantic theological elite over time, from its concern with evangelical orthodoxy in the nineteenth century, to the liberal Protestantism of the early part of this century, to the current efforts at meta-theology, might see basically similar groups guarding their prerogatives, the main one being that of arbitrating or integrating all other theological views.

There is more truth in this than I, for one, find comfortable to acknowledge. A key step takes place in the transition from the commendation of certain attitudes—careful study of other religions in their own terms, sensitivity to cultural differences, appreciation of the variety within a single tradition, concern for injustice—to the assumption that there is one general meta-position constituted by the sum total of such concerns. This is a universal claim subject to the same interrogation as any other. One of the obvious things this means is that it is open to the crude empirical test of whether people claiming such a meta-position have a monopoly on these attitudes or exhibit them to a greater degree than all others.

It seems to me a nice question which approach tends to the most invidious "hardening of the categories": commitment to a religious principle or truth of a normative sort, or commitment to a normative scheme for interpreting all religions. In fact the two things go together. A religious truth claim is associated in a loose or integral way with some field in which that claim is grounded. The principles of religious faith to some extent constitute the field of considerations within which they are found valid (though it appears that this does not mean automatic validation—that principles can themselves at some point be rejected by reference to this field). And any proposed field of validation, some ordered weighting of factors which may serve as warrants, implies a judgment in principle about what sort of things can be validated.

Bernard McGrane notes in *Beyond Anthropology* that four general paradigms have been used by European Westerners in rough succession to interpret "others" (McGrane 1989). The first paradigm viewed the difference in religious terms between Christian and pagan. The second paradigm developed in the enlightenment and framed the difference in terms of knowledge: others were distinguished by error and superstition. A third paradigm arose in the nineteenth century and construed the

difference as rooted in time: Western humanity was at a different stage of development than "primitive" societies. Most recently the dominant paradigm has become that of cultures, a framework that equalizes difference, rejects larger schemes that would interpret the variations into some meaning, and, in McGrane's view, tends to press all diversity into "mere" difference.

My sole interest in McGrane's interesting typology is the way that it illustrates a fundamental fact. Openness to others "on their own terms" is always a limited possibility, just as measurement at the outer bounds of physics is. The construal of difference in religious terms—Christian/pagan—no doubt introduced one set of blinders into the relationship. But it is also true that it allowed a certain kind of openness. The wise and virtuous pagan could be routinely recognized within such categories and even celebrated by persons convinced their Christian faith constituted a sufficient and positive difference. An age that put behind it this religious lens for difference might increase its appreciation of other religions and mitigate certain kinds of arrogance. But if the difference itself were now construed in terms of ignorance and knowledge, or primitiveness and development, new types of blindness and chauvinism came in to replace the earlier ones.

Nirad Chaudhuri, for instance, notes observations on Hinduism by religiously hostile missionaries which provide significant and accurate data lacking in the accounts of later philosophers and academics with other paradigms for difference, and so other blinders (Chaudhuri 1979, 109-112). Meta-theories like the pluralistic theories of religion implicitly presume that the next paradigm in line will in fact break this chain, will bring comprehensive sight rather than a combination of new vision . . . and new blindness. They have not come to terms with Raimundo Panikkar's axiom that a pluralistic system is a contradiction in terms (Panikkar 1987, 110).

If one brings to the fore a scheme for dealing with religious truth claims—as for instance requiring these to be based on "universally available data" and to be "in principle" agreeable to those of all faiths—one definitely tends toward a certain kind of openness toward various traditions. On the other hand, at the same time, one also absolutizes a *commitment* to interpret the convictions of each of these traditions from a particular religious viewpoint (the one which is, so to speak, the "shadow" of the field of justification proposed). Such a purported meta-position recognizes not alternatives but subjects. Varying approaches to religious diversity, including the pluralist one, may be marked by different *patterns* of openness and exclusiveness, but can hardly be simplistically polarized into those which are open and those which are not.

In denying that Christian faith can be taken as the norm for judging other traditions, pluralistic theologies have tended to presume that the norms they have accepted to judge Christianity in the modern West *can*

be taken as universal standards for reconstructing all faiths. They intend to affirm the various faiths in the strongest way. To do this, of course, they must first be assimilated to the terms in which religion can plausibly be affirmed. Since the right-minded person who is the judge of this plausibility remains a very particular kind of Western intellectual, this process looks very much like the process of the Western construction of Buddhism in its own image which Almond described above. The one looks as imperialistic as the other, unless some strong explicit argument is provided as to why the terms of modern Western thought are a superior and universal truth. But pluralistic theologians claim to reject on principle any privilege for standards drawn from within Western cultures.

Few however are willing to spell out the implications as clearly as Panikkar. He writes, "The modern kosmology [sic], which assumes that time is linear, that history is paramount, that individuality is the essence of Man, that democracy is an absolute, that technocracy is neutral, that social Darwinism is valid, and so on, cannot offer a fair platform for the dialogue. The basis for the dialogue cannot be the modern Western myth" (Panikkar 1989, xiii). Here Panikkar is a good deal more pluralistic and consistent than many of his companions may find comfortable. For the problem is that each of the major pluralistic theologies takes one or more elements of "the modern Western myth" as the absolute basis on which the religions can be interpreted into a unified scheme.

In each case it is a perceived failing or vulnerability of religion—paradigmatically of Judaism and Christianity—in the face of modern critique which becomes the basis for reconstructing all religion. It is hardly an accident that pluralistic theology, in its definition and treatment of the religions, takes care to inoculate them against just those objections theologians in the West have found so troubling. It would do no good to insist that all religions were as valid as Christianity—or that Christianity was as valid as other religions—if they were all understood in a manner that made none appear valid at all. It is in terms of what will count as validating religion per se that the pluralist theologians draw so powerfully on their particularistic cultural convictions. In fact, some of the pluralist theologians are quite explicit as to the way in which they have universalized what in origin can be seen as a Christian apologetic view. So, for instance, Smith notes with approval Karl Barth's distinction between faith and religion, observing that it is only necessary to extend the distinction on an equal basis to all traditions (Smith 1981, 117).

The question is whether the various religious traditions are equally enthusiastic about this care on their behalf, seeing that it entails a prior acceptance of the validity of Western interpretations of religion. To accept the affirmation of their faith given by the pluralistic theologies, those of other religions need to agree first that it is actually still their

faith which is affirmed when it is in the translated form these theologies give it. Second, they need to be willing for their religious life to be cast in the mold pluralistic theology has set for it. The offer to be inoculated against the dangers of modernity, made on the solicitous ground that modernity in its Western form is the destiny of every faith, is apparently an offer that can be refused. It can be refused either on the grounds that not everyone is required to replicate the West's history or on the grounds that the specific responses to modernity recommended are not highly convincing.

If those in other traditions are not willing to adopt these categories, they seem to lose the dialogical parity that pluralistic theologians earlier so strongly demanded for them. Such a view is expressed surprisingly often. At one conference a well-known pluralist theologian said, in good humor, to a decidedly non-pluralist Jewish theologian, the veteran of long years of interfaith discussions, "With your views, you shouldn't be involved in dialogue." "Nevertheless, I am," he replied, and suggested that it was perhaps the pluralist theory that ought to be adjusted and not the reality he represented. In any event, the Jewish theologian continued, when liberal Christians and liberals of other traditions get together to talk about their liberalism, he did not call that dialogue. This affable exchange was capped by another pluralist voice in the audience who allowed that though his Jewish compatriot might be able to dialogue "after a fashion," he would be unable to participate in authentic dialogue until he had adopted a thoroughly pluralistic outlook. Here it would seem that the old lamented triumphalist attitudes of Christians remain in vigorous health, if in different forms.

No doubt a primary motive of pluralistic theologies is to affirm the validity of various religious traditions. But it is an implicit primary assumption of such theologies that these traditions are without exception indefensible as they stand. Only as demythologized, adapted to the categories of critical historical thought, put in the context of Western understandings of epistemology, and measured against modern conceptions of equality and justice can these religions be pronounced valid. It could be no other way, since only in these terms can Christianity itself possibly be valid for these writers. Pluralistic theologies thus presuppose the truth of one version of normative Christianity in the intra-Christian debate. Though they resist the notion that one religion might be distinctively true in contrast to another, they seem committed to the proposition that within traditions—most particularly Christianity—one or some versions are decisively preferable to others.

In this indirect but determinative way, Christianity remains normative as a kind of photographic negative. The shape that Christian faith may take is determined by contemporary standards: the specific content inside the silhouette of Christianity may be washed out and replaced with the content of any other faith. But the boundaries of the image

remain set and there is no possibility of religions bringing their own profile to change the outline. Whether this is done crudely, like a face photographed inside a boardwalk cutout, or with exquisite skill at retouching, the principle remains the same. And it severely limits any independent critique the religions might offer on those contemporary Western standards themselves.

It is frequently remarked that enthusiasm for the pluralistic enterprise is more vivid among Christians than their neighbors. Some in the various traditions suspect that the effort is only a new and sophisticated form of proselytism. Others suggest that despite claims to offer the first truly common religious project, the enterprise in essence conscripts the religions to help deal with Christian or Western problems in Christian and Western terms. These criticisms are levelled against Christian advocacy of interreligious dialogue generally, not only pluralist perspectives. But we have already seen criticism raised specifically against pluralistic theologies on the same moral grounds that animated them.[2] The charge is that they represent a "commodification" of religion, an attempt to define away the world-shaping power of the faiths and make them each forms or "brands" of a common product. This "religion for the marketplace," as Lesslie Newbigin calls it, has less to do with respect for the faiths than their domestication into consumer choices that will not trouble dominant orders. It is not surprising that there is no great rush among religious traditions to adopt the constraints of the pluralistic self-understanding.

MAKING THE WORLD SAFE FOR RELIGION: THE APOLOGETIC TASK OF PLURALISTIC THEOLOGIES

Though the pluralistic theologies we have reviewed include passionate criticisms of the Christian tradition, they have a positive intent in drawing the true boundaries of an acceptable Christianity. The ringing denunciations can easily obscure the fact that the end result of these theories is to insulate Christianity from the attacks it has long suffered. The antidote to the toxic particularity that believes only its own faith can be right is the recognition that no major religion is at bottom wrong. If we are to respect the validity of the various religions, we can hardly fail to respect the validity of Christianity. In the pluralist schemes, the religions do not break ranks. If supposed the highest religion, Christianity would be a threat. But if Christianity were taken to be a false religion it would be a dangerous precedent; confirming ironically its own past exclusivist belief in such things. This is nicely illustrated, for

---

[2] See Kenneth Surin's argument in regard to John Hick and especially W. C. Smith, which is summarized in chapter 2.

instance, in W. C. Smith's extended argument that "idolatry" does not and has never existed . . . except perhaps in the religion of those who attributed it to others (Smith 1987).

The conclusions of pluralistic theologies which are presented as shocks to Christianity's self-importance also at the same time secure Christianity an apologetic victory it has been otherwise unable to win so decisively. Despite its religious wars, its implication in colonialism, its philosophical trials, Christianity must be fundamentally true. It must be an authentic response to the divine, for pluralistic theologies insist one can say no less of any great tradition. There is a kind of inclusivism in reverse here, a validation of Christianity based upon a proposed insight into the common religious truth of which it is one cultural expression.

In Christianity there is rough parity of response to "the Real" or realization of "faith" or pursuit of justice with that in other great traditions. The dramatic denunciations of Christian tradition offered by some pluralists apply only to that in Christianity which they at the same time insist is secondary and conditioned. In this their strategy differs not at all from the most traditionalist defenders who will insist that the evils of Christianity have to do only with incidentals. A truly radical rejection of Christianity or any other major faith is precisely what pluralistic theories seek to forestall by definition. It is not a metaphysical or a moral possibility on their maps.

Pluralist critique of Christianity, for all its vehemence, draws a line beyond which critique cannot go. Radical feminists who see Christianity as patriarchy plain and simple, demonic without remainder; Christians who believe that the religious end they seek is distinctive and will not be attained by those devoted to alternative aims; a Buddhist who sincerely believes Christianity is the product of a lower level of understanding, its adherents attaining at best a transient good: all these in the pluralists' view are wrong. Yet as we saw in Hick's treatment of naturalism, rejection of any major religion or of religion generally is treated as a covert form of participation in it. The common thread here is a consistent disinclination to face otherness. There are no intractable others, and those who claim there are, who even claim to *be* other, are mistaken.

This strategy is unpersuasive in two ways. What it claims to assure as the truth of all religion is too generic and too detached from the concrete particulars of the traditions to be satisfying to their adherents. It is too close to being a truth that is not recognizable as "religious" at all in terms that carry significance. Even for believers troubled by the acids of modernity, this is too thin a guarantee to replace the hopes of a concrete tradition. Second, it seeks to minimize the genuine venture of religious commitment. There are possibilities which may be realized if we choose one path and other possibilities, perhaps even mutually exclusive ones, that will be realized on another path. In addition, there is a real possibility that we and/or others may be simply wrong: mistaken or deluded. It is a positive value in my view to face these possibilities squarely, whether in the case of a single religious tradition or in the case of all of them collectively. Attempts to make of religious faith something that can be conventionally assumed appear to me both misguided in principle and futile in practice.

W. C. Smith in particular stresses the value of incontrovertibility for religion. We can focus most clearly on the true nature of faith, he suggests, when we are not troubled by uncertainties about its object or our destinies. This leads him to strip away from true religion everything about which there may be such differences. Hick in his own way makes a similar move, when he baptizes even consistent naturalism as a covert religious adjustment to the Real. Knitter likewise turns away from the "doctrinal" matters about which he sees religious disagreement as inevitable toward a search for a single, concrete definition of justice which would serve as the true focus of religion. This search for certainty, the retreat from seeking it in particular revelations or rational principles to claiming it in a postulate, an experience, or a practical method, is a shorthand history of modern Western thought. None of these proposed certainties are really proof against the suspicions they propose to overcome. The empirical situation of cultural and religious diversity is itself a primary factor in making increasing numbers of people *aware* that there are diverse options, that these options lead in varying directions, and that something is at stake in the difference.

The three themes emphasized by the three versions of pluralistic theology are all ones that have played a dominant role in Western modernity: epistemological doubt, dualizing subject and object; historical consciousness, limiting texts or traditions to their times; and a political vision of individual rights and equality which casts into doubt all social orders as conventions. Each, in other words, in its understanding of the religions emphasizes different elements of what Panikkar called the modern Western "myth." In Hick's case the elements are primarily philosophical, in Smith's primarily historical, and in Knitter's primarily social.

John Hick's pluralistic hypothesis forbids any religious tradition to claim its end is better or even different than another's. In his highly abstracted vision of religion's bottom line, no major faith can possibly be wrong. For Hick there clearly is no way to make this claim about religion's truth unless the statement can be insulated from the denials of modern critical thought, just as a claim that Judaism or Christianity in particular were true would have to be defended. In order to affirm the universal validity of religion it is necessary to put every religion in a defensible form.

As I pointed out in discussing his hypothesis, Hick's early career focused on a philosophical apologetic for Christian beliefs. Eschatological verification is a key concept he developed to defend these beliefs as meaningful truth claims, in the face of logical positivist charges that they were empty of any predictive content. In his pluralistic theory of religion this epistemological apologetic strategy, developed in the face of a modern Western philosophical movement, is universalized and absolutized. But do other religions choose to be defined and constituted in these terms? Even in the West, not all Christians by any means have agreed to do so. Are the standards proposed by the analytic philosophical critics who shaped Hick's work in fact universal ones, binding on all, and not themselves conditioned?

It would of course be possible to affirm the salvific effectiveness of varied religions (as some non-pluralistic theologies do) or even to affirm the separate and independent validity of all religions, on grounds that were not so insulated from modernity's criticism and which would offer some prospect of criticism *of* modernity. For instance, one might affirm the salvific effectiveness of several religions and hold that this implies the historical events any particular religious tradition deems essential to its life and faith (the death and resurrection of Jesus, the life and career of Muhammad) were actual events of history and took place substantially as believed. Among other things, this would inevitably lead to an ongoing discussion about the validity of the principles of Western historical study. Such a discussion is already suggested in the exchange between Hans Küng and Hossein Nasr described earlier. It has played a significant role in the development of Western historical thought in the past. Indeed, it would seem to be the kind of interaction through which religious diversity makes its most significant contribution to culture.

But that kind of affirmation of the faiths would open itself to possible contradiction. Hick's formulation makes these issues matters of indifference to pluralistic theology's affirmation of the truth of religion, since "both correct and incorrect trans-historical beliefs, like correct and incorrect historical and scientific beliefs, can form part of a religious totality that mediates the Real to human beings, constituting an effective context within which the salvific process occurs" (Hick 1989, 369-370). Certainly if those religions that invest decisive significance in historical events can be induced to accept this perspective, the field of determining what is a correct or incorrect historical belief would be left untroubled to the norms of secular historians.

The value of the immunities which Hick's theory grants to all religions is directly proportional to how acutely threatening the conditions they ameliorate are perceived to be. This is not the same in all cultural or religious contexts. To affirm the equality and truth of all religions can be seen as an apologetic step which greatly eases the ability to commend religion either generically or specifically in a Westernized context. Where there is political guilt and a widespread feeling that religious intolerance is a specially Christian vice, the ability to affirm that all religions are valid has high value. In the face of modern critical objections to religion, it is very attractive to be able to argue that the contradictions among the traditions need not be taken seriously and that all testify in common to a fundamental, if abstract, religious truth. In other religious traditions, or in other contexts, these matters might not receive such overriding priority.

There would seem to be little reason, for instance, for those who have not already accepted the hegemony of Western thought on these crucial points (or who are now questioning it) to submit to the reconstitution of their own traditions so as to be most consistent with that thought. This does not mean of course that the condemnation of Christian sins cannot be appreciated by those of other faiths in its own right. But the interpretation of their faiths themselves is another matter. I suggest that pluralistic theologies look toward the religions to play a consultative role in an unequivocally Western theological project. Tom Driver observes as a sympathetic participant in the pluralists' project that it would be the better part of wisdom to concede that their theologies tell us less about the religions than they do about "Western liberal religious thought at the present time" (Driver 1987, 206).

W. C. Smith is a particularly interesting case because, following rather euphoric estimations of modernity early in his career, he has issued some crusty rebukes to its pretensions. He regularly proclaims that modern rejection of a transcendent realm is a nearly pathological aberration in human thought. The overwhelming majority "of intelligent persons at most times and places, and all cultures other than the recent West, have recognized the transcendent quality of man and the world" (Smith 1981, 189). In his view, this blindness can only be pitied. He also, as we have seen, has sharp words to say about the modern university and its disciplines.

Yet Smith also sees this Western world, so oddly parochial in its secularism, as specially gifted with a historical perspective on faith. The dawn of a new consciousness has come, and it rises in the West. Historical perspective is the key to a new view of religion, one that will cast off as anachronistic many assumptions inherited from the past (whose right-minded consensus regarding the reality of the transcendent he invoked a moment ago to rebuke secularity). What this modern historical perspective uncovers is the intertwining of religions, the illegitimacy of boundaries between them and normative definitions of their centers. This truth of the unity of the world faiths, he says, is "newly discovered" (Smith 1981, 6). It has been revealed by means of the history of religions, that characteristic product of the West and its aberrant anti-transcendent thinking.

Actually, Smith's discovery about the religions had been well prefigured by some historians' argument, a generation earlier, that it was intrinsically impossible to trace and define Christian orthodoxy. There had been no normative Christianity, only different groups that had happened to come out on top politically at different times (see, for example, Bauer 1971). All boundaries were inherently dubious. A similar conclusion was eventually applied to Hinduism and other traditions, Hinduism serving as a paradigm example of the folly of insisting on a normative orthodoxy in a religion. There was more than a little irony in this, since in a prior phase of the history of religions these traditions had already gone through extensive constructive efforts to put them in the approved unitary form of a "religion" as then understood by Western study, which required precisely normative texts and doctrine. But this reformulation was not compelled primarily by the evidence of field studies of the faiths themselves. The impetus came again from much closer at hand: from Western philosophical and cultural trends.

The focus for Smith falls on faith as an existential attitude, a "quiet confidence and joy which enables one to feel at home in the universe and to find meaning in the world and in one's own life, a meaning that is profound and ultimate" (Smith 1979, 12). The uncanny resemblance of this, which we are told is the central and universal religious characteristic, to the existential form of Christian faith developed particularly in the Protestant West in the train of Kierkegaard needs little amplification. It arose specifically in relation to the intensive historical consciousness which Smith celebrates as his key to understanding religions, as a form of faith specially insulated from historical judgments. A gentle internal logic leads Smith to the discovery that this particular way of construing faith is the key to the underlying meaning of all religious traditions. It would have been inconvenient to discover that any religion's fundamental element was one less well suited to prosper under historical critique.

Paul Knitter has taken justice, a thoroughly this-worldly dimension of salvation, as the key to validity in all religious traditions. Any transhistorical referent for religion can be left aside to focus on the struggle against poverty and oppression. In this approach the apologetic dimension perhaps comes through most clearly. In Hick and Smith the faith traditions are implicitly defined into the forms of true religion allowed by modernity. Knitter more straightforwardly says any religion that does not make the struggle against structural social evil primary "is not authentic religion" at all, and he has no desire to affirm it.

All religions are true then, so far as they exercise a preferential option for the poor and eliminate suffering. Knitter and those with a similar approach are quite aware that a particular definition of "justice" from a single religious tradition or from any combination of traditions may serve the interests of some over others. They therefore see the various religious traditions—the "great world religions" which Hick and Smith tend to focus on, but equally importantly feminist, liberationist, and other challenging traditions within or outside them—as constituent voices in an ongoing cycle of dialogue and praxis that will serve continually to refine the end being sought. Since no existing ideal is adequate, criteria taken from the various ideal visions of the various religious traditions along with those taken from the agendas of concrete liberation movements must be used to construct a kind of heuristic guide to salvation, an interim definition of justice, to drive the process on. It is around this emerging truth-in-action that the religions and their members should unite.

Clearly the distinctive feature of this approach is a focus on structural and systemic change that affects the state of oppressed groups. This is not to be confused with those traditions (or any combination of them) of charity, renunciation, or social transformation that have existed among the religions historically. Whatever virtues these past responses of religious traditions to the evils of the human condition might have, they presupposed pre-modern social relations. For that reason, these pluralists conclude that no dialogue or combination among them as they now exist can be adequate for human life. The religions are all in need of reconstruction through Western social analysis. And they need to be reconstructed in such a way as to close ranks behind solutions to human injustice that also stem from particular aspects of that social analysis. The religions are important recruits, but they are recruits for a struggle regarding whose definition and strategy they are to have very little substantive say. The unity of the religions is not a fact but a future accomplishment, to be realized as they bring about what Knitter in Christian language calls "the Kingdom of God."

The primary sources for this type of pluralistic theology are in the Christian movements of liberation theology, in social liberation movements generally, and in the Western tradition of social scientific analysis which undergirds both, including but not limited to Marxist analysis. The need for various faiths to be reconstructed in these terms is stated quite plainly. The equality of the religions resides in the fact that people within them all have moved and do move toward partial realization of the justice which has been primarily revealed and named through these Western categories. But it is perhaps mostly based in the negative fact that all religions as systems are equally far from fulfilling that justice. Just as in the "Reality-centered" pluralistic theology of Hick the religions are not permitted to differ in their actual definitions of reality, and in Smith's faith-centered world theology the religions are not permitted to differ in the nature of their faiths, so in this salvation-centered perspective religions that might have a different conviction about what it means to be saved are left aside as inauthentic.

Knitter's is the most straightforward version of pluralistic theology. The vision of social justice which serves as his norm did not need to wait upon interreligious conversation for its validity to be assured in his eyes. It needs the assistance of other faiths if it is to be fulfilled. He is more than open to receive complementary perspectives from other traditions which will extend or revise the dimensions of the justice he already seeks. But he will accept no changing of the subject. And he is frank to say he has no time, not even time to dialogue, for those who simply do not see what true religion is. So long as all these certainties carry no explicit Christian labels, Knitter seems to feel he can proclaim their ultimacy to his religious neighbors with untroubled conscience. This is, to my mind, a plainly inclusivist approach, which maintains its precarious standing in the pluralist fold only by professing at times an agnosticism about the nature of justice which it does not feel.

THE RELIGIOUS PARTICULARITY
OF PLURALISTIC THEOLOGIES

All three themes developed in these pluralist theories of religion—epistemological, historical, social—intersect dramatically in the subject of salvation. Few aspects of Christianity were so at odds with the assumptions of modern consciousness as this affirmation of a human end beyond full comprehension by our present epistemological or experiential capacities, resting upon events in specific historical locations and periods, and ostensibly available on terms other than those of strict equal opportunity and merit. It is emblematic that the typology which has come to shape recent discussion—the categories of exclusivism, inclusivism, and pluralism—is one which makes little sense except with salvation, and even specifically a postmortem salvation, as the organizing factor. Presuming this univocal reference point, the typology's spectrum unfolds along a range of views on the extent and terms of access to this one salvation. Exclusivists regard their own tradition as in sole possession of religious truth and therefore as the sole path to salvation. Inclusivists believe the salvation which is available through their own tradition is also available within or through other religious traditions because the truth known in this home tradition is effectively if tacitly active there. Pluralists affirm that each religious tradition is independently and equally valid and reject any notion that one may offer secondary access to a salvation more explicitly known or realized elsewhere.

Now if the crucial difference between inclusivists and pluralists were over the extent of the availability of religious fulfillment outside the bounds of one religious tradition, the distinction would hardly be a watershed. A good number of inclusivists have affirmed on their own grounds that all religious traditions are paths leading to religious fulfillment. And yet pluralists generally see the divide between such views and their own as momentous, a "Rubicon." This is apparently because the basis on which inclusivists positively assess possibilities within other traditions is particular and not manifold. A Christian, for instance, may believe that Hinduism and Islam are paths of salvation because the God that Christians know and worship is also present, active, and available for encounter in these traditions.

There are at least two problems with such an inclusivist affirmation from a pluralistic perspective. First, it leaves us with all the liabilities of a specific religious referent like "God." This referent is subject to the critiques which have been levelled against it during recent centuries in the West. It thus can hardly be any more secure a basis on which to affirm the validity of other religions than it is to affirm the validity of Christianity itself. Pluralists may condemn the inclusivist's judgment as arrogant, but it appears they are at least equally concerned that the inclusivist claim is apologetically ineffective. To ground other religions' validity in the biblical God is to do them no favors, seeing how problematic that God is. The same can be said of any specific referent we might substitute from another tradition. In addition, this inclusivist position leaves Christianity as foundationally uncertain as it was before, importing no additional support from the other religions.

Second, to the pluralist the inclusivist approach perpetuates a dangerous religious triumphalism by maintaining that the salvific validity of the other traditions is actually grounded in a reality more adequately grasped by Christians than by members of those traditions themselves. Pluralistic hypotheses try to overcome these liabilities, seeking a religious referent insulated from the critiques of modernity and at the same time not identified with any specific religious tradition or combination of traditions. These hypotheses themselves seem inevitably to run afoul of the same problem, however, since they must involve a claim to understand the character of this religious referent more adequately than any religious tradition does.

Pluralistic theologies most often take one of two decisive steps at this point. Some like Hick and Smith move in a metaphysical direction. They press a radical Kantian divide between the true religious referent ("the Real," or "truth-Reality") which is utterly noumenal and the existential human response to it. All the concrete religious language and practice that characterize the Real or which express the subjective human orientation toward it are then seen in entirety as the products of culture and history. Others like Knitter or Suchocki stress the achievement of justice and social transformation as the fundamental shared religious task.

In the case of the strongly dualistic approach, there is one very dramatic result: the concrete historical religious traditions—"religions" as we actually know them—become secondary in all their specific elements. In the face of modern historical consciousness this is a great benefit, for one can give over completely to historical judgment all the concrete beliefs and practices of the faiths, without reservation or qualm. The results of critical study on these particular elements have virtually no bearing on the validity of their traditions. What Bultmann did for the New Testament is graciously done for all the religious traditions. This leaves Smith, for instance, free while wearing his objective historian's hat to make categorical decisions about the truth or falsity, validity or invalidity of any elements within the "traditions." At the same time he affirms nothing but the highest respect for the existential faith expressed in all these traditions, a faith which as a Christian he believes he fully shares.

From pluralist perspectives then, it is crucially important that concrete religious traditions exist through which persons can relate to "the Real." But nothing particular affirmed or practiced in any or all of these traditions is itself crucially important. Some pluralists might object to this conclusion and point to the generic affirmation of post-axial religions that a limitlessly better possibility is available to humans in relation to the Real. This claim, they may say, is both specific and crucially important: without some form of this belief people would not seek salvation and if it is not true, religion is an illusion. However, I have argued at length in earlier chapters that this affirmation is not a particular assertion at all—as Buddhism makes, for instance, in saying that cessation or nirvana is attainable, or Christians in saying that communion with God is attainable—but rather an abstraction from several particulars. The claim about a "limitlessly better possibility" or "the Real" cannot *substitute* for such particular claims but can only be derivatively confirmed by the validity of at least some of them.

Those "soteriocentric" pluralists who stress justice as their norm address head-on the modern critique of religion as a social narcotic, as itself the source of inequality, oppression, and dominance. Religion, as they define it, will not be subject to this attack. It will necessarily throw its weight on the social scales in such a way as to merit approval or at least attention from those who are least convinced or interested in religious transcendents. The standard modern Western critiques of religious traditions—that they do not sufficiently affirm the supremacy of the individual and the individual's rights in the personal sphere, that they support traditional or premodern views of gender and society, that they are not radical enough in their prescriptions for remaking social structures—provide a mold for true religion. "Authentic religion" is defined as that which manifests these modern Western commitments. As a result, this type of pluralistic theology effectively insulates religion against the modern critique that it is socially regressive, since that critique is rooted in the same set of commitments that are now normative for religion. Since the pluralistic axiom is that all major religions must be fundamentally valid, it follows that they must fit this mold. With this confidence, pluralistic theologies have no hesitations about assuming interpretive authority over majority voices within religious traditions and over critical, naturalistic voices from outside them: in negating one they also negate the other.

In these pluralistic theologies the basis for the affirmation of the equal validity of all faiths is carefully crafted in reaction to a perceived failing or vulnerability of religion—paradigmatically of Judaism and Christianity—in the face of modern critiques. It is hardly an accident that pluralistic theology, in its treatments of the religions, takes care to indemnify them all against just such objections. Someone like John Hick, who has struggled so long to reconstitute Christianity's claims in response to philosophical challenges to its meaning and truth, wants the other religions to share in the benefits of these labors. All the better that the means of achieving this immunity tend to discount the very religious differences that are problematic for pluralistic theology. The various religious traditions may not be so enthusiastic about this care on their behalf, seeing that it entails an inexorable assimilation of the religions into certain recent Western categories. This helps to explain the hesitation of those in various traditions to accept these theories as superior to their own accounts of pluralism.

As theorists of artificial intelligence work to develop computer programs which can translate one language to another, some opt for the use of a "middle language." In such a program, the sentences from Swahili are first translated into an artificial language or symbol system and then from that structure into French or any other tongue. The artificial or "middle language" is spoken by no one and has no culture of its own. Yet it controls what may be said from one language to another. The advantages of such an approach are obvious: rather than working out specific terms for translating each language into every other language, it is only necessary to work out a program which takes each language into and out of the middle language. For pluralistic theologies, I suggest, modern Western critiques of religion constitute a kind of middle language. It is an implicit axiom of these pluralistic approaches that the central elements or dynamics of each religious tradition must be filtered into the terms demanded by such critiques and then come out again intact in the equivalent forms of another religious tradition.

It is not surprising that when these authors aimed to affirm the vitality and validity of the great religious traditions of the world, they would interpret "affirm" in categories drawn from their particular religious and cultural setting: a setting in the Christian modern West, and predominantly within the academic world. To affirm other religions as true and efficacious meant to put them in such terms as could plausibly claim validity according to the canons operative in that context. This would not be so serious a defect had these writers not insisted so vehemently that it is illegitimate to impose standards that stem from a particular context as universal norms.

Pluralistic theologies are largely constructed so as to shield religion from the very forces that, its authors tell us, make such theologies necessary. Confessional perspectives cannot reasonably persist, these authors tell us, in a world come of age in its understanding of epistemology, history, and human rights. These critical developments cast suspicion on all traditions. But pluralistic writers each find ways of redefining "true religion" so as to preserve it from these challenges. Thus our writers are never more particular, more modern, more Western, than in their avid desire to overcome modernity's effects; they long to do away with doubt.

For Smith, lack of recognition of faith and the transcendence it responds to can only be due to aberrant thinking. It is dismissed out of hand by reference to the testimony of the vast majority of people in history, the testimony of tradition. For Hick, while it is admittedly possible to doubt the Real and its limitlessly better possibilities, this doubt can only be exercised in toto. That is, one can doubt that there is a single, fundamental generic truth to all religion (for Hick such doubting itself, it turns out, is an appropriate way to relate to the Real). But doubt regarding the specific claims of any tradition does not really touch the truth of religion. It only has to do with the cultural forms in which that truth is expressed. Both Smith and Hick adopt an apologetic strategy of safety in numbers; no religion which can muster some minimal adaptive human benefits (providing meaning, community, some moral guidance) can be disqualified by scrutiny of its particular assertions or features. All rise and fall together. For Knitter, it is possible to resist true justice—to be, as it were, on the "wrong side of religion" as one might be on the wrong side of history—but not to propose or practice faithfully any other notion of religion.

Pluralistic theologies have struggled conscientiously to avoid imposing explicit Christian categories on other religions. But it seems obvious that they have enthusiastically made normative, in the negative as it were, modern Western views on true religion. They have taken the simple existence of multiple religious traditions with utter seriousness as a fact. This is greatly to their credit. But the philosophies, the theologies, the views of history, the social thought of these other traditions and their societies are hardly taken seriously at all. The religions are salvific variations on a theme that the pluralists assume is already known. They are not even considered as the sources of alternative fundamental categories for approaching religious diversity itself, alternative to those of modern Western critical philosophy, understandings of historical process, and standards for justice.

One would suppose that the pluralistic ranks would be enriched by entries that took as central categories for defining and interpreting religions some which were culturally shaped by forces other than Chris-

West as measuring stick

where's the heel on your sweater? where's the yolk on this car? the tires for this book?

tianity and the Enlightenment, and which contrast with the accepted norms of Western modernity. This would give us some examples of how the faiths of pluralists and our own current cultural norms would look if recast to count as "true religion" on someone else's terms, to go with these numerous examples of how the other traditions are recast to count as true religion on pluralistic terms.

To give one Christian example, we might consider the work of Francis Clooney, S.J., in comparative theology (Clooney 1990). Clooney is a scholar of the *Mimamsa* tradition in Hinduism and more particularly of the Tamil devotional poetry that developed out of it. His method for exploring comparative theology is engagingly concrete. His aim has been to learn Indian languages, "their grammar and vocabulary, their patterns of thought and, finally, the content and modes of expression of the various religious texts" (Clooney 1990, 63). Clooney's emphasis in comparative theology is on the cross-reading of religious texts, so that for him as a Christian these Hindu Tamil poems become part of the biblical world. He goes on to articulate an inclusivist theological position which arises from this emphasis.

For my purposes it is sufficient to stress both the particularity and modesty of his approach. The meeting point he chooses is the word. It happens that this is a point very congenial to part of the classical Hindu tradition which puts great stress upon the hearing and the understanding of the Vedic words. Indeed, one can well imagine a "dialogue" which on Hindu terms would consist of hearing, studying, and interpreting together divine words, Vedic and Christian. From the point of view of this stream of the Hindu tradition, such interaction would proceed on a series of assumptions about the constitutive effect of divine words, the non-necessity of a "revealer," the ritual character and effects of the proper recitation of various sounds, and the specification of elaborate spiritual practices built up around these words, in written or oral form. Many of these assumptions would not be shared by Christian participants, who would bring some of their own about revelation, relationship, and history. Such a basis for dialogue appears to have no place in pluralist theories; it proceeds on assumptions that are deeply problematic in Western categories and therefore are defined as secondary in pluralist terms. But it does have the significant virtue of allowing a certain priority to each tradition's account of itself.

Clooney indicates that even prior to any explicit reflection, such cross-reading of other religious texts inevitably affects the Christian's understanding of the Bible. In this reading, as the other tradition's texts become inscribed in the Christian's biblical world, he says one cannot help but be aware that one is also being read by the text. That is, one is aware that there is another way of shaping the world, and that one's own texts and tradition can be inscribed within it, assimilated to its terms. This awareness is not possible, of course, if both have already been predigested in more dogmatic terms, if there is no room for real other-rationality.

It is not clear, Clooney says, what motive a Christian pluralistic thinker would have for reading carefully the texts of another faith as he does. The unwillingness to impose "*our* Bible on others is accompanied by an implicit self-protection against impositions *their* texts might make on us" (Clooney 1990, 78). The pluralistic supposition is that their texts remain theirs and ours ours while we "get there on our own," for reasons not tied to the explicit content of these texts or traditions.

This is only one example, and others could be given. The point is that it is very difficult to see what pluralist rationale can be given for a *need* to attend to the specifics of various faiths. The lack of such a rationale is understandable in light of the apologetic dimension of pluralism. These theories attempt to transform religious diversity from an apparent embarrassment for claims to religious truth into supporting testimony for one truth subsistent in all faiths. It is not surprising that the specifics that distinguish the traditions are pushed into the background.

This attempt to affirm the religions while de-emphasizing their substance is finally futile. Respect for a faith tradition that does not extend to its actual aims and practices is a frail force. Such affirmation, as we have seen, is quite compatible with an assumption of sovereign judgment over everything concrete in that tradition. But even more important, it is in these specific dimensions of the faiths that the real benefits of dialogue are to be found. It is the "surplus meaning" of the various traditions, over and above the generic, abstract content pluralists prescribe, that offers real hope for mutual transformation.

There is a great deal of discussion today about "post-modernity" and about the possible changes which may follow the dethroning of North Atlantic views of history, knowledge, and justice from their supposed universal status through a recognition of valid alternatives from other cultures. Insofar as such a transformation were actually to take place, pluralistic theologies would seem to be among the most likely casualties, defensively structured as they are around the presumed universality of the codes of modern rationality. Ironically, pluralistic antidotes to Christian particularism may prove to be much more culture and time bound than the theologies they condemn. The very religious traditions pluralistic theologies wish to affirm may find on the whole they have as much to fear from the pluralists' embrace as the exclusivist's denial.

The primary challenge to pluralist theories is to make explicit their case for the global normativity of the Western critical principles that determine their univocal definitions of religion. There are serious arguments to be made for the universal application of these culturally particular notions—whether it is Hick's Kantian metaphysics, Smith's existentialism, or Knitter's social theory—and for the resulting insistence that the faith traditions' accounts of the world do not belong on the same plane as these privileged beliefs. These writers generally avoid mounting such a case, for the obvious reason that to do so would be to join the inclusivist camp. But I believe explicit arguments for the validity of their religious views in preference to others would be welcome and appropriate. Pluralistic theologies are caught between an implicit need to provide such arguments and explicit principles that exclude them as illegitimate.

A JOB DESCRIPTION

As we come to the end of this critical review of key pluralistic theologies, it is time to look beyond criticism. The many positive elements in these theologies and the objections I have raised can both be summarized in several points of a "job description" for a different and hopefully more adequate approach to religious diversity. The overarching task of such an approach is to find a fruitful way of combining recognition of truth or validity *and* difference across the religions. In this sense, pluralists are committed to limiting their attribution of truth to what is convergent in the religions, while insisting that what is truly different is always truly secondary. Inclusivists, while much more likely to emphasize difference, are almost equally inclined to stress the truth of what is similar (in this case, another tradition's limited approximation of their own beliefs or practices) and to deny validity to what is different. A perspective is needed which can recognize the effective truth of what is truly other.

The job description for such an approach can be sketched by outlining major points we have already discussed. First and most generally, I have raised a question about the *status* of such theories of religion. The claim of these pluralistic theories to transcend confessional particularity and to provide a unique level of religious reflection above that carried on by others cannot be substantiated—whether it takes the form of a claim to postulate the most ultimate religious object, a claim to superior expertise in the most comprehensive field of religious data, or a claim to motivation by the highest moral standards. In their various ways, the religious traditions themselves make similar claims. Each one has itself arisen out of a situation of religious and cultural diversity and has taken on its particular identity through continuing encounters with difference. The Western, modern and Christian particularity of these pluralistic theologies is plain enough. They are religious commitments and perspectives among others. An alternative and preferable perspective would be more modest in this regard and acknowledge there can rightly be a pluralism of views on the same plane it occupies.

The second point has to do with the fact that pluralistic theologies severely limit the saving or constitutive truth of the faiths to a sphere so narrow and/or abstract from the concrete substance of religions and religious practice that it loses touch with these faiths as they are actually known and practiced. My job description for a more adequate perspective would seek a way to recognize much more extensively and concretely within the traditions truths and valid practices that are integral to religious fulfillments. This would involve, then, according the faiths much more truth *on their own terms* than the pluralist hypotheses. The capacity to at least recognize that these are other, alternative views which have the means to "read" and subsume us in their categories is an important one, not least because it allows more room for critical judgments that may be brought against us and the assumptions of our current context.

A third point has to do with interreligious dialogue, study, and encounter. I have noted that pluralistic views oddly offer little intrinsic reason for the careful and often tedious labor involved in study of or dialogue concerning the specific distinctive elements of various traditions. Knitter and others who focus on justice may offer a partial exception here, providing a compelling motive for interaction, but it applies to a limited range of issues and actively discourages attention to others, even if they are highly valued by the dialogue partner. The simple question is, what can the specific and special aspects of another faith tell us that is of significant importance? An alternative perspective should have an answer to that question which indicates what there is of substance to be learned in interreligious relation.

Fourth, the wider scope for discovering particular truths in the various faiths suggested in points two and three should extend up to and include the possibility of *divergent* religious ends or fulfillments. This is perhaps the most dramatic suggestion and the sharpest contrast with "pluralistic" principles though it is, ironically, a more pluralistic vision. If it is possible to articulate a consistent rationale for this possibility, this would be a desirable feature of an alternative perspective.

Fifth, the job description sketched so far would include grounds for crediting as valid and appropriate the various traditions' testimony regarding their own uniqueness and "one and only" character. Again, this would be a large step beyond the existing pluralistic theories in terms of respect for the religions in their own terms.

Sixth, the alternative perspective I am suggesting would acknowledge frankly the venturesome dimension of religious faiths. There are critiques which claim to negate the validity of religions, collectively or individually. I have suggested in this chapter that pluralistic theologies are apologetically crafted to neutralize such critiques, to limit their scope or literally to define them away. Many may not regard it as a recommendation for an alternative view that it recognizes the real uncertainty present in all religious commitment, an uncertainty these critiques highlight. Palatable or not, I argue that it is in the interest of the religious traditions to face these critiques as the thorough-going challenges they are, rather than to take collective refuge in pluralistic theories of religion. These theories grant a certain immunity from religious doubt but do so by largely giving up the relevance of the actual substance of the various religions.

A seventh point in the job description has to do with the practical and ethical goals of pluralistic theologies. The concern to remove Christian motives for oppression or persecution, the desire to foster nonviolence, mutual respect, and active cooperation among the faiths; these are admirable commitments. I have suggested reservations about whether either these commitments or their effective realization are unique to pluralistic views. But a proposed alternative should be expected to share these concerns and offer equal or better prospects for being practically effective in overcoming these evils.

Finally, it also remains to indicate how the proposal I make is to be grounded in explicitly Christian theology.

This is an ambitious prescription. I believe it can be filled.

PART II

Salvations

5

Salvations

A More Pluralistic Hypothesis

In expositions of pluralistic theologies of religion by their primary advocates one word never appears in the plural: salvation. This is the more dramatic since diversity is otherwise their constant theme. One writer, for instance, suggests it is wisest to affirm that God has different histories and different natures, that in fact there may be many gods (Driver 1987, 212). But in all the speculation and professed radicalism "salvation" remains a comfortable and unitary reference point. The prominent figures I have reviewed make salvation the universal, cross-cultural constant in interpreting religious traditions. John Hick adopts what he calls "the soteriological criterion" to test the validity of such traditions (Hick 1989, 299). Paul Knitter revises his theocentric approach to the theology of religions in favor of "soteriocentrism," with its absolute presupposition of a single "soteria" (Knitter 1987c, 187).

At first sight, the use of a traditional Christian term to designate the standard to judge all religions seems odd in those who explicitly warn us against such particularism. But they regard "salvation" as shorthand for one process taking place within all major religious traditions, though not normatively understood or described in any of them. Hick calls this process the "transformation from self-centeredness to Reality-centeredness," a process leading to a "limitlessly better possibility" for humanity.

The largely undefended assumption that there is and can be only one religious end is a crucial constitutive element of "pluralistic" theologies. Despite their appropriation of the title, these theologies are not religiously pluralistic at all. Difference in religious aims and ends is what they bend their impressive efforts to deny. I would suggest that more adequate perspectives are possible which diverge sharply at this point. Incorporating many of the concerns of the authors treated so far, such perspectives would differ not in *whether* they may affirm truth or validity in many religious traditions as opposed to only one, but in recognizing the possibility for much more extensive concrete and contrasting validity in those faiths than pluralistic accounts allow.

Hick's affirmation of the faiths, for instance, begins and ends in the realm of formal ultimacy. What is fundamentally affirmed as true in the religions is the existence of one ultimate "Real" beyond all substantive description, in relation to which a limitlessly better possibility of indeterminate character is open. The "mythological truth" which he grants to the actual substance of the different religions amounts to the claim that their beliefs and practices are true *insofar* as they are interpreted to represent Hick's philosophical content. But the "Real" and the "possibility" which Hick takes as the true religious object and end are entirely nonfunctional. They serve as actual religious ends for no one. As described by Hick they cannot specify in any concrete way what kind of person we should become to "adjust" to them. And yet the religious materials that actually do constitute human practice and experience are treated as fundamentally extrinsic to religion's truth.

What would a truly pluralistic hypothesis look like, one that was interested in affirming—as religiously significant—a much more substantial portion of the various faith traditions? This alternative would explore the conditions under which the various believers' accounts of their faith could be most extensively and simultaneously valid. It would open the possibility of affirming religious traditions as truthful in a much more concrete sense than pluralistic theologies provide. It would mean that the traditions themselves would not be superseded by the philosophical framework placed on them. The key to such a hypothesis is the willingness to consider more than one realizable religious aim. Such an approach would be consistent with the data pluralistic theologians review and could be supported by many of their own arguments, as well as others. But it would not require such sweeping and dogmatic postulates.

Gandhi wrote, "Religions are different roads converging to the same point," and asked, "What does it matter if we take different roads so long as we reach the same goal? Wherein is the cause for quarreling?" (Gandhi 1938, 36; quoted in Burch 1972, 111). To which we may well ask: What should it matter were we to reach different goals? Wherein is the cause for quarreling? (Burch 1972, 111). The refusal of pluralistic theologies to address this question is their primary failing. It is also, as I have argued above, a reflection of the very exclusivism they reject.

Grace Jantzen has pointed out the false unity that is implied in transporting the term "salvation" into interreligious discussion. She cautions against the assumption that "all religions have a concept of salvation at all, let alone that they all mean the same thing by it or offer the same way to obtain it" (Jantzen 1984, 579-580). In an important article, Joseph DiNoia faults both inclusivists and pluralists on this ground (DiNoia 1989, 249-274). Christian inclusivists traditionally focus on the manner in which those within other religious traditions may achieve a specifically Christian religious fulfillment. Pluralists stress a common goal or process present in the various faiths beneath their specific accounts of their own ends. In both cases, DiNoia maintains, the distinctive features of the traditions' varied religious aims fall into the background. They do not "survive their transposition to pluralistic and inclusivist theological contexts" (DiNoia 1989, 252). It would be much preferable to find a way to recognize the integrity of the religious traditions in their own terms rather than to denature them in either of these ways. Is such a perspective possible?

I believe it is. In this chapter I will focus on the philosophical dimensions of such an approach, paralleling the philosophical emphasis in Hick's theory. The first section will focus on the first stage in the "job description" for a new perspective: the issue of the status of the perspective itself. We are seeking a framework that will intrinsically acknowledge its own lack of neutrality, recognize that it exists on the same plane with alternatives, and yet have the universal scope pluralistic theories claim. We will begin by exploring a suggestive argument that has been developed in contemporary philosophy and then seek to adapt it to the issues of religious pluralism.

The latter section of the chapter will turn toward the second stage of the job description. The framework I suggest in section one would be consistent with a wide range of perspectives on religious diversity, those generally called "inclusivist." In section two I argue on behalf of a certain type of perspective within this range which I believe goes a step beyond inclusivism as usually presented and which offers the possibility of maximizing the credibility and significance of the various religions' self-descriptions. It does so by offering a "more pluralistic hypothesis": the contention that there can be a variety of actual but different religious fulfillments, salvations. Development of a specifically Christian perspective embodying these elements must wait until the following chapter.

DIFFERENT VIEWS OF DIFFERENCE

The theological argument revolving around exclusivism, inclusivism, and pluralism is crosscut by two different ways of conceiving the problem. In the first, religious commitment is largely understood in terms of the assertion of propositions. The power of such discussions rests in the fact that all faiths can be taken to entail propositional presuppositions. Thus Paul Griffiths in *An Apology for Apologetics* can make a very compelling case for the inevitable clash of categories which attends religious pluralism (Griffiths 1991).[1] Implicitly and explicitly, he maintains, religious faith itself appeals to some standard of rationality. Even though emphasis might be put on a practice, like repeating the confession "There is no God but God and Muhammad is his prophet," and a positive subjective attitude attained in this practice, it is still the case that both the practice and the attitude presuppose the truth of certain propositions about God and the prophet. Griffiths's argument is considerably strengthened by his recognition that this propositional dimension does not exhaust the content of religion. Apologetic engagement is unavoidable, he suggests, but only in certain circumstances. Interreligious encounter may involve propositional conflict and agreement but is hardly limited to them. At times they will be decidedly secondary considerations.

A second approach, by contrast, stresses constitutive, non-propositional elements: ritual, community, affect, meaning. As the first perspective would point out that these all in fact imply propositions, so this view would emphasize that propositions depend upon contexts. They not only meet or fail rational tests, but express values, serve functions. So W. C. Smith, as we have seen, makes his case for human "faith"—an existential attitude—as the universal substance of religion (see Smith 1979). Here the evaluative, dispositional aspects of religion come uppermost. Such faith always takes a particular historical form, and that form involves propositions. But these must always be understood in terms of their relation to faith and not the other way around. "One's faith is given by God, one's beliefs by one's century" (Smith 1977, 96).

In the two examples I have given, Smith argues for a common core of religion and Griffiths for incommensurability between faiths. But either *type* of approach, non-propositional or propositional, can be used to argue either identity or conflict. Some share Griffiths's propositional focus but argue for a universal shared cognitive content of the great traditions, perhaps in a common set of ethical prescriptions. A strongly cultural-linguistic approach like George Lindbeck's would incline, like Smith, to stress that faith cannot be identified with propositions, but would argue that the religions are incommensurable forms of life.

Most theological treatments of religious pluralism approach the issue primarily along one of these paths and do their best to take account of the other. Reasonableness and truth are the deep concerns of one; commitment and meaning the deep concerns of the other. My argument is that a fuller integration of the two approaches—showing the sphere and necessity of each element—may at the same time press us beyond the current options. Such a perspective will also help us to sort out the elements of particularity and universality woven through each faith tra-

---

[1] Griffiths draws significantly on the work of William Christian, *Doctrines of Religious Communities*.

dition. The basis for this integration is suggested by some recent work in philosophy.

In *The Strife of Systems* Nicholas Rescher outlines a view he calls "orientational pluralism" (Rescher 1985).[2] Although Rescher is explicitly concerned with recent philosophical debates about objectivity and relativism, his arguments intersect powerfully with the issues of religious pluralism. He specifies a way of philosophically respecting "non-philosophical" factors in our search for truth. He addresses the dilemma of how philosophy can reconcile its foundational commitments to truth with an enduring condition of pluralism on all major questions. He recognizes that in contemporary philosophy there is a tension between those who maintain the classic view that the discipline's *raison d'être* is the search for truth through rational analysis and those who hold that its true role instead is either technical—the clarification of the progress from premise to conclusion—or "therapeutic"—a constant category-loosening play of conversation which disabuses us of pretensions to truth. These two poles are significantly analogous to the two paths of approach to religious diversity I outlined above.

Since Descartes, skeptics have echoed his lament that philosophy has been "cultivated by the very best minds which have ever existed over several centuries and that, nevertheless, not one of its problems is not subject to disagreement, and consequently is uncertain" (Descartes 1968, 32). Contemporary philosophers, steeped in the sociology of knowledge, are hesitant to expect any end to the situation Descartes described. Philosophy thus faces its own problem of pluralism: there appears to be not one rational truth but many. This casts in question the validity of the entire philosophical project. Rescher's contention, in brief, is that philosophy as a discipline can accommodate itself to this enduring lack of univocal progress while at the same time retaining belief in a unified reality and commitment to the most vigorous doctrinal debate.

Rescher reviews and rejects three possible responses to the philosophical situation (Rescher 1985, 177). Their similarity to approaches in the discussion of religious pluralism is evident. One response he calls the unique reality view: reality has a determinate character and only one of the competing descriptions of it can be most rationally adequate. Another response he calls the no-reality view. There is no ultimate reality or at least none that can be known. Therefore philosophical "truth" problems are pseudo-problems which need to be reconceived, not answered or argued. The task of philosophers is to entice people out of their bondage to this mirage. A third response affirms a multifaceted reality. Each competing view gives truth, but none gives the whole truth.

---

[2] I express my appreciation to Owen Thomas, whose unpublished paper introduced me to Rescher's work.

Reality is the sort of thing that contrasting rational views can be right about. He quotes Nelson Goodman: "There is no one way the world is, but there are ways the world is" (Rescher 1985, 177).

In place of any of these, Rescher advocates what he calls "orientational pluralism." One and only one position is rationally appropriate from a given perspective, but we must recognize that there is a diversity of perspectives. The distinctive thing about his view is the insistence that a practicing philosopher rightly and inevitably proceeds by inclining to the unique reality view. Argument and inquiry can only operate from a perspective. From a given perspective there is ultimately only one rationally defensible conclusion. We seek to discover what this is, and insofar as we believe we do we may rightly hold that it is more valid than conclusions reached from other perspectives.

It is important to note how Rescher's position differs from the apparently similar affirmation that reality is multifaceted. Such an approach points toward a possible all-inclusive position by accumulation. The perspectival view, by contrast, affirms an irreducible plurality. Facets can be combined, while perspectives cannot. Perspectives are one (at a time) to a customer (Rescher 1985, 188; see "exclusion principle").

This "exclusion principle" is both personal as well as logical. While it violates the principle of non-contradiction to say that at the same moment I both see and do not see a train, there is no contradiction involved in saying that another person sees it and I do not. And there is no logical problem in saying a train is seen by two people at once—one from inside and one from outside—though it is not possible for the same person to be doing the seeing in both cases. Recognizing a diversity of perspectives allows us to say that contradictory statements can both be true at the same time, of different persons with different perspectives. It also allows us to say that two things which are not logically incompatible may in fact be mutually exclusive for any single individual or community at one time. So the "exclusion" Rescher has in mind deals as much with personal states that cannot both hold at the same time for the same person as with contradictory propositions.

Rescher roots his discussion in consideration of what he calls "aporetic clusters." These are families of contentions, each of which has a strong evidential claim but which are mutually incompatible: the underside of an Aristotelian syllogism. An example would be three statements widely held by the Greeks:

1) If virtue does not always produce happiness, it is pointless;
2) Virtue is crucially important;
3) Virtue does not always yield happiness (Rescher 1985, 25, paraphrased).

Philosophy arises precisely because we find ourselves situated in such thickets when we try to make sense of what already makes sense to us.

Each statement in the cluster is highly plausible but they cannot all be right. Nor, Rescher says, can we appeal to the evidence to decide the matter: what the cluster of statements expresses *is* the evidence, as best we can determine.

Something must be sacrificed—something with a strong appeal—if consistency is to be achieved. Different philosophical "doctrines" arise according to the path chosen. In the case above, one path to consistency is to deny (1) and maintain that virtue is worthwhile entirely in itself even if it does not produce happiness/pleasure. Rescher says this was the path taken by Epictetus and Stoics. Another option is to drop (2) and maintain virtue *is* pointless, like Plato's Thrasymachus. A third option is to deny (3) and hold that virtue is inevitably productive of happiness, a path Rescher attributes to Plato. The key point Rescher stresses is that this choice itself cannot be made purely on the basis of evidence and reason. It requires recourse to evaluative judgments or commitments.

Philosophy thus always presents us with overabundant material, an excess of empirically grounded, rationally defensible propositions. We can't have them all. Without such decisions philosophy can hardly begin. In deciding which to keep and which to let go, we depend upon an evaluation of priorities. Such judgments define the constraints of what *counts* as a solution. Epistemic values have to do with the paradigms we favor, with what we mean or want to mean by "knowledge" (Rescher 1985, 104ff.). These will be quite different, Rescher suggests, if our model of knowledge is taken from mathematics (Spinoza) or from literature (Derrida). It is these epistemic values which constitute an "orientation," from which "orientational pluralism" takes its name.

Rescher offers the following aporetic triad to illustrate his own view (Rescher 1985, 117):

1) Philosophical problems are legitimate and solvable cognitive issues;
2) Solution to philosophical problems is only achievable through recourse to cognitive values;
3) Recourse to values is illegitimate in rational inquiry.

Orientational pluralism drops (3). It holds that no philosophical thesis can be justified without adopting an evaluative perspective. To assert a thesis is also to commend adoption of the orientation in which its warrants rest.

Orientational pluralism plainly acknowledges that it is a thesis subject to all the conditions just described. It can be chosen and defended from among alternatives only by evidence combined with evaluative factors. We could drop (2) rather than (3) if we give a higher priority to certainty and judge the existence of ongoing differences more repugnant. From an orientation committed to the epistemic values of certainty and disciplinary agreement, a thoroughly rational case can be made for this view. Philosophy can be conceived and practiced in this way, in other words, but only by radically limiting its scope.

Orientational pluralism is not intended as a neutral, methodological description of how philosophy operates. If any such description is taken to have implications for the practice of philosophy, it is already "doctrinal." It is not "mere" description but judgment. Every account of the nature of philosophy is a position *in* philosophy. Orientational pluralism thus understands itself as an alternative to views like the one described in the prior paragraph, on the same categorical level. It is frankly normative and doctrinal. It says that its description of how philosophy operates is true, and that the recognition of a variety of tenable rational views is compatible with "doctrinal" commitment to one of those views— in this case to orientational pluralism—since such a diversity of rational possibilities is what this doctrine expects.

Rescher argues, in effect, that we necessarily assert the validity of our own perspective in the process of exercising it. It is both irrational and dishonest to argue otherwise. This is essentially the same point Krieger made in the discussion we described in chapter 3 about the encounter between the varying perspectives of the anthropologist and the tribal leader. Krieger suggested that there were three modes of discourse. The first two, argumentative and boundary discourse, correspond in a rough way to the two poles that Rescher treats as rationality and orientation. There is also a good deal of similarity between Krieger's third type, disclosive discourse, and Rescher's view. The prime benefit of disclosive discourse for Krieger was that it allowed the recognition of "other rationality" and yet maintained commitment to the universal value of one's own convictions. It is my contention that Rescher's work allows us to develop this insight more broadly than Krieger has done.

The case for orientational pluralism then has two fronts. On the rational side Rescher stresses the consistency with which it can apply its principles to its own case, a consistency lacking in many competitors, including pluralistic theories. One perspective on the nature of philosophy, for instance, maintains that evidential considerations alone will lead to a single rational conclusion. But this view itself is not agreed to be the single rational conclusion of the evidence. To claim that only purely rational arguments should be allowed is to adopt one kind of value orientation. To deny that other value orientations exist can be shown by evidence to be false. But to acknowledge that the evaluative context is a crucial factor in our conclusions is to contradict one's own assertion that evidence necessarily leads to only one rational interpretation. As Rescher puts it, "If you share my values then by rational rights you should share my position. If not, you can look elsewhere . . . indeed you must" (Rescher 1985, 238-239). The availability of other rationally tenable views is consistent with what orientational pluralism asserts in claiming to be the most adequate account of philosophy.

On the second front, supporters of orientational pluralism make frank evaluative arguments. Philosophy struggles between a rationally rigorous practice that risks becoming largely irrelevant to primary human questions and an engagement with those great questions which is frustrated by the failure to find agreed answers. Rescher suggests that his account of the options best allows us to understand and practice philosophy as a rigorous cognitive activity which also bears on large and live human questions (Rescher 1985, 264-265). There is no determinative rational argument that philosophy *must* be understood in this and no other way. But if it is to be understood in this way—if rationality and human relevance are both evaluative priorities—then Rescher argues that orientational pluralism is the single best rational account of it. It is the true account of philosophy from this evaluative perspective, the perspective Rescher holds and commends to others.

We may recall that Hick recommends his pluralistic hypothesis by appeal to an evaluative orientation. He claims it is the most effective way to secure 1) real cognitive content for religion, 2) substantial parity among the faiths, and 3) preservation of some standard to detect destructive religion and so avoid relativism.[3] Insofar as one shares these epistemic values, one's argument with Hick can be thoroughly rational (argumentative discourse, in Krieger's terms). The criticism of him in chapter 1 was largely carried out internally, on the presumption of such values. But, as will become clear below, I will also propose a shift in the orientation itself, stressing (1) more extensively than Hick does, and modifying the understanding of (2).

In summary, orientational pluralism insists there is only one reality and we are trying to know it. It is not committed to regarding other substantive views as equally valid, only as tenable from different perspectives. What is fragmented is not truth but justification or warranted assertability. The justification offered by a philosophy may be orientationally limited in appeal, but the claims themselves can be universal and unrestricted (Rescher 1985, 190). People who rationally hold contradictory views from different orientations are each justified in thinking the other wrong. "We can only pursue *the* truth by cultivating *our* truth" (Rescher 1985, 199). Philosophical positions are not opinions but judgments. And, as Rescher strikingly puts it, we are not in a position to concede that someone else's basis of judgment is superior to ours. Someone else's expertise or information may well be so. Such data enriches and expands the basis for our evaluation. But to acknowledge that others have better values or beliefs *by* which to judge is in effect to adopt their perspective and drop any other.

Why does recognition that diverse rational positions are appropriately held not contradict the conviction that one's own position is more

---

[3] See the discussion above at the end of chapter 1.

valid than the others? There is a common contemporary reflex which asserts that to privilege one's own conclusions is the same as denying that others are possible or reasonable. This is clearly not so. Suppose a person lives according to conclusions we accept as perfectly rational, but whose premise—that money is the primary end, for instance—we do not share. If we go on to say that this premise is acceptable for that person, though it would not be for us, we make this judgment on grounds of some kind inextricably bound up with goods we value. If we affirm the appropriateness of their pursuing that end while we pursue another, we presumably regard this judgment as more valid than at least some others, made on other grounds; for instance, the judgment that the money-oriented person must be coerced in some way to conform to our view. We make a rational judgment about how to deal with differences in orientation, and we make that judgment on the basis of our orientation. In this we behave formally no differently than the person who would insist that the financier change his or her ways. One negates and the other affirms the viability of this differing evaluative orientation, but we both do so by asserting the primacy of our own evaluative orientations. This is an embarrassingly plain and unoriginal observation. But it is rather regularly disregarded. We are unable to judge our own grounds of judgment to be anything but preferable to alternatives. This is not a legalistic but a thoroughly practical contradiction; *we* cannot act on two different orientations at once, even if we understand both are defensible. In the end, we are all inclusivists.

If we say we judge others' orientations to have the same value as our own, we are committed to regard the rational conclusions that flow from those orientations as equally valid, including the exclusivist conclusion that others' orientations do not have the same value. Again, this is not a logical debating point. It has a perfectly practical correlative: none of us do in our practice, speech, and thought grant the same value to the perfectly rational conclusions that stem from different orientations. If we insist that no privilege attaches to the perspective from which we judge, it seems we must claim that we have made this judgment itself without any reference to grounds or values that others do not share. W. C. Smith goes to precisely this extremity, insisting that nothing in religion ultimately should be accepted by anyone that cannot be accepted by all others, and for the same reasons (Smith 1981, 100-102). He, of course, must drastically qualify this principle, as we discussed, and postpone its realization to the future. In practice, pluralistic authors insist that others should, or will, or anonymously already do share their particularistic grounds of judgment. This is the standard practice of the inclusivism they condemn.

Philosophy as Rescher views it is a communal venture, "a competitive yet quasi-cooperative endeavor to build up as good a case as possible for a diversified spectrum of discordant possibilities" (Rescher 1985, 273). From the perspective of orientational pluralism, the diversity of philosophical systems is not a problem but a solution. It is cultural evolution's way of prodding, challenging people on the one hand to include as much evidence and as many values as possible in their understanding of the world and on the other to honor the fact that even in the face of the same evidence people can make different commitments and develop in different directions. Discussion and argument among the perspectives are the very lifeblood for each one.

Rescher writes:

> From Hegel's day to ours, philosophers of all persuasions have seen the strife of systems as something to be overcome—somehow to be put behind us once and for all. Some, following Hegel himself—that Napoleon of Philosophy—use the approach of conquest and annexation, of seeking to absorb all of philosophy into one great synthesis (Rescher 1985, 276-277).

But in Rescher's view philosophy does not aim at consensus so much as it collectively seeks for those in each orientation to develop the most sophisticated, most responsible, fullest understanding of the truth possible. Differing visions of truth are the primary allies in this process and communication with and about them its primary medium.

Rescher has attempted to reconcile the cognitive rigor of philosophy with the integral role of perspectival judgment. If he is on the right track—I believe he is—what would a similar approach look like in the area of religion? Clearly philosophy and religion are different spheres; the evaluative, perspectival elements that have been so problematic for post-enlightenment philosophy are unavoidably central in religion. Faith presents an analogous if heightened problem of balance between perspective and universality.

One important point is that Rescher's treatment is a largely individualistic one. It might be objected that in religion one's orientation is much less a choice than in the philosophical debates he discusses. Although the modern experience is one which heightens exactly this dimension in religion—the awareness that there are other options—still I readily acknowledge the weight of the communal aspect of religion. For our purposes, however, this does not change a great deal. Rescher's analysis is valid even if persons do not start *de novo* religiously. They certainly do not do so in philosophy, where communal traditions are also crucial. Much of what Rescher says can be applied to religious communities as well as individuals.

His argument illuminates portions of the current debate about the diversity of faiths. Many commentators remark on the ironic exclusiveness of pluralistic theologies in their claims to represent the only defensible understanding of religious pluralism.[4] Their representatives generally respond to such observations not by arguing for the objective truth of their account in contrast to the falsity of all others—a response which would more or less confirm the charge. Instead they tend to appeal to certain experiences, conditions, or aims which require some such explanation as they provide. These might include the encounter with noble persons of other faiths, the realization of the cultural conditioning of our own values, the need for peaceful human relations. The data that pluralists identify in this way is generally recognized by those who hold other views. There may be no debate about the positive moral qualities of a Gandhi or an Ambedkar, and yet pluralists will argue that there is no true recognition of these qualities that does not also extend to recognition of the rough equivalence of the faith tradition in which they arose to other traditions. What pluralists argue is that a different priority or weight should be assigned to these particular elements. In other words, they appeal to an evaluative perspective. Rescher's philosopher says, "If you share my perspective, then I maintain you should recognize my position is the most reasonable conclusion." Pluralistic theologians tend to respond to critics, "If you don't reach my conclusions, it is because you have failed to share my perspective and you ought to do so." This is quite what we would expect in orientational pluralism's terms.

There is a difference here, however, not to be overlooked. Philosophy is constituted by a certain commitment to rational argument and philosophers are traditionally those who accept that methodological commitment. The crisis Rescher addresses is a result of the breakdown of this methodological agreement. "Religion," despite its confident listing in our academic syllabi, designates no such discipline and the adherents of faith traditions make no such common methodological commitment. Thus the perspectival diversity that Rescher integrates into philosophy, against its ostensible grain, has a much more dramatic range in religion considered generally than in philosophy. If anything, this should make his conclusions even more applicable for religious life.

Accounts of religious diversity of any stripe—exclusivist, inclusivist, pluralistic—are at the same time second-level descriptions of religions *and* first-level religious assertions. Rescher points out that even in philosophy, where it might seem that there could be some consensual, meta-doctrinal account of the discipline as a whole (given the ostensible methodological agreement), this is not the case. Such accounts are inevitably themselves doctrinal in character. This condition is intensified, not di-

---

[4] See, for instance, Heim, "Crisscrossing the Rubicon," 688-690, for a summary of these views expressed in D'Costa, *Christian Uniqueness Reconsidered.*

minished in the field of faiths. It is not that we can't attempt and to some extent succeed in empathetically describing various traditions. But the minute one attempts to draw any kind of conclusion from these descriptions one has entered the doctrinal realm.

What do we mean when we say that others are justified to hold views contrasting with ours? We might mean that others lack knowledge or experience that we have, and in the absence of this they reasonably reach different conclusions. This justification would disappear as soon as they have access to evidence with which we are familiar. We might mean we appreciate that because others adopt certain evaluative judgments which we do not share, they reasonably reach different conclusions. And because there is no definitive rational basis to allow only one type of evaluative orientation, this justification is not likely to lapse. Each of these meanings makes sense to me. But I understand pluralistic theologians to contend for another meaning: that varying views can be justified as similarly appropriate to hold, *on the basis of specific reasons and evaluative judgments equally agreeable to all.* As far as I can see, this contention can be defended finally only through a full relativism (the agreed grounds being that no grounds exist to prefer one of the views over another) or a radical imperialism (attaining agreement by requiring that all subscribe to some particular set of grounds). The first defense is in fact simply an instance of the second.

Pluralists basically say that adherents of various faiths are right to view things as they do because such views are salvifically effective, in ways the pluralistic theologian understands and others do not. But pluralists hope that on this fundamental issue diversity will eventually die out and all will eventually see their particularities *from* the pluralistic perspective. In this sense pluralists do not countenance continued diversity. Their account of religious variety has no internal rationale for the continuation of accounts of that religious variety alternative to theirs. At this level they see no more valid reason why they should be one view among many than traditional exclusivist perspectives do.

To use Rescher's idiom, we could construct the following aporetic cluster:

1) More than one type of religious position is valid;
2) Pluralistic theories of religion are religious positions;
3) Pluralistic theories of religion should be accepted to the exclusion of all others.

Exclusivists and, in varying extent, inclusivists affirm first-order conflict or alternativeness among the faiths. They thus stress the similarity between primary faith and meta-theories of religion, in that both are partly constituted by evaluative orientations. As a result they affirm (2) and reject (3). Pluralistic theologians reject (2), usually not by denying some religious quality to their theories but by arguing that they are not religious in the same sense as (1). They claim a neutral or generic religiousness which transcends the actual faiths and is not to be classed alongside them. To make good on this claim pluralists bear, and consistently fail, the test of insulating their meta-theories from particularist structures.[5] Part one of this book has tried to make that case.

Rescher's approach by contrast treats his own view of what philosophy does as one of the contending doctrines in philosophy itself. According to his account, one would expect there to continue to be such contention and expect each doctrine appropriately to make its case over against the others. From this perspective, one can see why there are and continue to be different doctrines, while at the same time maintaining the preferable validity of one's own.

In making the argument Rescher does, he acts in complete consonance with his professed conviction. *Both* his argument for his own view against others *and* his affirmation of the appropriateness of other views than his being held—and claiming superiority over his—are fully consistent. To regard our convictions as "just like anyone else's" is to regard our convictions as the best and most truthful that we know, a better ground of judgment than the alternatives. To regard others' differing faiths as "as good as ours" is to regard them as making more sense than or being preferable to ours, but from a different perspective, one we do not share.

By contrast, the pluralistic views are caught in a quandary. To be consistent they must maintain that they are not religious views among other religious views. Or, if they acknowledge this, then they must apply their stated principles on religious diversity to validate the positions at odds with their own. Very few face this question directly: Is a pluralistic view bound to affirm exclusivisms as independently valid religious ways, with no intrinsic need of pluralistic modification? When a clear answer is forthcoming, it is always of an inclusivist sort, though pluralistic thinkers insist inclusivism is to be rejected. An orientational pluralistic perspective seems a significant improvement on this score, in both clarity and coherence.

Of course this objection is made: Why not see major faiths as *equally* valid, given their different perspectives, and rule out any contention among them? The orientational pluralist responds that it is perfectly possible to argue for the equal validity of varying faiths, as one doctrine among others. It is not possible to argue plausibly that this is a "non-doctrinal" position. This is the character of the argument between the pluralistic theologian and the orientational pluralist over the status of theories of religion: it is an argument over what kind of argument we are having.

---

[5] These are the criticisms which have forced John Hick, for instance, to shift the grounds for his pluralism from Christ, to God, to an ultimate "Real" resolutely purged of any particular features at all.

The orientational pluralist maintains that this is a doctrinal argument, which cannot be resolved except by recourse to evaluative perspectives, by adopting a particular religious faith among alternatives. Thus it is an area in principle likely to remain a field of rationally appropriate diverse views. For orientational pluralism the diversity of views about religious diversity is, like religious diversity itself, rationally justified and therefore reasonably enduring. Pluralists affirm religious diversity, but not the appropriateness of varying views of that diversity. They expect the matter to be settled at the meta-religious level in a way that they would not countenance among the faiths themselves. I maintain that the attitudes which theories of religion take up toward competing theories of religion replicate their true attitudes toward the religions themselves. Each of the religious traditions itself is also an alternative at this level, containing one or more of its own theories of religion which can be put alongside pluralistic ones.

The pluralistic perspectives view themselves as more valid than any other accounts of religion. This is an appropriate type of conviction (if concretely incorrect) from an orientational pluralist's perspective. But pluralists refuse to recognize any other orientations, from which alternative perspectives would be reasonable. What the pluralist in this sense maintains is that there are *no* legitimate perspectives from which it makes sense to have any other conviction. Such perspectives as may exist must be incoherent or immoral in some way. Thus pluralism repeats the dynamic of the strong exclusivism it opposes: those who disagree are not rational or not worthy or both.

Orientational pluralism combines a more thoroughgoing commitment to the warranted justifiability of pluralism in religion with a more positive view toward the actual practice of witness on the part of believers commending their visions to others. It is highly skeptical of readiness to attribute others' differing religious attitudes to pure irrationality, immorality, or bad faith. It also encourages serious attention to the evaluative viewpoints from which neighbors' faiths cohere, since the development of our own truth can only proceed by incorporating more of what we may come to view as valuable in theirs. This is part and parcel of our commitment to the universal import of the truth we believe we partially grasp (otherwise we could rest content in ours and leave others to theirs) and of our commitment to learn from as well as differ with those who construe the world differently.

The account which Rescher gives of the importance of discussion across philosophical systems has a great deal in common with an insight John Cobb offers out of interreligious dialogue. He believes that there is "one relatively objective norm" that can be inferred from the practice of dialogue (in his case, this is primarily Buddhist-Christian dialogue). He notes four features that he believes characterize at least those traditions that engage in such encounter. They make some claim to the universal value of their affirmations. They teach some measure of humility about our capacity to understand reality in its fullness. They tend to develop some level of mutual appreciation. And the norms by which they judge both themselves and others are enlarged (Cobb 1990, 86-87). The last is the key point in Cobb's estimation. The "relatively objective" norm which he sees arising from such encounter has to do with a religious tradition's "ability in faithfulness to its past to be enriched and transformed in its interaction with the other traditions" (Cobb 1990, 92).

From Cobb's view, there is no reason for religious traditions not to bring convictions of uniqueness and the universal validity of their special beliefs into dialogue or interfaith relations. These do not need to be dropped or bracketed. It is equally, of course, not the case that each instance or type of interfaith interaction needs to focus on such questions. What dialogue makes possible is for each tradition to develop the fullest and most rigorous and inclusive version possible of its distinctive convictions and life. Cobb assumes that this necessarily involves transformation for all the traditions. In fact, he is not hesitant to make a claim for Christian superiority—the claim that a faith centered on Christ will prove to have an unsurpassed capacity for precisely this kind of dialogue, inclusion, and transformation (Cobb 1990, 92-93). And he would view it as entirely appropriate for those in other traditions to make reciprocal claims.

Such a vision of dialogue seems very much in line with what orientational pluralism would imply in the religious area. This is a vision in which the religions' claims to distinctiveness and their impulse to witness are valued along with sensitive appreciation for different commitments. Somewhat ironically, then, orientational pluralism finds a good deal more in order with the faith traditions' actual perspectives on religious pluralism than do contemporary pluralistic views that ostensibly commend respect for the religions' views.

A REAL PLURALISM OF RELIGIOUS ENDS

So far, we have dealt primarily with the first stage in our job description: the search for a framework for viewing the religions which is modest enough to recognize its character as one religious perspective among many, yet open enough both to maintain its own universal claims and recognize those of others. I have sketched one such alternative. But we need to expand the scope of our discussion to touch on other elements in our job description. One of these key elements concerns the rationale for the importance of studying the particularities of the religious traditions. When we encounter such particularity are we encountering something of possibly decisive and significant religious import for us, or are we encountering variant cultural expression of the single actual religious path already expressed in another cultural manner in our own tradition? I have argued that the first hypothesis offers the more compelling rationale for exploring these particularities with care and intensity. The question, then, is what theories or theologies of religion will allow for the maximum truth value in the specifics of the traditions and will most significantly ground the importance of concrete knowledge of them?

Consider the following set of statements:
1) Religious truth is one;
2) Religious truth is called by many names, experienced in many forms;
3) Cultural and personal categories are constitutive of our knowledge and experience of reality: all experience is "experiencing as";
4) Religious aims and fulfillments are various.

This is not exactly an aporetic cluster: I maintain that there is no necessary conflict among the four convictions. However, pluralistic theologians generally deny (4) while my perspective requires at least some interpretation of (1)—as may be appropriate for a trinitarian!

(1), (2), and (3) together indicate primary elements of "pluralistic" approaches which remain constant whether religious truth is mainly seen as a noumenal "Real" beyond our experience (Hick), an existential character of our experience (Smith), or a concrete imperative for our behavior (Knitter). (2), (3), and (4) together describe the most radical pluralism, an effective polytheism.

The tension between (1) and (4) is roughly analogous to the tension between rationality and value orientation in philosophy which Rescher addresses. I suggest that an adequate perspective on religious pluralism requires a similar attempt to give both their full due. In my view the key to such an effort is an emphasis on the fulfillment of various religious ends.

We know that there are a number of proposed religious ineffables: referents in various religious traditions, whether beings, structures, or conditions, which are deemed to be of ultimate significance and to be very inadequately grasped in human concepts, though not necessarily strictly noumenal.[6] These referents are described and approached through patterns within religious traditions, patterns including elements such as

---

[6] I use "ineffable" here in an attenuated sense, similar to that in which we may say that a certain kind of pain is ineffable; short of actually experiencing it, no description gives anything like a full understanding of it. Yet we know very clearly what kind of thing is being talked about. We are in no danger of confusing it with the mass of non-painful experiences, and in little danger of confusing it with at least some other kinds of pain.

art, concepts, music, rituals, and relations. The traditions and their patterns differ from each other in varying extent. According to these faiths, there are states of religious fulfillment which have already become actual for at least some human beings in connection with the ineffable referents (righteousness, nirvana, the *tao*, God). While even under these circumstances of fulfillment the referents may remain ineffable—unable to be fully described—they would be actual for those human beings who participate in them. *What* is actual for them, whether it is one and the same thing, as Hick suggests, and whether or not even those persons are in a position to be able to determine such questions, we simply do not know. Certainly if we are to credit the various religious accounts of their aims, the presumption is that they are different.

What metaphysical assumptions would be consistent with regarding many of these varying accounts as substantially and concurrently truthful? To put it another way, what hypothesis might we frame if instead of constructing metaphysical premises to mandate the oneness of religions we explored the conditions under which they could be variously and distinctively true? The minimum needed would be the supposition that the noumenal realm is such as to support the attainment in some measure of the diverse religious fulfillments we know otherwise to be the objects of justified religious belief. In other words, there must be at least one religiously significant reality, whether it is Hick's "Real" or the biblical God or the Advaitin One or the condition of enlightenment. It could be that there is only one such actual being, structure, or condition, which unites or subsists in the various ineffable religious ends. But it could also be that there are in fact various realities in the noumenal realm which are religiously significant and which ground diverse religious fulfillments (for instance, both some form of personal deity and a condition similar to that described as nirvana). For our purposes at the moment it is not necessary to choose between these possibilities. We do not require a claim to know or postulate the true reality beyond every religious ultimate. We are only asking whether there are conceivable metaphysical conditions under which the religions could be giving accounts of human religious ends which are both truthful in their particularistic elements and also substantially different from each other. If we hypothesize that some such conditions do exist, then the possibility would exist in principle to acknowledge in the various traditions not merely some abstracted common object or attitude, but the concrete availability of some or all of the specific religious fulfillments they affirm: ineffable reals like enlightenment or communion with God. These are actual human possibilities.

From this perspective an open set of varied religious ends may be available for realization. This is so both within the historical horizon of human life, and eschatologically, though there may be some differences between the two. For instance, it may be that there are some religious fulfillments, irreducibly distinct within the historical frame, which ultimately collapse together in some further state. But this hypothesis does not presume that all faith fulfillments do in fact reduce to one, either in the historical frame or eschatologically. Individuals and communities live their way through a cloud of live, alternative possibilities and, in their passing, make some rather than others concrete—as the act of detecting an electron "collapses" a quantum probability distribution into an actual location or velocity.

Before considering some of the obvious objections to such a hypothesis and developing it further, let us note several of its features. First, it directs us unavoidably toward the religious traditions themselves and their accounts of their religious aims. It is the religions as they actually exist—as patterns and complexes of life directed toward particular visions of human fulfillment—that are the objects of affirmation, not a principle abstracted from them, of which they are secondary cultural forms.

Our job description gave a high priority to the capacity of an approach to religious diversity to find validity in religions' concrete features and therefore to ground the intrinsic value of study and dialogue that deal with this "thick" texture of the faiths. The hypothesis that grounds exist for the realization of particular religious ends impels us to take the testimony of the traditions and their believers with a good deal more seriousness than in Hick's case. On his hypothesis, once we know that a religion mythologically represents a transcendent ultimate and a limitlessly better possibility, and its adherents in some proportion manifest some signs of self-transcendence, we know all about it *religiously* that we need to know. This neither requires nor even encourages any detailed, continuing familiarity with its substantive account of itself.

On the other hand, the hypothesis of multiple religious ends "relativizes" each faith path in a rather different way. It affirms that more than one may be truthful in their account of themselves, and that these truths are distinct. That is, it relativizes the religions precisely by actual relation to each other. This contrasts with the relativizing of traditions on Hick's hypothesis by referring them to his postulated absolute, which as such figures in no one's lived religious life.

Second, this approach would seem much more consistent with Hick's stress on all experience as "experiencing-as" than his own hypothesis. All of our experience is crucially constituted by the contexts we have for it. This includes, we would think, the experience of religious fulfillment, both here and now and eschatologically. If Hick's evaluative orientation grants a high priority to the belief that religious fulfillment is equally available to all, this hypothesis satisfies that value no less. But it does so in line with the insight that as long as we are humans, our experiences are not in fact the same except as we bring to them some of the same elements of construal. It presumes religious fulfillment is available to all but not that there must be only one identical fulfillment, as Hick and others hold. In fact, the thesis that there are different religious fulfillments seems to meet this concern much more effectively while also giving more weight to the religions on their own terms.

Given the history of intra-Christian discussions of religious diversity, it is not surprising that religious ends are often treated primarily in terms of the postmortem fate of individual persons. Indeed, when Hick rejects non-realist interpretations of religion because they are insufficiently optimistic he himself seems to be leaning heavily on the assumption of an enduring substantial self: he insists those persons who have died unfulfilled in history must not be lost (Hick 1989, 207-208). In his major work *Death and Eternal Life* Hick himself seems to emphasize that postmortem experiences of human consciousness would also bear the shape of the categories an individual's history had brought to it (see Heim 1992, 207-219).

As I pointed out in chapter 1, Hick's own vision of eschatology appears to expect that the experiences of the world to come could only be taken by the human subjects involved as concrete confirmation of *particular* religious expectations. This would not require any thoroughly literal conformity to the detail of such expectations. To take one of Hick's examples, experience of communion with a personal God and a risen Jesus would confirm a Christian's expectations beyond a reasonable doubt, with or without robes and wings. If in fact such events are significantly conditioned by our prior practice and commitment, then it would seem there is good reason to credit the "one and only" testimony of various religious traditions. It is unlikely that one can attain to an end in any other manner than by following the way that aims at or near it in preference to other possibilities.

The case is, of course, even more dramatic if we consider religious ends insofar as they are realized in the historical frame. Here the very evidence Hick wishes to bring forward to demonstrate "saintliness" and moral transformation in the various religious traditions displays at the same time the different textures these exhibit in contrasting religious settings. The examples are clearly not identical, however similar selected items from varied cases may be. Even if there is some sense in which all those in question have sought to be "good," it still appears that one would have to choose between one way of being good and another. It is also clear that people in various traditions pursue and claim to participate in religious fulfillments other than or in addition to moral transformation. The thesis of an identical religious end for all can be proposed with rather more impunity for the world to come than the current one, but in neither case is it persuasive if we are serious about the cultural-linguistic component of all experience.

In order to participate in the distinctive dimensions of Buddhist religious fulfillment in this life, there is no path but the Buddhist path. And the same is true of each tradition. Indeed, this can be seen as a complementary truth to the fact that at another level any serious attempt simply to understand the character of a faith tradition requires immersion in its "one and only" history, practices, texts, and beliefs. Here again, the hypothesis of multiple religious ends coheres with an emphasis on the importance of a religion's concrete texture.

The testimony of religious experience from the different traditions would also be direct evidence in support of this hypothesis. It is just such experience which Hick argues at length the believer is justified in trusting (Hick 1989, chap. 1). But the religious experiences which believers rightly take as ground for affirming specific religious ultimates and ends, Hick coopts as evidence for a reality he characterizes, the Real, beyond any such specific description.

How can Hick make the specific accounts of varied goals count toward justified belief in a single noumenal Real as the true goal referred to in each case? Only by contending that since the accounts conflict, the only options are to reject them all, to choose some as true and others as false, or to adopt some form of his pluralistic hypothesis. Since Hick rejects the first two and claims the last is the only other one compatible with the evidence of religious experience, he can argue that in a loose sense it is supported by that evidence.

So, for instance, Hick will say that nirvana and communion with God upon death are contradictory beliefs. Then he contends we have only three options. All such religious faith is nonsense; one is true and the others false; or the true content of religion is on a plane far above the terms of such contradictions. But this all depends on a non-pluralistic assumption. Nirvana and communion with God are contradictory only if we assume that one or the other must be the sole fate for all human beings. True, they cannot both be true at the same time of the same person. But for different people, or the same person at different times, there is no necessary contradiction in both being true.

It is interesting to note that the reality of multiple religious ends could hold on a number of different metaphysical assumptions, which makes the hypothesis particularly amenable to incorporation in differing religious perspectives on religious diversity. Michael LaFargue has recently proposed a "critical pluralistic" theory of religion which has significant affinities with the suggestions I have made (LaFargue 1992, 693-713). I do not accept his thoroughly experientialist account as a stopping point, but it illustrates one type of theory that falls within the broad hypothesis I have sketched. He offers a powerful case for multiple religious ends if we limit ourselves thoroughly to the historical plane.

LaFargue's perspective is truly pluralistic in that while he presumes that "religion" has to do with a distinctive categorial region or subject matter—what is of overriding importance in life—he rejects the notion that it has to do with a single object, structure, or end. Religions are not different ways of relating to the same reality. They are different systems in the same subject area (LaFargue's example is the difference between a Euclidian and a non-Euclidian geometry, both in the field of geometry). He has a radically experiential view of religion. Religious faith is basically an experience of the overriding importance of some good. Knowing, for instance, that Buddhist enlightenment is the one thing needful is a matter of such experience. Religions are differential systems of meaning built around such distinctive experiences, "differential" meaning that the terms of the system are all self-referential. Differential, system-dependent definitions are "the *only crucial and essential* determinants of the meaning of the elements of a given religion" (LaFargue 1992, 710).

One of the useful elements of LaFargue's theory for our purposes is his description of the category of "goods." His "goods" and differential systems are roughly analogous to Rescher's orientations and rationality. Whereas Rescher treated value orientations as individual choices, LaFargue emphasizes that particular religious goods exercise a claim on us. There is an experience of their compelling right to our response or reverence. This is a valuable modification in the model we took from orientational pluralism.

Leaving aside other significant aspects of LaFargue's theory, I pass directly to his conclusion:

> In this view "God," "Nirvana," "Tao," etc. have irreducibly different meanings. These are not meanings possessed by realities (or a single reality) that can be defined apart from the meanings. These meanings are the foundation of the valid claims made by these realities on the devotion of believers. To this extent they are *constitutive of the being* of God, Nirvana, and Tao as objects deserving religious commitment.
>
> This theory displaces the emphasis religious apologetics has tended to place on superior religious *certainty* about ultimate norms, and replaces it with an emphasis on the superlative "goodness" which these realities represent for the ideal believer (LaFargue 1992, 713).

Thus for LaFargue the actual reality of these religious ultimates can be critically substantiated "in concrete cases for specific individuals, and for groups sharing a common experience" (LaFargue 1992, 713).

LaFargue's view of religion resolutely resists the dualism so central to Hick or Smith. Religious objects are thoroughly integrated with the means by which they are responded to and received. Religious ends are constituted by the meanings that the faiths bring to them. In distinction from LaFargue, I want to stress that in my view the religious objects or ends are not "nothing but" meanings constituted by human culture or creativity; that they are constituted in significant measure and remain so seems clear.

The orientational pluralism hypothesis I have suggested so far offers an account of the status of theories of religion. I have argued further on behalf of a particular type of religious perspective within this larger framework, a type that allows for the realization of various religious ends.

Let us consider now some examples of religious theories of religion consistent with my approach: two statements contrasting Buddhist and Christian views of "salvation." Here is a Christian writer:

> Buddhists do not attain Christian salvation, since their Way does not lead to that personal relationship with God which is salvation. They attain a high degree of compassion and inner peace; and their unselfish devotion to the truth as they see it will surely fit them to receive salvation from a personal God when his saving activity becomes clear to them (Ward 1990, 16).

Here is a Buddhist writer:

> Liberation in which "a mind that understands the sphere of reality annihilates all defilements in the sphere of reality" is a state that only Buddhists can accomplish. This kind of moksha or nirvana is only explained in the Buddhist scriptures, and is achieved only through Buddhist practice. According to certain religions, however, salvation is a place, a beautiful paradise, like a peaceful valley. To attain such a state as this, to achieve such a state of moksha, does not require the practice of emptiness, the understanding of reality. In Buddhism itself, we believe that through the accumulation of merit one can obtain rebirth in heavenly paradises like the Tushita (Dalai Lama 1990, 169).

These are classically inclusivist views, which interpret other faiths ultimately in the categories of the "home" religion. What is striking in these two cases is the additional factor that the *reality* of the religious end sought by another religious tradition is acknowledged in some significant measure, in very much the terms of that tradition itself. However, that state is regarded as penultimate, leaving open the further possibility of achieving or not achieving a state which the home tradition regards as integrally related to the truths or reality it regards as ultimate. Within each of the perspectives I quoted, and certainly for anyone who compares them, it clearly makes sense to speak of salvations. There is no necessary contradiction in these two accounts of possible human ends, though there is a decisive divergence in the two evaluative frameworks for these ends and there may be contradictions in the metaphysical assumptions associated with each framework. Both accounts could be flatly wrong. But there is no logical reason that both cannot be descriptively correct. In fact, if one of the writer's characterizations is correct, it implies the substantial truth of the other. By contrast, the pluralistic view is that both authors are in error, because they insist on distinguishing real differences within what pluralists believe is an identical religious end.

Both writers might agree in broad terms to the existence of one "salvific process," but they would mean by this that it may be possible to move in succession from the pursuit of the aim of one tradition toward that of another. This is emphatically not the same thing as insisting there is one and only one religious fulfillment. Ironically, it is just this kind of mutual recognition of *concrete* substantive truth in another tradition that Hick wants to rule out. It would imply difference, and he insists that the ends described in the various traditions are not actual at all but rather mythological signs, inducing the proper attitude in us toward the noumenal Real.

I have argued that all theories of religion are either exclusivist or inclusivist in nature. Orientational pluralism is consistent with advocacy of virtually all varieties of inclusivism. The key element is the recognition of other orientations and the defensibility of other views from those orientations. Such inclusivisms may well—and often do—assume that the other defensible views will ultimately dissolve into recognition and realization of the religious end of the inclusivist's "home" tradition, if their adherents are to achieve "salvation" at all. The more limited class of inclusivisms I am commending extends pluralism a crucial step further. Although they continue to see their tradition's religious ultimate at the center, they are willing to entertain the possibility that penultimate goods (from their view) could endure as the religious fulfillments of those who pursue various religious ends. Just as orientational pluralism recognizes that conflicting reasonable cases can be made from different orientations, a pluralistic inclusivism sees no compelling reason that these differences could not be maintained through the historical and eschatological states of religious fulfillment themselves.

SOME OBJECTIONS CONSIDERED

There are at least two major objections to this more pluralistic hypothesis. The first has to do with the obvious question: Which is more ultimate? To take the example of the Buddhist and Christian writers quoted above, is there something more fundamental behind both of the ineffable reals these traditions take as their aims? The possibility is not ruled out. But my hypothesis avoids such a postulate, on the grounds that such an answer is precisely what religious traditions provide and that to provide another is to set up *as* a religious tradition, in preference to the others (see Ward 1990, 17, on "revisionist pluralism").

Plainly, I hold that my hypothesis *is* theological in the same way that Rescher's orientational pluralism is doctrinal. It is not religiously neutral. My fundamental religious commitment is Christian. For this concrete reason I am interested in a theory of religion whose adoption does not displace that commitment or, as it happens, the analogous commitment of those in other traditions. My hypothesis is rooted in an evaluative orientation (in my case constituted as far as I am able by Christian faith) which affects the direction of my rational argument. I contend that all arguments are in fact based on the combination of these two elements and thus reflect particularistic commitments. This leads me to recognize that with different value orientations and sound reason people may argue for other views—such as pluralistic ones. At the same time my approach holds that it is appropriate and consistent for each of us to argue that our accounts are preferable to the others.

Some pluralistic writers disparage exclusivist and inclusivist religious commitments on the grounds that they amount to little more than tribalism, privileging a faith or judgment for the arbitrary reason that it happens to be mine. At one level the point is well taken; conclusions reached on limited evidence are always fallible. No one can make good the claim to have a "God's-eye view." On another level the objection is ludicrous: Whose basis of judgment am I to privilege if not my own? If I privilege another, it has become mine in that very act. An appreciation of my limitations should lead to a recognition of other tenable orientations toward the world; the alternative is arrogance and self-delusion. This recognition should not lead to a denial that from my orientation some commitments and conclusions are more adequate than others, and that in many cases I am convinced these apply not for me alone, but for all others as well; the alternative is dishonesty and self-delusion.

In philosophical terms the options are open. There could be many ineffable reals, and only one of them truly ultimate in the sense of excluding or being the ground of the others. There could be in fact only one actual ineffable real, subsisting equally in the fulfillment of the various religious aims and equally described or not described by the various traditions. Or there could be many coexistent ineffable reals, none of them truly ultimate. Any of those metaphysical conditions could be consistent with the contention that, for instance, Sunyata and God are both ineffable and both real, and that human realization of the one and communion with the other are actual experiential possibilities. Thus both could be functional religious ultimates. Whereas Hick is committed to saying that "Sunyata" and "God" are mythological cultural forms which represent "the Real," my hypothesis presumes that they are real religious ineffables available to their seekers, while not foreclosing the possibility that one may ultimately be subordinate to the other or both to some other absolute.

The same objection might be put slightly differently by complaining that my hypothesis allows those in individual traditions to continue to regard their referent as more ultimate than that in another tradition: as with the Buddhist and Christian writers quoted above. It certainly does. Even more pernicious to some, it presumes that adherence to different religious truths will eventuate in distinct fulfillments. Hick's hypothesis requires those who accept it to regard its referent—the Real—as more ultimate than the actual referent in any tradition, a fact not much mitigated by the coordinate claim that it actually *is* the referent of all the traditions. This is an inclusivism that differs only in being more mandatory than most: one inclusivism to replace the many. If the objection is that my hypothesis would permit the two writers I quoted above to speak as they do, I fail to see, either on the grounds of practical inter-religious harmony or philosophical consistency, why I should want a theory that forbids them to do so.

The convictions they express are an aspect of religious pluralism which cannot be stamped out unless the pluralism itself can be stamped out. They correspond to the human capacity to seek differing religious fulfillments. My contention is that the way forward in religious pluralism is to focus on the substance of the particular possibilities advanced in the varying traditions, not to reduce them to one possibility. The way forward is to live positively with otherness, not to suggest it is too dangerous to be real.

The second objection has to do with contradictions between the fulfillments in the various traditions. Does not my hypothesis involve too much affirmation, appearing to agree with systems whose accounts of the way things are cannot consistently be true? It is important to recognize that the hypothesis affirms the reality of different experiential states of religious fulfillment; it does not require that all of the elements a tradition associates with attainment of that state are also the case. One religious fulfillment may be associated in its tradition with an affirmation of the eternity of the universe, another with affirmation of the creation of the universe. One may be associated with a theory of the self and another with a theory of the no-self. To regard the religious fulfillments as real does not entail accepting in their entirety both sides of these oppositions. The inclusivist perspectives quoted above are examples of this inevitable discrimination.

There are real metaphysical differences, real ontological questions with real answers. Hick claimed that these answers (Is reincarnation real? Are there heavenly Buddhas?) are irrelevant to salvation. I suggest that the resolution of such questions in one way may not preclude the achievement of a variety of salvations or religious ends, but is decisive as to how these fulfillments are ultimately ordered.

Let us return for a moment to the cluster of statements we discussed earlier:

1) Religious truth is one;
2) Religious truth is called by many names, experienced in many forms;
3) Cultural and personal categories are constitutive of our knowledge and experience of reality: all experience is "experiencing as";
4) Religious aims and fulfillments are various.

The commitment to 1) in the cluster above—one world and one consistent truth—means that my pluralistic hypothesis, like Hick's, views questions of fact to have resolutions. Reincarnation takes place or it does not. Jesus rose from the dead or did not. Hick's point is that, true or false, such matters are salvifically irrelevant. I argue on the contrary that one's commitments about these matters and others are integrally constitutive of the distinct religious fulfillment that is realized, if any are. Further, at least some of the factual differences implied in the diversity of these commitments have a crucial bearing on how the various religious ends relate to each other.

Last of all we can consider the practical benefits which Hick sees flowing from his hypothesis. This discussion has to do in major part with our evaluative orientations, since Hick and others commend his rational hypothesis in significant part by appeal to such values. Therefore it becomes a crucial question whether my alternative hypothesis serves these values as well or better and whether other values might be suggested that exercise an important claim.

If accepted, Hick believes his hypothesis provides reason for people in all religious traditions to take up an attitude toward their differences that would preclude conflict and bigotry. Second, it would appear to provide a great apologetic breakthrough for religion per se by removing the accusation of arbitrariness brought against each actual religious tradition. The same salvific process is going on in each tradition, leading to the same limitlessly better possibility. Salvation does not depend on anything that can't be known with certainty, anything that could be missed by an honest mistake. Birth and cultural location then do not privilege some with regard to religious fulfillment and disadvantage others. Therefore people can pursue any particular religious tradition without concern that their choice has affected the result which may be expected for themselves and without any anxiety over the possible fate of others.

I believe the pluralistic hypothesis I have proposed rules out as much as Hick's does any dogmatic assertion on the part of one tradition that all others are simply wrong. Equally with Hick's, it presupposes that the achievement of a religious fulfillment cannot be limited to one tradition alone but is available in many. Even more cogently than Hick's, it maintains that these fulfillments are available precisely through the traditions that seek them. As to whether one approach is better than the other in terms of restraining conflict and supporting harmony, this turns on the fundamental question of whether we can only respect and appreciate what is identical, or whether we can equally respect and appreciate what we recognize is real but different. I believe the long-range hope for life in pluralistic societies rests on the latter.

My hypothesis no less than Hick's can stipulate that "honest mistakes" or cultural location will in the end bar no one from achieving religious fulfillment. But must humans seek and achieve only one end? This is what I question. Does *every* religious tradition in fact have a distinct and realizable religious end? Unlike Hick's hypothesis, mine does not resolve this question; that can only be done by assessing the various religious accounts and their specific convictions and grounds. However, the important point here is that although my hypothesis does not predetermine that humans must seek and achieve only one religious end (whether one not specifically thematized by any religion, like Hick's, or one belonging to one or some set of traditions), it presumes that religious aspirations cannot be finally thwarted by circumstance or inadequate knowledge. The number of religious ends available to humanity is a separate question from the terms under which these ends can be achieved.

The cooperation and mutual respect between the traditions which Hick desires are desperately needed. However, I am much less sanguine than he about the power of his ideas to bring about such conditions. I agree that good relations among religious groups seem to require not simply respect for others as people and toleration of their faith as an aspect of their humanity, but some positive respect for the others' religion itself—in its integrity and practice. Hick would say that this must include positive respect for the other religion's *truth*, or else we are doomed to conflict and bigotry. My hypothesis expects to find truth in religions, certainly the major faiths which Hick has taken as the premise of his hypothesis. We do not differ on that fact so much as how much and how many truths we expect to find. Hick presumes all these religions are right about one big thing, which none of them has normatively understood but which they all mythologically represent. And he believes that some may turn out to be correct on certain specific matters which are of no ultimate religious significance. I suggest that the traditions are more concretely correct about distinct religious ends available to humanity than Hick will allow.

On the apologetic front—and this is much more an implicit than explicit element in Hick—there is a significant difference. His hypothesis rules out fundamental critique of religion in a way that I cannot accept. The insulation of the faiths against such criticism provides a protection that I, as one religious believer, do not want and comes at a cost to the traditions that I (as an insider in my own and a student of others) do not want to pay. Each tradition may have its own more or less extensive scope for "mythological" truth, for image and representation. But each also has elements that, if they prove to be illusory, preclude the concrete religious fulfillment that is sought. Likewise, I do not regard it as a virtue in Hick's theory that it assures us we need not pause over any concern that another religious path might offer some ultimate benefit different from our own. This is a matter of judgment. Those who want the assurance of the old exclusivist condition—there is only one way— in its fully modern form will prefer the pluralistic theological view at this point.

My hypothesis of multiple religious ends, salvations, is a simple one. But it offers a perspective little canvassed in the contemporary discussion of religious diversity. Plainly it will meet criticism from several sides. But I would close this chapter with two responses to that criticism. Some will object, out of ostensible respect for the value of all religions, to any hypothesis that religious fulfillments are actually distinct and conform more closely to the tradition's own expectations than to pluralistic theories. To them I would pose a simple question. Which faith's concrete religious end do they believe it would be a misfortune to achieve? Some within faith traditions will object to the possibility of a religious fulfillment intermediate between their own and some negative state of annihilation or punishment. I would ask them whether the value and power of their religious end are not of such intrinsic depth that they can be warmly, effectively commended even in preference to other goods.

Several more elements in our job description for a perspective on religious diversity remain to be treated. But they can be addressed more easily if we move to the third stage of my argument. In the next chapter I will indicate the nature of a specifically Christian perspective embodying the principles I have suggested and take up some objections to my hypothesis which are of a more historical than philosophical nature.

6

Plenitude and Trinity

A Christian Perspective on Religious Diversity

The last chapter made two primary points. The first concerned the *status* of theories of religious pluralism. I argued that these theories are in the same epistemological position as the religions themselves and cannot claim a "God's-eye view." Second, I argued in favor of one class of inclusivist approaches to pluralism, those that recognize a diversity of religious fulfillments. This chapter has two central purposes. The first is to outline a Christian perspective that is consistent with the principles I have described. The second is to consider the validity of these principles from a more historical perspective, in contrast with the more philosophical discussion in chapter 5.

I have argued that inclusivist religious approaches which recognize diverse religious ends constitute the most adequate set of responses to religious diversity. Similarly, I will argue that the Christian theological perspective I outline is one of the most adequate Christian approaches to religious diversity. In both cases the orientation from which I work is a Christian one, an orientation constantly subject to the enlargement and transformation described by John Cobb in the last chapter. In line with the orientational pluralism I have described, it is appropriate to argue in this manner for the universal validity of my position in the first instance, and the preferability of my view among Christian alternatives in the second.

I do not propose that either of these views I hold must be adopted by others as necessary conditions for dialogue. There are other religious orientations, and other Christian orientations, from which other defensible conclusions can be reached. In line with the orientational pluralist perspective, it is precisely dialogue with those who may have different premises or reach differing conclusions that I most desire. One of the most fruitful contributions to my growth in the Christian life is encounter with a religious pattern of universal scope which cannot be fully assimilated in my terms. This offers the challenge of having to "cross over" imaginatively and spiritually to see the world, however imperfectly, from another orientation. It is some limited grasp of the reasonableness of another reading of the world, in the terms of that faith, which can most powerfully bring home the claim of the values and evidence that are privileged in that tradition. If I have hope of enlarging my own understanding of truth, of deepening my own practice of faith, this is among the most valuable gifts I can receive. Yet it is a gift I am in no position to receive if I believe that there are no crucial differences in our lived readings of the world, that I never encounter any real alternatives.

NEITHER HEAVEN NOR HELL

Classically inclusivist Christian positions hold that adherents of other traditions may relate savingly to God either *apart* from their specific religious practices (for instance, because of their observance of some natural morality) or *through* concrete elements of their own religious tradition which are implicitly directed toward God. Perhaps the most prominent advocate of this last possibility has been the Roman Catholic theologian Karl Rahner.

Rahner's view is set within a very sophisticated theological anthropology.[1] But two crucial theses summarize his position. The first is "Christianity understands itself as the absolute religion, intended for all men, which cannot recognize any other religion besides itself as of equal right" (Rahner 1966, 118). The second states that non-Christian religion "contains also supernatural elements arising out of the grace which is given to men as a gratuitous gift on account of Christ. For this reason, a non-Christian religion can be recognized as a *lawful* religion (although only in different degrees) without thereby denying the error and depravity contained in it" (Rahner 1966, 121). Thus various traditions can be seen as structural means of salvation for their adherents, but only because they mediate grace that comes through and is fully disclosed in Christ.

Such inclusivism grants that the same truth and benefits available in the Christian tradition can effectively be found within at least some other faiths. It claims that they are not found in those faiths to the same degree of fullness as in Christianity and that there is no *alternative* reli-

---

[1] For a more extensive account of Rahner's thought, see the work by Gavin D'Costa, perhaps the most distinguished contemporary exponent of Rahner's approach to religious pluralism, *Theology and Religious Pluralism*, chap. 4.

gious truth there. What is not directed to the full Christian aim is not true or real. It is just at this point that I propose a change. I suggest that Christians can consistently recognize that some traditions encompass religious ends which are real states of human transformation, distinct from that Christians seek. There are paths in varying religious traditions which if consistently followed prove effective in bringing adherents to alternative fulfillments. The crucial question among the faiths is *not* "Which one saves?" but "What counts as salvation?"

On the one hand this requires a significant revision of traditional Christian outlooks. Christians have generally recognized some grounding in principle for other faiths in a common revelation in creation, while disagreeing whether this foundation could be practically effective apart from special revelation. But those on both sides of this disagreement have tended to assume that this foundation could have no actual use but attainment of the Christian end. That there could be a basis for achieving *other* ends was not considered in any terms except those of perdition. The fundamental challenge of my proposal for Christians is to reflect on the possibility of the providential provision of a diversity of religious ends for human beings.

As Joseph DiNoia puts it, Christian theology can affirm "the distinctiveness of the aims fostered by other religions without prejudice to an affirmation of the unique valuation of the Christian community or of its doctrines about salvation" (DiNoia 1992, 91). Such distinctiveness raises the question of a providential role for the religions in the divine plan other than or in addition to serving as channels for salvation as Christians understand it. These are roles "that are now only dimly perceived and that will be fully disclosed in the consummation of history for which Christians long" (DiNoia 1992, 91).

On the other hand, the alternativeness of these ends to Christian aims allows and even requires a judgment from the Christian perspective that subordinates them to the consummation of the Christian life. To realize something other than communion with the triune God and with others in the continuing relationship of created being is to achieve a lesser good. It is not the abundant life that Christians know and hope for in Christ. There is no reason to avoid this judgment, as long as we grasp that others make reciprocal judgments. The new factor we have added to the picture is the expectation, to be tested by encounter, that these reciprocal judgments may in fact be grounded in their own distinct religious fulfillments.

The discussion of religious difference shifts then from a sole focus on flat issues of truth and falsehood, or degrees of these, to include consideration of alternatives: not "Which religion alone is true?" but "What end is most ultimate, even if many are real?" The cessation of self, the realization of an absolute actual self which is "non-dual," communion with the triune God, living on only in our effects on historical posterity: let us presume for the moment that these and other aims are actual possibilities. These are real experiential human states, significantly constituted by the practice and aspiration of the person who attains them. They are not identical.

What is true in one tradition or sphere of human life must cohere with what is true elsewhere. Therefore, it is reasonable to believe that those faith fulfillments which are live possibilities have some ontological ordering as well. But that issue can be distinguished from the experiential availability of distinct religious fulfillments. Whether or not it is possible for an individual or community to regard two or several ends as equally desirable, it is highly questionable whether we can shape our lives in pursuit of more than one at once without dramatically changing each. The persons that we become through our concrete choices and religious practices may not only increasingly realize a distinctive aim, but may in proportion to that realization manifest a more unswerving desire for that end among all others.

A religious end or aim is defined by a set of practices, images, stories, and conceptions which collectively has three characteristics. First, the set provides material for a pervasive pattern of life. The "ultimacy" often spoken of in definitions of religion is here given a quite concrete interpretation; it is not some single dimension of life that is addressed but all its features, sublime and mundane. Second, at least some of these elements are understood to be *constitutive* of a final human fulfillment and/or to be the sole means of achieving that fulfillment. For instance, for Christians, there is a texture of such elements making reference to Jesus Christ, and Christ is believed to be integral to the fulfillment itself. Most Buddhists may maintain that all the instruments used to follow the dharma way are ultimately themselves dispensable, even the eight-fold path itself. But it can only be discarded *after* being used, and nothing else is fit to serve the same purpose. Third, for any individual or community the pattern is in practice exclusive of some alternative options. The set of stories and practices in its nature involves choices. "The ascetic life leads to peace" and "the sensual life leads to joy" may both be true reports. But one can practice the observance of one more comprehensively only at the expense of the other. For our purposes it makes no difference that some may make the tantric claim that some combined practice of asceticism/sensuality will lead to peace *and* joy. This is itself a claim, a pattern, and a practice which, if followed, rules out either of the other two paths.

The relations among religious ends are as diverse as the ends themselves. Some fulfillments may be similar enough that the paths associated with them reinforce each other to some degree, as typing and piano playing may both train the fingers. Other ends may simply pose no obstacle, one to the other, save the intrinsic division of finite time and effort: say marathon running and single parenthood. Yet others diverge so sharply that a decisive step in one direction moves away from the other: strict nonviolence and participation in armed revolution.

There is an interesting dynamic balance in the relation of religious ends. The more similar the aims, the more sharply issues of the fulfillment or supersession of one path to that end by another arise. If the aims were in fact identical—say the end is word processing—there are few who would not take sides between computers or typewriters as the more adequate road. In such circumstances, however, the common features of the religious aims provide a compensatory shared ground on which to struggle and work toward agreement. On the other hand, the more incommensurable religious ends appear, the less the question of supersession seems even strictly applicable. Though having less concretely in common at this level, there is a somewhat proportionally lessened impetus for denial or substitution. These dynamics are key elements in understanding religious conflict and the possibilities for mutual understanding.

"Salvation" or religious fulfillment for any religious community is integrally related to a comprehensive pattern of life. Any particular religious tradition would regard someone as "saved" whose life had been most fully shaped by the distinctive pattern it fosters. Even if the person in question had his or her life formed entirely outside explicit relation to this particular religious tradition, the person would be perceived and evaluated on the basis of the pattern provided by this faith tradition. Religious ends are not extrinsic awards granted for unrelated performances, like trips to Hawaii won in lotteries. No one is unhappy "in" nirvana or arrives at it unready, because the state of cessation is an achievement the path makes possible. It is not "enjoyed" until one has become what the path makes you.[2] The way and the end are one.

Though most faith traditions project the final fullness of their ends into a transmundane context, this constitutive relation between the end and the path certainly allows us to speak of a diversity of salvations in the historical plane. The evidence for this diversity is very strong. Edward Conze, a scholar of Buddhism, read through a Roman Catholic collection of lives of the saints and reported "there was no one of whom a Buddhist could fully approve. This does not mean that they were unworthy people, but that they were bad Buddhists" (Conze 1962, 82; quoted in DiNoia 1992, 34). W. C. Smith looks at the religious history of humanity and concludes that everywhere people were finding the same salvation, by which he means release of some sort from despair and self-absorption. This is a peculiarly unrealistic kind of report, resolutely abstracting as it does from the actual kinds of fulfillment recounted and celebrated in the traditions and the varying terms used. Believers

---

[2] This paragraph paraphrases several points made by DiNoia in a very helpful discussion of religious aims. See DiNoia 1992, 6-7 and 56-58.

do not report "despair-diminishment" as the nature of their religious end, except as an integral aspect of something more concrete from which Smith averts his eyes. We can agree with him on the widespread experiences of religious fulfillment, but argue it is both more accurate descriptively and less dismissive of the faiths themselves to recognize these fulfillments as diverse.

From a Christian perspective this requires the somewhat unfamiliar admission that other religious fulfillments may be both distinct and quite real. At the same time Christians may rightly continue to view the achievement of these alternative religious ends as something to be avoided, even in cases carrying some measure of the meaning of "damnation." That is, they are not positive evils (though such evils may also be live possibilities), but they are aims different than the best that Christians know and hope for.

Is such a diversity in human destiny consistent with Christian convictions? Plainly Christian sources, from scripture on, tend to stress a twofold distinction (the saved and the lost). With time, however, consideration arose for at least some diversity among the saved. And such diversity was often also imagined among the lost, as in distinctions made between the destiny of unbaptized infants and others of the lost (see Sanders 1992, 287-305). That is, within the overall twofold pattern, distinctions were made in each category. The possibility of alternative religious fulfillments can be viewed as a third division, a category that could be classed on one of the two sides or the other, depending on whether the emphasis is on the absence of the distinctive end Christians seek or on the intrinsic character of the alternative.

The possibility of a more thoroughgoing diversity in the future of humanity is in some measure authorized by the trinitarian vision of God and a notion of the divine plenitude. That is, it rests on the conviction that the most emphatic no of the human creature to the end of loving communion with God meets always some variation of God's merciful yes to creation.

PLENITUDE AND TRINITY

The principle of plenitude debated in the theological tradition maintained that the infinite nature of God mandated proliferation of the greatest variety of *types* of being. A universe that includes a stone, a human, and an angel is better, then, than one with three angels. Those like Aquinas who held such views clearly understood some levels of being as superior to others, but suggested that the *existence* of each level was equally important (see Lovejoy 1974, 52).[3] As a strictly logical proposi-

---

[3] This eventually led into arguments about the necessity of evil, which go beyond the scope of this discussion.

tion, the principle of plenitude always drew its advocates into knots of perplexity, confronted with the question of whether all possible modes of being were necessarily owed instantiation in the creation of a good God.

The philosophical and theological tradition was mesmerized with notions of being and possible being; plenitude was a kind of formal perfection to be attributed to God. I suggest a rather different and restricted meaning of plenitude, based not on a formal philosophical quality of God but on an economic expression of the fullness of God's love and relational nature. From this perspective it is a reflection of the divine plenitude that the human freedom which God has created may actualize itself in a number of ways.

It is already a commonplace of Christian thought that the fulfillment of communion with God, though shared by all the redeemed, may be various in its forms, even as the inner life of the Trinity is diverse. Dante's *Divine Comedy* reflects this in his vision of the circles of paradise. Beatrice explains to the poet that the figures they encounter on their travels through the levels of heaven are not truly separated spatially from each other or from God. They all dwell together in the empyrean realm:

> And all share one sweet life, diversified
> As each feels more or less the eternal breath.
>
> They're shown thee here, not that they here
>   reside,
> Allotted to this sphere; their heavenly mansion
> Being least exalted, is thus signified.
>   (Dante Alighieri, canto IV, lines 35-39, 82)

There are, of course, similar circles in Dante's hell and purgatory, diversified by attachment to various sins in the first case and by commitment to varied preparations for heaven in the second. Dante's cosmological vision presumes a kind of plenitude; the ensemble composed by these various possible levels of being (a matter in principle separate from their realization) is to him one of extraordinary justice, mercy, and beauty. God is glorified by the existence of such diversity, and by each particular in it.

An eschatological plenitude would further develop some of these same elements to suggest that the human realization of ends other than communion with the triune God could also be to the glory of God. From a Christian view such ends would no more be optimal ones, in terms of ultimate possibility, than Dante's vision would be to a Buddhist or a Vedantan. That each soul should receive its dearest desire, when each soul has had fullest scope to form that desire, is no reproach to the divine love and no diminishment of human hope. A similar type of reinterpretation can appeal to the classical Augustinian notion that, as God creates only good, the alternatives to full response to God can only themselves be disproportions of the good.

From such a revised Christian perspective three types of religious option appear rather than two: lostness, penultimate religious fulfillments, and communion with the triune God. The real possibility remains that a person may not actualize any viable religious end, may find not an alternative fulfillment but rather none at all. There are human conditions, contemporary or eschatological, that no valid religious view claims as consistent with its end. On this point there is ample room for common cause among the faiths: spiritual and practical cooperation to overcome these conditions, even from differing perspectives.

There is an enormous difference between this lostness from all religious fulfillment and the achievement of *some* religious fulfillment. Christians can affirm an eschatological plenitude whereby, for instance, those who give themselves to the "divine abyss" of emptiness can be seen to have realized a facet of the divine plenitude. From my Christian view this is a secondary good, since I believe that communion with God in a fuller range of God's being is possible. But the end is neither unreal nor evil; it does truly offer release from the round of human suffering. Our place in the great tapestry of the consummation is alterable, but each one glorifies God in some measure. This Christian conviction would be analogous to a Buddhist's confidence that a Christian's spiritual fulfillments could only uphold and be consistent with the dharma.

Is the realization of such diversity necessary to the fullness of the divine glory? Eschatological plenitude consists in the *range* of such fulfillments available to creation, not in any requirement that each one be realized in some fixed ratio. Human freedom shapes the diversity of fulfillment the eschaton exhibits. If all human beings eventually participate in the triune life in a network of relation among unique created selves, this would constitute a variety at least as deep in its richness as that represented by the panoply of various religious ends. And surely Christians believe the divine plenitude would be diminished if none were saved in the Christian sense. But no fixed proportion between these possibilities is necessarily specified by Christian eschatological hope.

Within Christian tradition there were debates over God's obligation to save humanity: Is God's justice or love compromised if some are not redeemed? Our new framework casts this question in a changed light. We could certainly affirm that God would be just if all the world attained a Buddhist religious end rather than a Christian one, even though what Christians believe a fuller opportunity for humans was not realized. Communion with the triune God is thought to encompass dimensions of other fulfillments, to be better because more consistent with the nature of the ultimate, and so more inclusive.

We cannot deny that other religious fulfillments have something, in their intensity and exclusivity, that is not present by definition in the end Christians seek. Christian religious fulfillment cannot be inclusive of an exclusive focus on either a feature of created being or a divine facet to the point of eliminating others. The divine love which overflows with such plenitude also sustains the diversity of ends that can flow from it. Persons who individually or communally fix upon a real aspect of divine creation or being and make their universe revolve about that center are "let be" by the divine love. There is no invocation of an arbitrary end to such pluralism.

This continuing conviction on the part of Christians that theirs is a distinctive and preferable religious end is itself a ground for the recognition of distinctively different religious fulfillments in other traditions. The two go together. This reinforces the arguments on behalf of an orientational pluralist outlook which I offered earlier. Christians may and should continue to argue that the patterns of life and thought relating to communion with the triune God can be crucial sources for developing perspectives on *common* areas of human life, whether political or economic. Religious convictions are of public and not only private significance. This is an issue we will take up at greater length in the next chapter.

Divine plenitude is a philosophical concept. For Christians its application is based on a more fundamental conviction regarding God's triune nature. The Trinity is a distinctively Christian template for diversity. Plenitude has to do with the provision of diverse possibilities for creation. Such an idea could be deployed within various religious perspectives. It takes on a particular complexion when rooted in the Trinity, deriving primarily from the freedom in relation of the three divine persons—a freedom in relation whose image is a watermark in creation.

The relations of the triune persons have a steadfastness which is not that of causal necessity but of unswerving constancy of character in freedom. Thus from a Christian perspective the plenitude of the universe and of human possibilities within it offer a reflection of its triune source. But this does not mean that all viable human ends are fully oriented to that source. John Hick speaks of the "epistemic distance" which God keeps from us in order to empower free response. We could view the plenitude of human ends in a similar way. A relation without any alternative, or no alternative but a punitive one, is not a relation in the full sense. It would be like choosing friends or mates when you belong to a generation of two. In the view I suggest there is a distinction within the plenitude of religious fulfillments between those ends which explicitly do not seek to relate to the triune God, and those which do.

Raimundo Panikkar and Gavin D'Costa, in rather different ways, make the case that the Trinity is the key for interpreting the theological significance of religious diversity. Panikkar does so as a professed pluralist, D'Costa as an inclusivist. Precisely because of their trinitarianism, however, it seems to me that this border nearly vanishes and both point us beyond such divisions.

D'Costa argues that the Trinity provides the deep Christian grammar for relating particularity and universality. It is "only on the basis of this particularity that we are able to affirm the universal agency of God's redeeming activity" (D'Costa 1990, 17). That is, the specific identification of God's presence in Christ is the reason for believing that God's activity is ongoing in all of creation. To affirm Christ's oneness with God is at once to affirm that God is not only in Christ. "The Trinity safeguards against an exclusivist particularism (Christomonism) and a pluralist universalism (theocentrism) in that it stipulates against an *exclusive identification* of God and Jesus, as well as against a *non-identification* of God and Jesus" (D'Costa 1990, 18).

The fullness of God's mystery is never grasped by us. It is hidden in the Father and source, overflows in Christ beyond the measure of our means to receive it, and is continually active in all of creation through the Spirit. "*All* history, both past and to come, is potentially a particularity by which God's self-revelation is mediated" (D'Costa 1990, 19). Christ is the concrete particularity *by* which Christians know this about the potential in all of history and *in* whom, in the unity with the divine Word, this self-revelation decisively takes place. The scope of divine activity in all of religious history widens in proportion to the decisiveness of God's self-revelation in Christ, not the reverse. Christ is normative, not absolute, the ground by which we can be open to other faiths and see that the Spirit blows where it will. If Christians confess the coeternality of the Spirit and stand equally under the Spirit's judgment, then the conviction that the Spirit works in other faiths makes relation with those faiths vital and not incidental for Christians.

Since the Trinity also discloses loving relationship as the fundamental mode of being, love of neighbor is an imperative for Christians. If Christ is understood in trinitarian terms, then the self-giving love of Jesus is normative for believers, requiring dialogue and justice-making. D'Costa argues that "non-Christians must have a narrative space within Christian theology and practice so that their histories and stories can be heard without distortion" (D'Costa 1990, 19). Discipleship entails working together with all creeds to overcome oppression. Attentiveness to our neighbor's faith, in order to learn what the Spirit may be doing there, and praxis for justice are *co-essential* with Christological devotion in the Christian life. There can be no firmer basis for such concerns within Christianity, D'Costa says.

Raimundo Panikkar's thought is rich in allusion and hard to simplify. Although he groups himself with the pluralists, he stands apart from them on several key points (see Panikkar 1987, 89-116; Panikkar 1973). He unapologetically puts forward a specific ontological view of reality and insists that there can be no "passing beyond" the particular grounds of the individual religious traditions.

This is highlighted in Panikkar's variation on John Hick's image of a Copernican revolution in religion. The pluralists' claim for a universal system is a contradiction in terms, Panikkar says. The shift needed is to a "theanthropic vision, a kind of trinitarian notion, not of the godhead alone, but of reality. The center is neither the earth (our particular religion), nor the sun (God, transcendence, the Absolute . . .). Rather, each solar system has its own center, and every galaxy turns reciprocally around the other. There is no absolute center" (Panikkar 1987, 109).

In a passage that summarizes this vision, Panikkar says

> The perfect self-mirroring of Being is truth, but even if the perfect image of Being is identical to Being, Being is not exhausted in its image. If the Logos is the transparency of Being, the Spirit is, paradoxically, its opaqueness. The Spirit is freedom, the freedom of Being to be what it is. And this is, *a priori* as it were, unforeseeable by the Logos. The Logos accompanies Being; it does not precede it; it does not pre-dict what Being is. It tells only what Being is. But the *is* of Being is free. The mystery of the Trinity is the ultimate foundation for pluralism (Panikkar 1987, 109-110).

If Trinity is the ground of all being and becoming, then *some* difference like that among the religions is not ephemeral but permanent. This rules out an eschatological expectation that in the end all religions must be one. "The incommensurability of ultimate systems is unbridgeable. This incompatibility is not a lesser evil (that would be to judge only by the logos), but a revelation itself of the nature of reality" (Panikkar 1987, 110).

Panikkar takes the Christian belief in the Trinity, transmutes it into a kind of philosophical cosmology that looks beyond confessional Christian formulations—though emphatically never denying its particularistic roots there—to view reality itself as metaphysically triune. He then turns this cosmology back upon Christianity itself to call it to recognize the legitimacy of being one among many faiths. Although the faiths are incommensurable, this "does not preclude the fact that each religion may be a dimension of the other in a kind of trinitarian *perichoresis* or *circumincessio*" (Panikkar 1987, 112).

Panikkar outlines three forms of spirituality which he loosely identifies with the three classical *margas* or ways of India: action (karma), devotion (bhakti) and knowledge (jnana). These correspond in his mind to the divine as icon, person, and mystery. Only with a particular form and quality can the divine direct life; only as relational may it be loved; and only in undivided union may it be known. These three are indissolubly different, and Panikkar suggests it is "only a trinitarian concept of reality which permits us at least to indicate the main lines of a synthesis between these three apparently irreducible concepts of the Absolute" (Panikkar 1973, 41). The crucial thing about such a synthesis is that the differences between religions remain part of the ultimate irreducible diversity of reality itself.

It is interesting to note that in a book published nearly at the same time as Panikkar's work on the Trinity, George Bosworth Burch covered some very similar ground. Following an analysis that agrees to a great extent with Panikkar, Burch swerved slightly to one side for a strikingly different result (Burch 1972). He argued frankly for a plurality of absolutes. The three absolutes he identified—Freedom, Love, Truth—are largely analogous to Panikkar's three forms of spirituality. But rather than argue that they cohere in a single absolute, Burch suggested that they are strict alternatives. His argument was that *absolute* freedom, love, and truth are incommensurable and do not encroach or impinge on each other in any way. Each could be absolute, in its purity, without displacing the others. The three occupy the same space but do not intersect: a trinity of non-relation.

In this view there are not merely different religions but different kinds of religion, with incomparable goals. Accordingly, one should recognize other ways as equal in the sense of being alternatives freely chosen and realized, not errors to be tolerated. Though human beings find themselves in similar conditions, in the same world, Burch argues that there are different paths that lead from the world, or into different aspects of it. The nature of reality is such as to allow humans to maximize, as it were, different dimensions. The difficulty of our condition comes from a mixture of suffering, sin, and ignorance. The religions differ primarily in fixing on one of these and seeking to purify life of it: Buddhism being an instance in the first case, Christianity in the second, and Advaita Vedanta of the third.

In Burch's view, any attempt to combine the three leads only to religious frustration. For a person can embrace two religions only at their lowest levels, "as a person can plant their feet on two mountains only at their lowest points" (Burch 1972, 110). The logic of the faiths is neither *not* (exclusivism) or *and* (some kind of unity of the religions, whether pluralist or inclusivist) but radically *or*. There is no necessity to deny the validity of other traditions, but every reason to expect that our destiny hangs upon our adherence to one as opposed to another. People walking by these alternative paths do not interfere with each other, quite the contrary. The more they develop their particular purification, the less ground for conflict exists between them.

Living in accordance with religious commitments, our life is formed by them. They make us who we are. Just as orientational pluralism suggests, Burch says we can judge how well we have abided by our commitments, but we cannot judge the grounds for the commitments themselves. We could no more judge what our life might have been like as a Methodist instead of a Sikh than we can compare the children we might have had with those we did.

The vision that I have sketched earlier in fact draws on elements of the views of D'Costa, Panikkar, and Burch. It corresponds to Panikkar's approach on many points: pluralism is real, not superficial; any theory of the religions must arise from a particularistic ground among them; a Christian inclusivist account of the faiths which allows them to be themselves is possible only on trinitarian grounds. Burch has a kind of "Trinity" in which three absolutes have gone their own way and have no mutual relations. I reject what amounts to three separate unitarianisms, but I do adopt his bracing conviction that there are diverse religious ends. Like D'Costa and unlike Panikkar, I maintain a stronger link between the Christological and the trinitarian doctrines.

Panikkar and D'Costa agree in commending a frankly particularistic approach to issues of diversity, and in taking Trinity as the focus. They differ in the extent to which they believe the Trinity can be "spun out" into categories which have dropped the explicitly Christological context. The normativity of Christ, which Panikkar also affirms, undergoes transformation in his thought into an ontological "Christic principle."

One of the primary concrete implications I see of this difference is that Panikkar views all fundamental religious differences as manifestations of the inner trinitarian relations. It is the complex interaction of the various religions as irreducibly different that is itself, for him, the full reflection of the divine. I would maintain, however, that the various religious ends are free to diverge more than this. At the least it is premature to conclude that religious differences amount only to a difference over which trinitarian person to focus on. This is too monolithic a Christian inclusivism, leaving no space to recognize constitutive religious visions that are distinct from or parallel to trinitarian convictions.

Panikkar's view is in truth a frankly inclusivist one, distinguished by its use of the trinitarian dogma to justify the enduring validity of religious differences and by its formulation of that dogma in terms highly abstracted from Christian roots, terms chosen to resonate with other traditions. It takes the significant step beyond most pluralist theories of recognizing enduring difference, but it insists those ultimate differences are all Christian differences, as it were: inner trinitarian differences. Thus in a very sophisticated way it remains impossible for there to be any true alternatives *to* the Christian vision, any otherness than its constitutive otherness. I admire Panikkar's thought as a Christian attempt to encompass the faiths. But it is quite unclear in its treatment of religious ends, and the theory of religions it embodies does not provide space to recognize a *non*-trinitarian reading of the world as anything but a partially trinitarian reading of the world. I believe our perspective on religious diversity is much strengthened by a dose of the thorough-going pluralism that Burch suggests in the eschatological realm and which LaFargue illustrated in the last chapter with regard to the historical realm. My approach tries to honor both.

At many points, however, my hypothesis has strong affinities with Panikkar's project. He says:

> Vis-à-vis the religions of the world, a Christian pluralistic attitude will affirm the Christian tenets, but without forgetting the limitation and contingency of the subject who formulates them. In other words, it will never proclaim "the true belief is x." It will always confess: "I believe x to be true" (the true belief). The "I believe" cannot be severed from belief. Nevertheless, this does not prevent me from affirming that I believe that others are wrong and even that their views are so harmful that I may feel obliged to combat particular errors—though not as absolute evils (Panikkar 1987, 111).

I would take this to be consistent with the perspective of orientational pluralism that I have elaborated in the previous chapter. Indeed, I believe that orientational pluralism adds something to Panikkar's statement. He stresses the tentativeness of individual subjectivity: I believe this is true. Rescher rightly indicates that we can also stress a less individual and more objective claim: on the basis of a specifiable evaluative orientation, I maintain this and no other view must be true. This is a communal affirmation and not just a subjective one. It can be checked, contested, and confirmed by others who share the same evaluative orientation. The conditioned character of conviction cannot be denied, but neither is it the case that this amounts to a purely individual subjectivism if there is criticism and debate within and among different orientations.

The fact that Panikkar is virtually alone among the pluralist theologians in taking a thoroughly trinitarian view is highly significant.[4] I believe it is not an accident that on this basis he proves the most open among his colleagues to real difference. The very goals which pluralistic theologians seek are only attainable in a recognition of actual pluralism, in ends as well as means. Most pluralistic writers tend to agree— Hick being the most prominent example—that incarnational Christology is the primary obstacle for Christians in relating rightly to other faiths. In so readily cutting the nerve of trinitarian doctrine, such approaches may have removed their own principal resource. As Christians, in failing to explicitly use our own particularistic grounds, we undermine true pluralism.

---

[4] See Rowan Williams's appreciative essay on Panikkar, "Trinity and Pluralism," in D'Costa, *Christian Uniqueness Reconsidered*, 3-15. I am indebted to Williams's essay for highlighting this aspect of Panikkar's thought.

DIVERSITY WITHIN RELIGIOUS TRADITIONS

Recognition of diverse religious ends leads us to renewed appreciation for the crucial significance of faith choices and development. We can expect a religious fulfillment to be in line with the "one and only" path that leads us to it. Our religious practices and decisions are important because they shape importantly differentiated lives and futures, rather than necessarily washing out in a single convergent process. Although we have first sketched this vision in terms of postmortem destinies, it holds equally well if we consider religious diversity entirely in a historical frame. Indeed, one of the recommendations of this approach is the way in which these eschatological and historical dimensions are made consistent with each other.

What has been said above eschatologically applies even more emphatically to proximate historical forms of religious fulfillment: living a Christian life, following the dharma. The meaning, de-centering of self, moral discipline, and hope persons experience on such paths are permeated with the concrete elements of a tradition. The lives that lead to the rewards of a Buddhist monastic, a devotee of Ba'hai, a Hindu brahmin priest, or a Baptist deacon have unique textures. It is not hard to note generic similarities: textual devotion, communal structures, ritual practices. But for those who would themselves attain to a religious fulfillment, the generic elements are irrelevant. They will need a particular text, a specific community, discrete rituals.

But are people obliged to choose these only in existing standard-issue combinations? What about the argument that religious traditions are not pure and well-defined options but in fact often permeate each other? Even if the diversity of religious ends is a reasonable assumption, what are we to make of the powerful contentions of W. C. Smith and others that empirical study of religious history reveals just the opposite: a seamless, single religious quest?

The unifying reality Smith finds in the traditions is a contentless, existential attitude, "faith," which is visible as such only from a modern, Western standpoint. Thus the unity of religious history is a function of the perspective from which it is viewed. Inclusivist strains within many faiths also see a unity to religious history, a unity grounded in their distinctive religious object and perceptible from their angle of vision. Smith's thesis consists in an eloquent call for others to share his evaluative perspective and an unconvincing claim that believers of the past already did.[5] But he is entirely right in pointing out the lack of sharp borders between religions. As a historian, Smith again

---

[5] As, for instance, in his extended argument that "faith" as used in the New Testament has the same intent as in his construction.

and again indicates that the traditions have been more intimately interconnected than contrasting rosters of doctrines would lead us to suspect.

This fact in itself cuts against the common pluralistic contention that diverse religions represent responses to an identical reality, aspiration to the same end, and vary only because of the different cultural contexts in which they arise. If religious traditions have been closely intertwined and in many cases actually arose out of similar cultural contexts in the same period (as Buddhism and Hinduism in India or rabbinic Judaism and Christianity in Palestine), then it seems less plausible to attribute their distinctions to cultural destiny.

The Protestant pioneer in the field of religious pluralism, Ernst Troeltsch, is widely known for concluding that Christianity was the supreme religion—for Europeans. Christianity is a relative phenomenon which "could, as we actually find it, only have arisen in the territory of the classical cultures and among Latin and German races" (Troeltsch 1969, 84). What Troeltsch made of the ancient Indian, Coptic, and Syrian churches or would make of a Christianity today centered in Africa and South America is unclear. His historical consciousness, which rightly pointed to the specific character of Christian development, ran perilously close to tautology. Christianity, or any other religion "as we find it," could only have a character consistent with passing through the cultural contexts it actually has passed through. This tells us nothing about its capacity to enter or be valid within yet other cultures: some faiths have dramatically exhibited this capacity and some have not. It would be more accurate to say that cultures may have a prevailing religious drift, but that even within a culture with a very strong current there is significant space for development in varying directions. Here we may give full value to W. C. Smith's observations on the diverse elements seeded through all the traditions, observations that tend to undercut Troeltsch's more dogmatic conclusion.

In fact there is a tendency among the strongest pluralist thinkers to veer between two options. On the one hand, like Troeltsch, they may tend to view religious diversity as a natural segregation, not unlike the way that the vast religious diversity within Hinduism historically configured itself in reinforcement of caste distinctions. Though these pluralistic theologians may maintain there is some ineffable religious end or essence in common, they hold that religions and cultures come in historical unities and people can only authentically adopt them as such. From this view a Chinese Christian, like a Swedish Hindu, is both odd and a bit unfortunate. A contrasting tendency is to contend with W. C. Smith that there are no real borders between the faiths at all, that they are a unified historical process, a single religious quest. Both tendencies err in what they deny.

I noted earlier that Christian inclusivists traditionally looked to other traditions only to find there the "incognito" elements of the gospel that might lead people to Christian faith. The proposal I have made adds a dimension for recognizing the distinctive truth and separate ends of other traditions. But room remains also for classical inclusivism.

Each great religious tradition can be seen as a strong spiritual wind, bearing those in its path or in cultures it shapes toward a definite religious end. However, there are currents within the prevailing wind and each individual or community trims its sail in some manner to meet the breeze. We all "tack" within the religious weather available to us, with results that can take us in distinctly different directions.

As classical inclusivists have argued, it is entirely possible to progress toward an alternative religious end *within* a dominant tradition, whether or not one actually is converted to a different religion in one's lifetime. It is frequently remarked that most major faiths appear to have developed a number of analogous dimensions. We can see for instance that elements of Christian faith have similarities with the personalistic theistic devotion of South Indian *bhakti* traditions and the bodhisatva figures of Mahayana Buddhism. In like manner we may note gnostic and monistic streams that recur within Christian history and find resonances in South Asian religions. This observation agrees with W. C. Smith's point that not even a single tradition is unbrokenly one in its faith resources. Rather than concluding that all the religious traditions are variations on a single theme, however, it seems to me more likely that what we see is testimony to the diversity of human religious possibility.

Short of some doctrine of double predestination, Christians are committed to the universal availability of salvation in Christ. It is precisely the fact that no religious tradition is monolithic that makes the inclusivist argument viable. Nowhere is any person without the religious means to move *toward* the religious fulfillment Christians seek. And within the Christian traditions, it is entirely possible for persons to move toward *other* goals. Affirmation of distinct religious ends does not require a belief that the traditions themselves are individually homogenous. As historical entities, the religious traditions are great fields of diversity. For a pluralist, these internal differences can have no substantive significance; if the differences between the faiths themselves are secondary, how much more so those within a tradition? From my perspective, these internal divergences are distinctly meaningful ones, differences that in their farther reaches connect with the wider pluralism.

The perspective which pluralistic theologies advocate that people in all traditions should take up is itself an interesting case in point. A "pluralistic" Christian or Islamic or Buddhist view will represent one strand within each of these faith communities. Pluralists insist that this one among the diverse streams within each tradition should be adopted and the others excluded. So they are arguing that this particular difference internal to a faith tradition is not simply a matter of a variant cultural form for the same religious truth. It represents a crucial divide in religious life. But if they are correct, this contradicts their own account of the secondary nature of religious differences.

One primary effect of today's intensified global communication is more ready contact among sub-streams of the various traditions which find strong mutual affinities. When Christians of a gnostic inclination and neo-Vedantans proclaim the unity of all religion, they have done so by a thoroughly inclusivist move, carefully selecting a version of the "other" that most closely mirrors themselves. It is often remarked that many of the issues of greatest religious conflict today run as much across the religions as between them, whether the issue is the status of women or monism versus pluralism. Most formal interreligious contacts reflect this "sociology of dialogue"; who talks with whom about what is largely a result of self-selection.[6]

We may pause here for a moment to consider the implications of the Christian perspective I have sketched for interreligious dialogue. Observers catalog different forms of dialogue, many of which are almost unanimously affirmed: dialogue oriented to mutual learning and removing misconceptions, dialogue fostering cooperation in social action, dialogue seeking to enhance personal relationships. Disagreements proliferate when expectations for dialogue beyond these aims are proposed. The framework that I suggest envisions three different kinds of judgment about religious truth that can arise in dialogue. Participants may conclude that there are elements of error and evil in another's belief or practice (at the extreme, this would mean the denial that there is a valid religious aim at all). They may conclude that they see in another tradition elements authentically relating to the same religious fulfillment sought in their own. They may conclude that they recognize in the other tradition a religious end which is both real and alternative to their own. In most cases any participant's tentative position will mix judgments of all three kinds.

Dialogue is severely constricted if these dimensions are not all actively in play. The contemporary typology, exclusivist-inclusivist-pluralist, revolves around only the first two. Pluralists and inclusivists tend to agree in emphasizing the second dimension, arguing over the extent to which a single religious end may be attained through different faiths while downplaying the third possibility (and in the case of the pluralists the first as well). Only with a broader set of options can the integral uniqueness of the dialoguing traditions be recognized and the depths of mutuality plumbed.

Including the dimension of different religious ends is important in several respects. It challenges faith traditions to account in their own

---

[6] Chapter 4 outlines what kind of self-selection is involved in the movement toward pluralistic theologies itself.

terms for the reality of other religious fulfillments. Just as significant, the recognition of this dimension entails an understanding that points of view exist from which our religious end itself can reasonably be seen as secondary or penultimate. This is a crucial feature of the orientational pluralism that I outlined in the last chapter.

Full attention to all three dimensions maximizes the impetus for dialogue and expands our appreciation for its legitimate varieties. For instance, we need not suppose that dialogue must focus on what is common between faiths. We can understand that often the attraction of dialogue is precisely to learn what is truly different. And yet, given the real possibilities of "tacking" within the traditions that I have suggested, we can readily see why two different interactions between the same two traditions may reflect strikingly different levels of commonality, depending on the orientation of the parties involved within their own faith. Suspicion of or hostility toward "syncretism" is often rooted in divergences that exist already within religious communities and are carried into the interreligious arena.

I should point out that from my perspective religious apologetics remains a viable and honorable discipline.[7] Though we recognize there are other religious perspectives from which varying conclusions can be reached, it is appropriate for each to make the case for the universal and preferable validity of its perspective. It is this impetus toward the universal which forces us to take the reality and the truths of varying traditions seriously.

Coordinate with accounts of their religious ends, faith traditions make philosophical and empirical claims. Investigation and argument about these are possible, and sometimes necessary. We have reviewed the various arguments of pluralistic theologians as to why such differences should not be regarded as of fundamental religious or salvific importance. By now the nature of my agreement and disagreement with their views should be clear. I agree that most doctrinal matters of this sort are not resolvable now to the rational satisfaction of all parties, though some of them may ultimately be so. And their truth or falsity may not definitively affect the achievement of *some* religious fulfillment through the faith of which they are a part. The crucial point is that such issues do substantially determine the *nature* of the religious fulfillments actually achieved, and their ontological relations. Dependent co-arising might not be an accurate metaphysical account of being, and yet an "experiential" religious fulfillment described by the category of nirvana may yet

---

[7] I use the word "apologetics" to encompass both "negative" arguments that there is no incompatibility in the primary convictions of a religious tradition and "positive" cumulative arguments that one religious tradition's conceptual scheme is superior to another. For a fuller discussion see chapter 1 in Paul Griffith's *An Apology for Apologetics*.

be an actual human state. It could be that there is neither a triune God nor a created universe, and yet that Christians do experience communion with a personal divine being.

The point is that realization of one of these "salvations" may well leave the metaphysical questions undecided, and yet answers to those questions will determine the ultimate status and character of those fulfillments. There is no cogent reason to assume that all of us—the vast majority *against* their prior conditioning and desires—will experience only one among these religious fulfillments or some undefined condition "beyond" any of them. It is possible that all religious persons will experience only illusion in this life and extinction in the next. What I claim is that our religious choices and formation do differentially determine our religious fulfillments in this life and, if there are such, in the next.

RELIGIOUS CHANGE: COSMETIC OR CRUCIAL?

If the traditions themselves are so multifarious, does this not finally put in doubt the distinctive religious paths I have claimed? If some Christians, for example, "tack" toward a Hindu fulfillment more than a biblical one, does it make sense to speak of a distinct or specifiable Christianity (or Buddhism or Judaism) at all? What I hope my analysis has made clear is that "orthodoxy" in this perspective emphatically does not have to do with arbitrary standards erected by religious authorities. It has to do with distinctive forms of life constitutive of a certain type of human fulfillment. The "orthodoxy" of an ascetic spirituality does not consist in any group's decrees about what shall be acceptable but in the relation between a human state liberated from bondage to bodily impulses and certain patterns of practice. Thus, for instance, should the vast majority of persons within the Christian tradition "tack" entirely toward naturalistic and secular convictions, their position can be viewed as "non-orthodox" in Christian terms simply because it is a *different* orthodoxy. The path chosen constitutes a different human form of life and fulfillment. There is no serious religious path which is not "orthodox," that is, which does not relate integrally to some end. Inclusivisms of all sorts often find amid the heresies of other traditions the putative orthodoxy of their own.

It is quite common in the United States today to encounter people who practice aspects of several religious traditions and who profess to be essentially equidistant from these faiths. Some will describe the religious end they seek in terms much in tune with the high-level generalities of Hick or Smith, testifying that multiple religious practice puts them more fully in tune with reality, leaves them less enclosed in self, encourages them to be more active in support of the good as they understand it. There is much to admire in many people I know who fit this mold. And the presence of a certain number of persons who insistently resist exclusive affiliation with one—or sometimes any—religious tradition does reinforce our sense of the heavily blurred borders of the faiths.

But there is an ironic limit to this effect. A group of people "in but not in" several traditions at once blur the boundaries. Should the number become large enough, it is no longer possible to avoid the recognition that this is a religious way in its own right. The population of seekers and pilgrims circulating always in the border lands is continuous with the seekers who circulate within a tradition's many streams. But when people begin to claim and to experience distinctive religious benefits, to suggest that their practice is a more effective path to a commonly sought end, or to distinguish their religious aim with particular descriptions, they are no longer "unorthodox" but represent an embryonic orthodoxy. History is replete with examples. A contemporary instance would be Ba'hai or many Unitarian-Universalist communities, in which people's exclusive practice or recommendation of Islam or Buddhism (or any single such faith) in preference to others would be the behavior perhaps most likely to threaten their standing in the religious tradition to which they now belong. Both communities are examples of groups who draw new boundaries by denying the validity of others. Christian history in North America offers several instances of denominations which began precisely as movements to transcend denominational distinctions.[8] The profession to be the only ones who do not claim uniqueness has long stood alongside other claims to religious uniqueness.

It is quite true that all kinds of overlap and similarity may be found from religion to religion. It hardly follows, as some suggest, that this means there are no substantive differences. We can draw no fixed boundary that sets off Buddhist orthodoxy from heterodoxy, no fine line that separates all Buddhists from all Hindus. Nor, notoriously, can we draw a fine line that sets off "religion" from other human realities. Life and history are in this sense one seamless, continuous system, just as W. C. Smith suggests. This intermingling of the traditions is a reality.

To consider how to evaluate it, let us take an example of a quite different sort. Marshall Hodgson, in *The Venture of Islam*, reviews the perennial historical argument over the "rise of the West," the beginnings of modernity in its scientific, economic, and social dimensions (Hodgson 1974, 34-36). The more that we know of the world's cultures, Hodgson suggests, the harder it becomes to say clearly why modernity happened

---

[8] This was, for instance, the perspective of Thomas Campbell, at the origins of the "Campbellite" or Disciples movement, as it was later of the Christian and Missionary Alliance.

in Europe. Elements that seem crucial in a convincing account of the causes for this development can upon close examination prove to be found in significant strength in other cultures as well. And any elements which can be successfully isolated as entirely unique to the West seem hardly sufficient to account for the scope of the transformation that took place. If this can be said of one of the most far-reaching historical changes in human life, it should lead us to question the assertion that because we can see human history is knit together in an intricate fashion, nothing decisively different happens in one part in contrast to another. If this is not a conclusion we would accept in history generally, why in the history of religion?

How would we regard a perspective on political life which insisted that its history must properly be seen not as an interplay of a vast number of distinctive visions, from Chinese state structures to Native American tribal systems, but rather as a single, seamless historical quest to realize a single universal human quality, "socialability"? At the least, we would recognize that this was but one possible perspective. It embodies a number of evaluative choices, choices to look at societies at a highly abstract functional level, to regard their self-understandings as secondary to one's own modes of analysis, and to decisively privilege static categories over change. Dramatic transformations do not register on this screen except as variant forms for an abiding function. Yet such an example appears quite analogous to pluralistic writers' modes of interpretation.

On another front, it might be objected against my hypothesis that we have no good reason to think that the religious ends sought by Christians or Hindus today are the same as in earlier centuries. Now, in principle there would be no problem in combining the affirmation of a diversity of fulfillments with the possibility that these could change within a single historical tradition. But I do affirm a continuity in the distinctive nature of the Christian end, and expect a similar continuity in other traditions, so this is an important question. In fact, I regard it as a benefit of the view I commend that it opens religions precisely to this kind of question and the uncertainties that go with it. From my perspective, the issue of continuity is a religiously significant one, and yet it is a question that pluralistic theories shield the religions from through the assumption of an unbroken unity of all religion.

I have argued strenuously that features of religious belief and practice are constitutive of the fulfillment achieved. Therefore the continuity Christians themselves manifest in the complex of elements—including scriptural texts, images, doctrines, liturgical practice—out of which their religious life is composed provides the strongest basis for presuming that the end in question retains its character. Within the horizon we can imagine, religious fulfillments always bear the texture of the constitutive elements humans bring to them. Since as a Christian I believe my fulfillment is also constituted by elements the triune God "brings" to it, the complex of constitutive human elements may vary considerably from one person or time to another and yet still attain a fundamentally common end. This implies the point already made in this chapter: salvation is presumably not perfectly identical for any two people. There is plenitude within and without the Christian condition of religious fulfillment.

Each religious person's or community's evaluative orientation and rational investigation (to return to the features of our discussion of orientational pluralism) are in a constant dynamic relationship with each other and with religious practice and experience. It is the interaction of these elements that make possible the "tacking" that I spoke of earlier. This dynamic process accounts for the seamless quality of the religious landscape as a whole. But this in no way means there are not distinctive thresholds seeded all through this landscape. To extend Panikkar's image, there is an enormous field of possibilities within the gravitational pull of a galaxy, but various combinations of velocity and direction will take one ultimately outside that field to effectively lodge within another. Our astronomical study of the material universe is capable of postulating a "center" of the universe at some point amid the galaxies. But this center is a mathematical position, derived from the disposition of stars and planets in space. There is nothing actually, decisively there. It is the matter in the galaxies (and the suspected hidden "dark matter") which exercises the active attractive forces. In the religious universe, too, it is the actual traditions that offer the living attraction. Whether in the furthest distant future all the religious galaxies may collapse together in a "big crunch," and whether this would be the attainment of a common religious end, a common annihilation of religious ends, or a consummation more in tune with one vision than another, we have no religiously neutral way of knowing—anymore than we can theorize about the end of our physical universe from any location but the portion of the particular galaxy in which we are now.

We may consider the question of the continuity of religious ends another way. There will be recurrent pressure in a faith's history for it to assimilate to its cultural surroundings in order to survive. The dangers of over-assimilation are not just a theoretical loss of religious purity. A tradition may adapt itself to make achievement of its distinctive religious fulfillment more intelligible, plausible, and effective. But if it loses touch with a distinctive religious end at all, then its passing is assured. So the development by which a tradition endures does have a kind of presumptive authenticity in that the developments would be unlikely to be effective unless they maintained contact with a distinctive religious end. If they turned toward another alternative, the tradition would probably not survive as a distinct tradition but be subsumed. The sociological career of Western Christian groups that have veered toward a secularly reductionistic view of their own content would appear to bear this out (see Stark and Bainbridge 1985, esp. chap. 1; Berger 1992, chap. 2).

In short, I believe that the presumption of diverse religious ends comports very well with the reality of steady flux that the historical view of religion presents to us. To turn the question around, I believe that the seething field of change we find within and among the faiths has a much deeper significance than pluralists are willing to grant it. For instance, Smith for the most part emphasizes diversity as a way of disparaging the notion that there are such things as distinctive religions at all, stressing that even one person's faith is not the same from one day to the next. But what then is the motive and reason for this constant religious change, the multitudes of renewal movements, sects, sub-traditions? The consistent pluralist response is that this must involve a steady exchange of the *cultural forms* in which people choose to grasp the same religious reality, no more. The sociological dynamism of religious life in this sense may be psychologically or socially but not religiously significant.

This is a curious conclusion. Are people who shift their religious allegiance or practice, in the conviction that they are constituting a different life for themselves, really expressing nothing but taste, changing nothing but the instrumental means by which they achieve the same end that could have been achieved before? Did those who struggled for liberty of religion in the past give their lives for the right to a more culturally comfortable form of the one faith? Is the freedom for faith a fundamental openness that permits materially alternative paths of human fulfillment and decisively different shapings of cultures and civilizations, or is it essentially a matter of fit? In the latter case, the crucial decisions about society and ethics must be made essentially for nonreligious reasons. If religious differences do not point to at least some divergent human ends, historically and/or eschatologically, then these differences, rather than providing a basis for choosing among behaviors and social structures, must themselves be objects of choice and adjudication on some other basis than the religious fulfillment involved.

This is not at all to say that there is some fixed set of options, that no new religious ends are possible. I would argue that the most realistic—though improbable—use of the pluralistic schemes we have discussed would be precisely as the foundations of a new religious option. This is unlikely both because the ground has already been claimed in more compelling forms, from neo-Vedanta to Ba'hai to the Unification church, and because pluralist theories generally resist concrete distinctive practices. But at least in abstract form these theories offer accounts of the religious end which could be put among others.

We can return in this connection to our earlier consideration of multiple religious practice. In such cases persons or communities blend elements in their own religious life from several traditions. In one sense this is just a more conscious and extensive example of what goes on constantly in the historical development of the traditions, as Smith illustrates. If such practice shows any enduring power, it takes one of two turns. It may become a kind of renewal movement within a religious tradition, assimilating elements from other traditions—probably in the face of charges of syncretism—into a scheme that gives priority to features of one "home" faith. The most common form of this in modern Western countries is probably the eclectic assimilation of elements from various religious traditions into a "home" secularist faith. The second option is for the multiple religious practice eventually to become a new religious movement itself, and in time a new faith.

Some instances of multiple religious participation seem particularly suggestive for this discussion. Messianic Jews, persons claiming to be at once Jews and Christians, are subject to condemnation or suspicion from most Christians, most Jews, and most pluralists. Such an attitude on the part of pluralists particularly might seem odd at first, since messianic Jews would seem to have realized—albeit in a limited sphere—the unitive truth of religion which pluralists preach. Even those convinced that Judaism and Christianity are two ways of walking the same path appear to believe it is important they walk separately, and that something of the distinctiveness of the two traditions is compromised in this hybrid movement. Interestingly, such messianic Jewish communities generally stress precisely the identity of the religious end of the two traditions and therefore see no reason why those who recognize this identity should not meld the two traditions and their practices and beliefs.

Obviously there are particular historical reasons why messianic Judaism is such a sore point between the two religious traditions. But the uneasiness of many Jews and Christians is also rooted in the expectation that the movement will eventually take (or already has) one of the two turns I indicated above, either of which would compromise the balanced equality or unity of the two traditions. Many members of the movement, for their part, tenaciously resist the suggestion that such an evolution is inevitable and try to maintain continuity with both communities.

A more common analogy used to address religious diversity is the case of Christian ecumenism (e.g., Hillman 1968). The ideal of such ecumenism is precisely an intra-Christian "multiple religious practice" in which Christian communions would recognize and share their sacraments, ministries, and confessions. Just as divided Christian denominations come increasingly to recognize each other's validity as part of the one body of Christ, so the argument goes, the religions should recognize each other's stature as parallel responses to one truth.

This ignores the fact that Christian ecumenism seeks unity through a grammar of particularity. It integrates continuing diversity on the basis of a clarification of a shared distinctive life. Two examples of this would be the *Baptism, Eucharist and Ministry* and *Confessing the One Faith* documents of the World Council of Churches Faith and Order Commission. Only by stressing some of the specifics that set Christians apart from others are certain intra-Christian divisions rendered acceptable diversity.

Christian ecumenism is not a sound analogy for religious pluralism, unless an analogous "grammar of particularity" can be articulated that is to serve as the uniting factor. John Hick and W. C. Smith's candidates on this score—the "Real" and "faith"—are explicitly empty and offer no real prospect of serving the purpose required of them. Paul Knitter's proposal on the liberation theology of religions will be taken up in the next chapter.

Beyond this fundamental point, it seems that the difficulties of Christian ecumenism may be even more relevant to our subject than its hopes. Certainly among many Christians the ecumenical dialogue has led to a situation where on some topics—say questions of what the Christian scriptures say in reference to Mary the mother of Jesus or in reference to baptism—the answers given by Protestant, Orthodox, and Roman Catholic scholars would largely agree. And many consensus statements have been produced and ratified by two or more denominations, covering issues that historically divided them. The practical results of these statements, though real, have been limited.

The fact that modest change follows upon such Christian ecumenical agreements can be attributed to two factors: the specific answers figure into different religious patterns of life in the different churches, and the grounds of judgment on which the agreements were reached often vary. Thus an agreed statement on the place of Mary in the Christian scriptures has a different meaning for an Orthodox Christian steeped in a type of Marian piety and valuing tradition than it does for a Baptist who has taken no devotional notice of her and who regards scripture as a definitive standard. The mere acknowledgment that certain views or practices are acceptable is a far cry from their active incorporation as a constitutive part of one's own religious life.

If an agreed statement of this sort is to have real effect—let us say it is to authorize certain joint Orthodox-Baptist liturgical practices in reference to Mary—then it will have to be received by each community as valid on its own terms. That is, Baptists will accept the argument that it is valid because of the scriptural justification only insofar as that authority continues to be decisive for them; likewise, Orthodox will accept modifications in their usual practice because of a case made from tradition only insofar as that continues to be a convincing authority. The Christian ecumenical hope is that in this process each tradition's norms can themselves be enlarged and enriched, that scripture and tradition for instance could come to be claimed by both communities as coordinate forms of one shared norm. This hope is deeply rooted in the particularistic elements held in common by Christians. The whole modality of ecumenism is to build upon what is most specific and most common, whether the Lord's Prayer or the Nicene Creed or the eucharistic meal of bread and wine and scriptural words, or the baptism in water in the name of the Trinity.

If one or both of the Christian communions in question change for reasons unrelated to their specific faith traditions—out of indifference to religious practice altogether, for instance—then this is not truly ecumenism and the result will hardly be unity. The reception of agreements and decisions to practice unity becomes effective insofar as the communities genuinely perceive them as integral to the pattern of Christian life and fulfillment. The process of dialogue has in many cases fed a renewed confessionalism among Christian bodies, precisely for this reason. It is the distinctive confessional orientations of the Christian traditions that are the instruments of unity. The historical modes of Christian confession are the only voices through which broader Christian unity can be affirmed and validated. This remains true, whether the orientations in question are primarily "denominational" in nature or have to do with differences over questions of justice, mission, and contextualization. Even with its rather extensive concrete commonalities, with much more than a purely formal agreement about the "ultimate" that all worship, the Christian ecumenical movement demonstrates the integral role of particular commitments. This, it seems to me, is the most telling lesson it offers for the interreligious context.

In this chapter I have attempted not only to outline a Christian approach to religious diversity, but also to indicate how that approach responds to further aspects of our job description. I believe that a diversity of religious ends can be interpreted and defended on Christian grounds. Among the Christian alternatives, this perspective provides the greatest scope for attending seriously to the religious traditions in their own terms and also offers a profound motive for interreligious relation.

One very large part of the job description remains, however. What of the concerns for justice and peace? Whatever its philosophical coherence or its respect for otherness, can this perspective effectively renounce past evils and struggle against contemporary ones? Can it compare in this respect to the unique value that pluralistic theologies claim for themselves? This is the topic for the next chapter.

7

Justice and Difference

If authentic diversity of religious ends is both philosophically and theologically cogent, a crucial question remains. What is the practical effect of such a perspective? In this chapter we turn more intensively to that issue. The discussion of religious pluralism is strongly motivated by concern over historical conflict and violence among the religions. The ethical dimension of pluralistic theologies is their most compelling feature. It is crucial to ask how well my proposal fares in this area. The fundamental question we must ask is whether *difference* is the necessary source of such evils, so that it is substantial religious difference we must deny or minimize.

There are two sides to the issue. The first has to do with healing religions' vicious tendencies, their impetus toward domination and scapegoating. How do we face specifically religious sources of conflict? The second has to do with enlisting the religions to oppose evils other than narrowly religious ones. Paul Knitter and others voice an imperative for religions both to stop creating violence or oppression themselves and to work effectively to overcome other sources of injustice.

This is obviously a rather delicate operation, since there are few if any capacities that can be turned only to good ends. The dynamics that can make religion destructive may be some of the same ones that make it redemptive. If the faiths are a force for transformation, we may not always view the transformation as fruitful. A key test of pluralistic theologies and their alternatives, particularly with respect to issues of justice, is their ability to provide a substantive understanding of religious change, within and among the traditions.

RECOGNIZING TRUE ALTERNATIVES: THE ROOT SOURCE OF RELIGIOUS EVIL?

The first dimension to consider is specific conflict among faith traditions. Is the idea that there could be some material reason to change

185

one's faith commitment itself a poisonous root of interreligious violence and prejudice? Is the affirmation of diversity in religious fulfillments itself an oppressive act because it allows people to advance convictions about distinctive and preferable modes of human life, permits
evaluative judgments that some religious ends are superior to others?

We can begin by asking whether it is empirically the case that wider
differences between religions foster greater conflict. What would the
human condition be like if there were but one faith tradition? Suppose
we were all Muslims or all Christians or all Buddhists. Would that lead
to an end to religious conflict and violence? The evidence points in the
opposite direction. The vying sects within a broad tradition usually already agree, as pluralists would have the religions agree, that they seek
the same general religious end. In addition they share many of the same
instruments to that end. In fact it appears to be a rough rule that the
more a common end is agreed upon and the *more* of the means are held
in common, the sharper may be the resulting conflict.

The Western Christian approach to religious pluralism has been most
fundamentally shaped by intramural wars of religion which pitted Catholic against Protestant, and sub-sect against sub-sect. Like Christianity,
Islam can probably count as many martyrs at the hands of coreligionists
as it can at the hands of others. The cases of Buddhism and Hinduism
are routinely presented as counterexamples. And it need not be denied
that violent conflict within these traditions over credal matters has been
less prevalent, though by no means absent. Oppression may have taken
different forms—violence because of caste or purity offenses rather than
"doctrinal" ones, say—but spheres of relative Hindu or Buddhist religious homogeneity have not been oases of peace either. As Wendy
Doniger points out, the rationalization and acceptance of differences
which modern interpreters often celebrate in Hinduism have historically
been inherently structured as separate but unequal (see Doniger 1991,
228-231). The rainbow of religious diversity within Hinduism was in
some measure legitimated precisely because it correlated to positions
of relative suffering or advantage allocated by karmic destiny. It thus
was a prime authorization for social conflict among the groups so defined. Within as well as among religious traditions, Doniger says, it is
necessary to "walk a razor's edge between denying diversity and
hierarchalizing it" (Doniger 1991, 231).

People of the same faith tradition find ample grounds for religious
conflict. This casts obvious doubt on the effectiveness of the pluralists'
strategy for ending such conflict by establishing some parity among the
traditions. Nor does it seem that closely related faiths are less likely to
set their adherents at odds than more distant ones. The relative calm of
Buddhist-Christian dialogue, say, when compared to Jewish-Christian
dialogue reflects this dynamic. Encounter with a dramatically different
and previously largely unfamiliar tradition (as Christianity with Bud-

dhism) may result first in deep uncertainty even over the categories by which to establish similarity or conflict. The more history that is shared, including one might say the more scripture that is shared, the more difficult the issues. It is quite possible to have a rough agreement about religious ends—and Jews, Christians, and Muslims must have more such concrete agreement than any pluralistic vision could hope for all faiths to have—and to be dramatically at odds.

The reason for this is not hard to grasp. Both religious practice and religious fulfillments are culturally-linguistically "thick." Faith traditions do claim to place us in touch with a reality behind or beneath that of ordinary experience. But whether or not one can ever have direct contact with such transcendence, life is not lived in that condition.[1] People who follow different traditions live discernibly different lives. Faiths as we actually find them on the historical plane are patterned around concrete images, beliefs, practices, and ends. Pluralistic theories regard these as secondary forms of religious life. But they *constitute* religious life and faith, insofar as these have any tangible reality, accessible to the practitioner or historian.

Even where people have clear formal agreement about ultimate religious aims and authorities, wide gulfs can open up when the actual practices and instruments of religious life diverge significantly. The proximate religious fulfillments of this life take on different character for the charismatic, the mystic, the ritualist, the moralist, who share the same tradition. Such differences often cause conflict and this conflict can escalate to denials that people actually are on the same way or share an ultimate end in common. The so-called Abrahamic faiths—Judaism, Christianity, Islam—can be viewed in this light. Though these traditions share in some measure a vision of the end of the religious life, their differences over what constitutes the way toward it arguably amount to distinct alternatives for any individual or community life. It is not clear, then, that conflict can be correlated in some way with the degree of religious difference. Denying substantial difference does not look likely to end the conflict.

We could consider another possibility. Perhaps it is not difference that is the primary source of tension but the dynamic of religious change itself. Does the core difficulty rest not in recognition of real differences among the traditions but in the live option of migration among them? This would appear to be a possible pluralist response. Perceiving other religious paths, within or outside my tradition, as live options for me may lead to experiences of uncertainty, curiosity, attraction, or experiences of threat and hostility. Does conflict arise from this perception of alternativeness, from the knowledge that people do not have to "stay

---

[1] I leave aside here the question of whether such mystical experiences themselves are culturally conditioned. With Hick, I believe that they are.

put" religiously and from the thought that others might have something I do not? If this is the case, then it may be the idea of conversion itself that is most dangerous, the belief that religious change can have decisive effects.

Though rather baldly stated, this is a crucial issue for pluralists. Much is made of the fact that most people follow religious paths into which they were born. If only those in one faith tradition can be "saved," then this fact can well be used to fault exclusivists with the unfairness of the divine providence they celebrate. But for pluralists the religious status quo seems implicitly to acquire normative status. The dynamic of religious change is seen as a source of conflict precisely because its premises can only, on pluralist views, be misguided. Persons alter their religious commitments in the belief that an alternative possibility is available to them. From pluralistic perspectives changes from one faith to another are not necessarily harmful (how could they be, given the unity of the faiths?), but the attitudes that prompt them usually are. That individuals should adjust their historical equipment for relating to the Real can be accepted on psychological terms as a purely personal matter. From this view religious ends themselves can never be a valid ground for such change (since they do not ultimately differ in the traditions). By example, the act of conversion runs the risk of inflaming the illusion that substantial differences exist and that they matter. My proposal, in stressing the significance of varying religious aims, would thus be guilty of fomenting more conflict among the faiths by reinforcing the dynamic of religious change.

None of the pluralists we have examined is seeking a single world religion. None sees any valid reason for one tradition to grow at the expense of another. In fact the major substance of the transformation that is required in each tradition is the recognition that this status quo is not only circumstantial but inviolate. So much stress is put upon the historical traditions as culturally determined responses to an ineffable reality that it would seem hard to understand how anyone could properly adopt an expression that was not his or hers by heritage. Troeltsch's conclusion that each culture had its appropriate faith is echoed in these formulations.

Should adherents of the world's religions be universally converted to pluralist views, they would affirm the equivalence of various faith/culture pairings. Judgments of better and worse, for the wholes if not the parts, would be ruled out and so too, pluralists contend, any motive for religious hatred. It does not disconcert these writers that there is little in history to corroborate their expectations of such a situation. They expect a new phase of human history. In this phase, religions, as distinctive realities, will cease to be players in the human project. Instead "religion" will become a single force, in its essential spiritual dimension.

I argue on the contrary that an adequate theory of religious diversity must include a positive account of religious change. The ideal of a frozen pluralism is unrealistic and impossible unless enforced by some central dominant power. The true music of pluralism can only be a dynamic, a melody in which there are shifting notes, dissonance, and harmony rather than the overtones of a single octave. Why should we expect that the religious situation as it happens to be when pluralistic thought arises is the one which is optimally permanent? My point is not just that this expectation is unrealistic. It is the stronger contention that the ideal of a religious status quo is one that cannot be realized or pursued except by an exercise of power.

From a broad perspective, change is at least as prominent as stasis in regard to religion. At least two-thirds of the world's people belong to faiths that did not exist two thousand years ago (Christianity, Islam, and "nonreligious"). At least a third follow paths that did not exist fourteen hundred years ago and at least a sixth paths that hardly existed two hundred years ago (see Barrett 1989). And this vastly understates the matter, since it ignores the constant currents of exchange among the traditions which may leave no net change, as well as the even greater numbers who migrate from one path to another within a tradition. Increasingly, people are born into cultures that contain multiple religious options. Insofar as the trends of modernity continue—the same alterations of communication, transportation, economics that have brought religious diversity forcefully to our attention—we can expect the dynamics of religious change to accelerate.

Pluralists generally put great emphasis upon the "axial age" traditions as paradigm cases of what they mean by "religion." Only passing notice is given to the survivals of what Hick calls "world maintenance" *primal* faiths. Their swift submersion, engineered today more by modernity than missionaries, calls forth nothing like the outrage reserved for conflicts among the axial faiths. One great global religious change has taken place—the displacement of nearly all existing religious traditions with axial age faiths—with the explicit or tacit favor of pluralists. It is all over, from Hick's view, but the "mopping up." Why might we not expect changes of a similar magnitude in this accelerating human future? At times pluralists speak as though their theories represent just such a transformation. Conversion must be appropriate, if only in the one instance of conversion to pluralistic convictions. If so, then by their own testimony religious change is a crucial factor—in a substantive and not just cosmetic sense—and affirmation of this importance must be legitimate, rather than an intrinsic cause of religious evil.

Unless human nature itself changes, the religious geography of the future and therefore a significant portion of the social geography as well will be marked by continuing transformation. This will be embodied in movements offering people different religious fulfillments than they currently experience or expect, in this life and beyond, or renewed and preferable paths to the end they already seek. Unless the vision of interreligious respect is to remain the property of a small elite, based on a very narrow cultural foundation, it will have to become an integral feature of specific faiths which prove themselves capable of flourishing in this landscape of change and renewal. The project of taming missionary faiths is futile, not least because it is itself a fervent missionary project. Faiths do not survive without a particularistic appeal. The paradoxical challenge of religious mutuality is to code it into traditions which are yet vital enough in their singularity to flourish in the economy of faiths.

Pluralistic perspectives are already adopted by minorities in various religious traditions, accepted by those who regard this as a preferable religious path and desire all others to adopt it as well. As one way of being a Jew, for instance, this will prove durable and satisfying, attract others and reproduce itself, or it will die out. If it is to be enduring, people will need to see some distinctive religious reason to be a pluralistic Jew rather than another type of Jew or something else altogether. But a distinctive religious reason for such a choice is what pluralism itself tends to deny. In other words, there are only limited ways the ideal and practice of mutual respect among the faiths can spread. They might spread as the doctrine of a new missionary faith, an evangelistically effective variant of the essentially Western pluralist theories we have reviewed, displacing existing religions. On the other hand, they might spread within evangelistically effective versions of those existing religious traditions, which each would have developed its own distinctive imperatives for respect among the faiths.

I am firmly convinced that the attitudes and concerns that motivate pluralistic theologies can best be advanced on particularistic grounds. This conviction is obviously reinforced by the conclusion argued extensively in chapter 4 that pluralistic theologies themselves are advanced on particularistic grounds. For Christians, this means grounding respect for religious diversity in foundational convictions regarding Trinity and Christology. For Buddhists, it means grounding them in foundational convictions about the dharma. The aim is for the imperatives of mutual respect, dialogue, and cooperation to become part of the DNA of the traditions themselves. As long as these imperatives remain attached only to theories *about* the religions, which believers are expected to apply generically to their own tradition, they will be marginal at best. Even were there to be momentary "successes" of this sort, they would constantly be reversed by the revitalization and renewal movements that are nourished by religiously specific roots. This also means that it is precisely the inability of those from different traditions to agree on all the specific reasons for interreligious mutuality that make such mutuality itself viable.

David Novak makes this point from the Jewish side of Jewish-Christian dialogue when he says that the affirmation of a higher universally evident truth that encompasses and transcends the *partial* truth of each community means "singularity, then, collapses into particularity: a part of a larger whole. And this higher truth is alone capable of being a source of rational action because it alone can be the criterion for distinguishing between better and worse. In our world today, such a higher criterion invariably turns out to be secularist." This agenda then "relegates both Judaism's Torah and Christianity's Gospel to a corner of historical obscurity where they pose no threat or challenge to the status quo in the world" (Novak 1989, 140).

Given the dynamic that Novak describes, those in any tradition that adopt the "higher truth" standpoint can expect to be regularly displaced by movements recovering and affirming some form of distinctive fulfillment in that singular faith tradition. I believe that the hypothesis I have sketched in fact offers a sounder basis for overcoming interreligious conflict, a basis itself diversified in the faiths and reflecting the very variety that is to be respected.

I do not want to leave this aspect of the question without making one more point. Despite their intentions, pluralistic perspectives in fact prejudicially serve some sides in religious conflicts over others. These authors have sensitized us to the way in which distinctive religious aims can be interpreted as occasions for religious oppression, for denigration of other traditions. They have however shown little awareness of the way in which their own perspectives could primarily serve dominant traditions. Pluralist convictions that deny one faith any distinctive final fulfillment in comparison with others would seem to set the stage for an unrestrained assimilation of all minority or imperiled religious groups. There would be no *religious* reason not to become a full participant in whatever was the socially dominant tradition in a given country or area. All things being equal, who would not reasonably prefer to be a Muslim in Egypt, a Catholic in Spain, a Buddhist in rural Thailand?

We can consider one historical precedent. Some of the Muslim Sufi orders pioneered approaches similar to those commended today in pluralistic circles. They advanced teachings that there was no essential difference among religions, properly and esoterically understood. In certain areas of the Muslim conquest where Christians were a large portion of the subject population, Sufis taught that Christianity and Islam were equally valid faiths and that Christians need not leave their community in order to be saved. Equally, of course, they taught that there could not be anything decisive or unique about Christianity which was lacking in Islam. Christians were thus encouraged to hold to Jesus as their savior if they wished, while recognizing this was an instrumental and not a universal truth. As the historian William H. McNeill notes, "Such doctrines, obviously, facilitated conversion to Islam since not the repudiation of Christianity, but of Christianity's claim to exclusive truth was alone at issue" (McNeill 1963, 551).

The results of such attitudes survive still in places where Muslims and Christians hold in common certain shrines and saints, whose origin in one tradition or the other can no longer be surely determined. Here is surely a dramatic example of the amicable overlap of religions. But the most significant and predictable historical result of this approach was the conversion of most Christians to Islam. In a society where considerable disadvantage attached to being Christian and considerable advantage to being Muslim, full acceptance of the belief that there was nothing of crucial distinctive truth in one's own tradition would lead quite easily, in a generation or two if not immediately, to adopting the dominant tradition.

The reputations of the Sufis as at once the great latitudinarians and the great evangelists of Islam are not as contradictory as they might first seem. As another writer said of the Bektashi order, "The concessions of Bektashism to Christianity and of Christianity to Bektashism seem at first sight exactly balanced. Christian churches adopt fictitious Bektashi traditions and receive Bektashi pilgrims: conversely Bektashi *tekkes* adopt fictitious Christian legends and receive Christian pilgrims. But the apparent equality is only superficial. The ultimate aim of the Bektashi was not to amalgamate Christianity with Bektashism on equal terms, but to absorb Christianity in Bektashism" (Hasluck 1929, 585-586).

The purpose of this example is not to criticize the Sufi orders or Islam. The practices just described stand out positively in comparison with most European Christian attitudes toward Muslims in the same period. My point is that far from being the resolution of religious conflict, pluralistic theories are inevitably only one more instrument in it, an instrument that readily serves the purposes of traditions already in dominant or majority positions. They can be appreciated when they replace violent instruments, but they hardly are impartial. This dynamic can be seen elsewhere as well.

The particular anger with which many in the Jewish community regard messianic Jews—in contrast even to other evangelistic efforts directed at Jews or to groups of Jews that are not actively observant of the tradition—relates to the claim that one need not cease being a Jew to accept Christ. As the Sufis asked Christians only to give up the idea of Christ as a decisive difference, while remaining Christians, messianic Jews ask Jews to keep everything of their tradition and give up only the idea that it cannot be amalgamated with another tradition's fulfillment. Jewish theologians who criticize this claim argue concretely for the integrity of their faith. But they also sharply point out that this kind of "equality" is a death knell for a group resisting assimilation in a dominantly Christian culture. The notion that religious differences are not of crucial significance must undermine the position of religious minorities trying to maintain their identities and propagate their beliefs, much more than that of majorities. Even with complete legal liberty, there is a social cost to being different, and one will naturally be less inclined to bear it if there are no religious grounds for doing so.

The extinction for a time of Buddhism in its native India was assisted by a broadminded insistence by Hindus that it was a variant form of Hinduism, to be tolerated in all respects save the claim to be distinct. Similar difficulties attended both Buddhists and Sikhs in their struggles to attain the status of independent religious communities under modern Indian law. The current waves of Hindu fundamentalism are further proof, if any is needed, that the doctrine that varying religions are cultural forms for relating to the same religious reality may offer a perfectly serviceable rationale for oppressing religious minorities, since only one form is regarded as truly authentic for a given culture.

Indeed, the ordinary grounds for religious freedom would appear to require reconsideration if a pluralist perspective is adopted. In the United States, it has been argued since the passage of the first amendment not only that an established church is dangerous to the civil polity, but that religious consciences should not be coerced. The crucial point arises if we ask why it is thought harmful to coerce religious conscience. What, specifically, is the harm in doing so? The answer has been that religious freedom is the "first freedom" because it is the most encompassing and ultimate determination of a person's fulfillment. These are decisions so momentous for persons and communities, and their effect so dependent on the sincerity of the commitment, that they must be made by individuals within their elective community, not by legal fiat. The importance of the freedom rests on the assumption of crucial differences in religious means and ends, and of the depth of the perceived consequences.

It is a precedent still controverted in law that it is an unconstitutional infringement of religious liberty for people participating in a state-sponsored event (a high school graduation, for instance) to be made even tacit participants in a religious exercise carried out at the behest of the state authorities. If we ask not for the narrow legal precedents for this position but for the reasons those precedents make sense, it seems they depend on some perception of harm in such a situation. I suggest this perception presumes a very important difference in religious aims . . . or at least the legitimacy of people believing in such differences. If what is in question is a different cultural *form* of a common religious quest, then it is hard to see either what harm such a practice could be thought to do—it can only enrich our religious experience—or why objection to a steady rotation of such public religious observances is not simply rank cultural bigotry.

In fact, those who argue in favor of such official religious observances generally stress exactly these elements: either they advocate a prayer or practice of a highly generic quality—which presumably is intended to point to something like Hick's "Real"—or they advocate a rotation where different particular traditions take turns, presenting over time the sum total of the cultural forms this adjustment to reality takes. I suspect that there is no cogent basis to resist these arguments which does not recognize the integrity of distinct religious ends.

The heart of the issue regarding interreligious conflict has to do with whether justice and peace can be served by substantial as opposed to accidental difference. The variants of pluralistic theology see difference as inimical to peace. Though they recognize diversity, they each find some foundational area in which to emphasize identity. Generically they call this area salvation; specifically they call it adjustment to the Real or faith or justice. All difference is then subsumed as variation on this unity. Although all three disclaim "essentialist" views of religion and criticize religions' attempts to define their own orthodox cores, they are committed to a distinction between content and form much at odds with most descriptive approaches to religion that insist on the integral relation of the two. Hick and Smith implicitly and Knitter explicitly struggle with the one kind of difference that fits uneasily into this strategy: religious patterns and groups differ in their receptiveness to and support for these pluralistic approaches themselves. If the difference between accepting or rejecting pluralistic views is one of fundamental importance, this would appear to be confirmation that there are valid objective grounds for religious conflict. If that difference is not a crucial matter, this relativizes the pluralist project itself.

I suggest that my hypothesis is at least as effective as those advanced by pluralistic thinkers in combating the evils of religious pride. In fact it encompasses the possibility of a much more positive mutual recognition than is conceivable in pluralist terms. I look toward reciprocal affirmation of substantive rather than formal or "mythological" truths among the faiths. Since it assumes the possibility that various religious traditions may offer both truly realizable and concretely different religious aims, my approach requires that such mutual recognition deal with particular and not only abstract features of the faiths. Knowledge of and contact with the specific elements of another tradition are necessary because they are integral to what is to be recognized, not merely expressive "forms" for a subsistent salvation.

Most important, this perspective maintains the integrity of otherness. Great emphasis is put by pluralist writers on the absolute necessity to articulate the grounds of the possibility of talking together, otherwise we are condemned to lives of mutual isolation. *That* there are such grounds is a belief important for dialogue and relation. But participants may bring their own construal of those grounds. Honor for otherness is as important as convictions of commonality. Any who do not approach encounter with the readiness to acknowledge otherness up to and including another basis for encounter itself have severely constrained their partners and the results.

To make "justice" the compulsory subject of dialogue, for instance, is unjust. It is unjust on its own terms, for not wanting to hear what any of the poor and oppressed it claims to privilege may have to say about anything they might think important or ultimate besides their oppressed status as we have defined it. It is unjust for ruling out of dialogue the very kind of interchange that could reveal our commitment to "justice" as particularistic and limited rather than universal. This is why I argue so strongly for the three dimensions of interreligious judgment: error, convergence, and *effective* difference. My friends do not honor my humanity if they pretend that I cannot go astray, that I cannot arrive independently at truths we share, or that I cannot achieve or settle for a life they do not.

The conceptual and religious space for an authentic other is the same space that allows us to recognize that we can *be* the other. We can be read, interpreted, and inscribed in other projects than our own. Unless we have means for another person or tradition to get free of our affirmations, perhaps even more than our condemnation, we effectively preclude any recognition of their reading of us. My contention is that without such space, misunderstanding and social violence will continue.

So far, we have considered only the question of conflict among the religions. I have argued that the claim of pluralist theories to be the sole effective means to end the evils of religious conflict is not plausible, both because greater religious agreement does not preclude such conflict and because these theories themselves can function practically as instruments of religious conflict. The presumptions and practice of religious change are not necessary causes of religious violence or intolerance. This is only one aspect of the issue, however. The "liberation theology of religions" addresses a much broader concern than narrowly religious conflict. It asks of each religious doctrine or practice, and of each theory of religions, what contribution it makes to the global struggle for concrete human well-being. We will devote the balance of this chapter to that challenging question.

WHOSE JUSTICE? RELIGIONS AS SOURCES AND SERVANTS OF SOCIAL VISIONS

The focus shifts now from interactions among the religious traditions to the impact of those traditions on the social orders around them. The liberation theology of religions suggests shifting emphasis from the varying ultimates of faith to the shared crisis in front of us: poverty, violence against women, racial hatred, states' terrorism against their own citizens. The religions themselves and their contacts with each other should be devoted to ending these evils. Any alternative construal of the nature or priorities of religious diversity is a form of complicity with these oppressions.

As I have suggested earlier, this is the most straightforwardly inclusivist form of pluralistic theology. Knitter's liberation theology of religions states particularistic universal claims which it is willing to defend against alternatives and which decisively guide its practice. And I have no criticism for it on that ground. However, to return to my argument for orientational pluralism, the liberation theology of religions in fact becomes exclusivistic in its refusal to recognize other orientations as having some legitimacy. I have discussed this in chapter 4. The questions I would take up here have to do with *what* the religions are thought able to contribute to liberation and with the exclusivist views of justice.

The struggle for justice, Knitter says, is too big a job for any religion alone. All the faiths need to be enlisted in this effort. But who defines the effort into which the religions are then to be enlisted and what exactly will they bring as their distinctive gift to the job? If we return for a moment to the issue of conflict between faiths, we can note that one effective way to defang religions would be to deny that they have any distinctive power at all. Some pluralistic theories of religion come perilously close to this option. To prevent people from doing bad things in religion's name, we could try to convince them that religions—the concrete beliefs, rituals, and lifeforms—have no particular significance, but only a generic one. Conflicts are pointless because anything it is possible to disagree about religiously can't be of enough significance to be worth the conflict. The difficulty is that while this generic meaning may not be totally vacuous, it is certainly close enough to provide no specific social direction.

Rising outrage over religious chauvinism coincides in our society with a general disinclination among many to regard faith as genuinely causative, a doubt that religion has any independent, substantive influence on behavior. It is somewhat hard to determine the extent to which people kill and oppress each other for specifically religious reasons, when most religious behaviors are already understood to have nonreligious motivations. Some pluralistic theories themselves reinforce such views by arguing that all *particular* religious practices are thoroughly determined by cultural factors. It is only in the far reaches of mystical contact with divine mystery or in the depths of subjective individual dispositions that one enters the truly religious realm. To paraphrase W. C. Smith, God gives us faith; culture determines *what* that faith will be.

The nerve of religious superiority is cut by denying that anything concrete which would distinguish one faith from another is properly religious at all. This may leave undisturbed many other motives for oppression, but it removes the religious one by the fiat of definition. Those other motives are troublesomely effective. The Mongols, who seem to have been quite pluralistic in their respect for various religions, were not for that reason inhibited in brutally annihilating non-Mongols. The lack of specific religious hostility was, one imagines, of limited comfort to the victims.

The heyday of Western colonialism coincided with a questioning of Christian exclusivity that had been initiated by the enlightenment. As Lesslie Newbigin points out, "The explosion of European power into the rest of the world during the nineteenth century was much more a matter of the export of Europe's political and scientific ideas and its science-based technology than of its religious beliefs and even Christian missionaries were heavily involved in exporting European secular thought and practice through their schools, hospitals and 'development' programs" (Newbigin 1990, 136). The history of colonialism did not only demonstrate the way theology could reinforce cultural imperialism. It demonstrated equally well how belief in cultural superiority could substitute for religious conviction in the service of domination.[2] Imperial Europe was well on its way toward being pluralist in religion: the categories had already been established for Christian differences. It was decidedly not pluralist in respect to reason and science (Newbigin 1990, 136, paraphrased).

The moral imperative not to regard our own faith as distinctively truthful collides with the expectation that religion is to be enlisted in the struggle for liberation. Faith can only be expected to have an effect in that struggle if religion is an independent and significant force in its own right to shape individual and social life. And it is such a force presumably only because of the believer's conviction that it makes a decisive difference. In molding life through specific religious practices, adherents commit themselves to what they regards as of overriding importance in life, of enough significance to justify, if necessary, their conflict with the dictates of family, ruler, or self-interest.

Newbigin stresses this in remarking on the difficulty pluralistic theologians have in justifying their unequivocal conviction that some religious positions are "intolerable." Langdon Gilkey pins his hopes on "relative absoluteness," a practically absolute commitment to a certain set of values upon which we will act, leavened with the acknowledgment that it is impossible to claim these values are more fundamentally rooted in truth than all others (Gilkey 1987, 47). Newbigin's apposite response is that steady inoculation with such a view is likely to steadily diminish

---

[2] Observers as different as Orlando Costas and Lesslie Newbigin made this same point. See Orlando E. Costas, "Reply," in Gerald H. Anderson and Thomas F. Stransky, *Christ's Lordship and Religious Pluralism*, 166-167. W. C. Smith also noted that the shift in the missionary movement from evangelism toward cultural uplift was in many respects a retreat from genuine religious encounter. See "Mission, Dialogue and God's Will for Us," *International Review of Mission*, 364-365.

the risks run out of commitment to these "relatively absolute" truths. The Nazis are Gilkey's paradigm case of what is religiously intolerable. But Newbigin points out that the formula "practically absolute commitment to values that are less than universal" translates quite readily into the "blood and soil" of the *Volksgeist*. Fascism did not have to be advanced by appeal to universal truths: it was the special genius of the German people, the internal logic of their historical development, which Nazis claimed was to be absolute *for them*. To call such commitments and those that would oppose them both "relatively absolute" is to change nothing about which is more likely to be chosen. If it has any differential effect, it probably supports the side with the most power. Belief in and appeal to a transcendent order which can relativize the present established powers is one of the few resources the weak have against the strong. To say that one should regard such resistance as having, at best, a relatively absolute source is in fact a boon to oppressive powers. It is true that such a belief does deny oppressors one tool—the attempt to cloak their power in metaphysical terms—but this is rather like denying rich and poor alike the right to sleep under bridges. The powerful have many other tools, the weak painfully few.

Knitter suggests, more by allusion than explanation, that the animating force of faith can somehow be transferred to preferred social causes, rather like an electric outlet into which a new appliance is plugged. To think of the religions in this way, as a kind of power reserve, is to presume a dichotomy that few faiths themselves would recognize between commitment and its content. The energy and motivation that flow from a religious orientation are not independent variables, separate from the actual meanings and practices they happen to be associated with. Religions are not battery packs that can be wired into connection with the practices or views we have decided need supporting.

Such a supposition seems to reflect the deep private/public division enforced on religion in the West. The substance of religious traditions must remain private matters. What is permitted in the public realm is religion as motivation, as resource and personal empowerment for actions with an otherwise secular purpose. The devout Muslim family that feels a vocation to adopt a handicapped newborn or the Christian woman whose faith impels her to help welfare mothers organize to seek better treatment by the state may be publicly admired. If the first seeks to change abortion law or the second to change welfare law for explicitly religious reasons, they will be censured for violating this distinction. In fact, here as in many other areas it seems that pluralistic theories have ratified the secular dogma that the specifics of religion are private, conditioned matters that deserve no standing in the common realm.

The assumption that religion can be dichotomized in this way undergirds much contemporary talk of "constructing" theologies to serve certain ends, whether averting nuclear holocaust or fostering ecological consciousness. But why should we expect a religious shrine constructed with the primary intention of encouraging, say, economic egalitarianism to attract more attendance or higher commitment than a political meeting with the same intention? This instrumental approach to the religions seeks to tap a motivational power and commitment in them, while skirting the issue of whether the actual sources of renewal and empowerment the traditions rely upon are real. As faith commitments actually exist, the power and renewal flowing from them come inextricably mingled with the substance of the particular religious aims and objects.

If the historical substance and texture of the religions amount simply to culturally determined versions of the same religious process, then it is hard to see what distinctive guidance or truth they might have to offer for the public concerns of economics or politics. If the religions are by definition themselves dictated by cultural forces, it would appear that they could have no decisive direction to provide to their cultures. This is particularly so since economics and politics increasingly operate as integrated cross-cultural systems. If, as we are told, religions are culturally determined expressions, then it seems that any particular religion's influence on such a multicultural system would be sharply limited because by definition the religion represents only a narrow cultural scope. This would seem to leave no other social function (as opposed to a personal function) for these religious forms than to serve as a conduit through which religious motivations might flow into social movements organized on another basis, a civil religion function.

If in fact the liberation theology of religions is not simply a call to substitute its specific social agenda for the tenets of the faiths, then it is seeking a series of parallel transformations in the traditions, where each on its own grounds gives greater weight to the social concerns of liberation. Such a project can only advance through real engagement with those specific grounds themselves.

This brings us to the question of how justice and liberation are to be defined. I have noted already that pluralistic theologies spare no energy in investigating the cultural determinants of the forms of the various religious traditions, but are comparatively reticent about such a genealogy of their own views. They generally prefer to refer them to global developments, new stages in human consciousness, or simply to preface key affirmations "We now know that. . . . "

Chapter 4 indicated that exegesis of both the "we" and the "now" in such statements reveals the cultural and religious particularity of such views. This is true of the liberation theology of religions as well. Knitter claims that the traditions are more alike in their soteriological starting points than in their doctrines. There is a certain undeniable truth to this, if it means that the various traditions all developed in awareness of human suffering and transience. But Knitter swiftly transmutes this into an assumption that some constant condition is currently available as a reference point for all traditions. But the "human condition" is only available to those in the traditions and to pluralistic theorists in an already interpreted form. The very distinction Knitter makes between soteriologies and doctrines is a prime example.

John Milbank has argued effectively that Knitter's assumption can actually be reversed. He contends that the major religious traditions did indeed originate in face of a similar social context: the context of a society divided into a three- or fourfold class structure. Milbank suggests that the traditions were *differentiated* by their responses to this social problematic as much as by their varying postulates of a metaphysical sort (Milbank 1990a, 185-186). It is the very commonness of the social question they face, in other words, that helps explain why the religions must be understood as radically different *social* projects.

Milbank points out that nearly all the major religious traditions can be seen as outgrowths of the "'imperial,' nomadic adventures of the Indo-European peoples" (Milbank 1990a, 180). He sees the various empires associated with these adventures as ambiguous developments. Rather unfashionably, he notes their positive dimensions. They broke down local tyrannies, tribal conflicts, and pure parochialisms. The multicultural religious traditions that arose within them were under constant pressure to reinvent their own principles in ever more universal terms. Milbank faults pluralists for continually treating the traditions as "tribalisms," when in fact they represent the longest-standing attempts in human history precisely to face and overcome mere local or clan chauvinisms. The religions are thoroughgoing social projects. They are as distinctively divergent in this as in any other dimension.

Thus, for instance, there is no reason to think Christian incarnational doctrine an occasion of more likely conflict among the religions than the existence of the church as a theological/social community. In India, for instance, Christological and trinitarian doctrine have long been a favorite ground of Christian-Hindu speculation. But the more rending historical issues have arisen around baptism and communion, disjunctures between the practices of the ecclesial community and the social norms dictated within the Hindu tradition. From this perspective, Christianity's "metaphysical" beliefs about Jesus are considerably less decisive than its social practices of table fellowship in contrast with purity codes, or its requirement of baptism in face of the family and caste connections this might break. In the Indian context one's employment, marriage, and social rank hinge on these latter elements in a way they never would on a "doctrinal" issue in Knitter's terms. And yet this social project that is the church is of a piece with what Christians mean by faith and salvation. A similar and reciprocal thing might be said by a Westerner who had found refuge from the individualism and egalitarian autonomy of his or her culture by adhering to a Hindu guru, living in an ashram with strictly constrained roles and dress for women and men, a clear spiritual hierarchy, and definite mensal and cultic codes. Here too, a social project is inseparable from the religious aim.

Milbank contends that "an embracing of modern secular politics and legality is what is going on in the praxis solution" (Milbank 1990a, 182). Agreement in the sociopolitical sphere across religious traditions "nearly always betokens the triumph of Western attitudes and a general dilution of the force of traditional religious belief" (Milbank 1990a, 184). When the full difference of another religious outlook is seriously pursued—as in attempts at some version of thorough Islamic practice in Western countries—tension quickly escalates, precisely at the level of the religious social project.

> For the Western toleration of a diversity of religious beliefs and practices (so long as this means merely practice of *rites*) assumes a concomitant secularization of law, politics, knowledge and for the most part education, which often renders impossible a complete modern manifestation of religions in their guise as social projects. Practice, therefore, turns out to be no neutral meeting ground, but rather the place where the other religions and even Christianity itself to some degree, have been most engulfed by the dominance of secular norms (Milbank 1990a, 184).

From Milbank's perspective, the attempt to make "justice" the rallying point of the religions is misguided in two ways. Since what it really means is an attempt to enlist the religions in the causes of human rights, feminism, anti-racism, environmental concerns, and perhaps socialism, it is implicitly committed to disguising or suppressing the differences among the religions as social projects. Even where there might be significant coincidences in social outlook across religious traditions, if they are of an anti-modern sort these will be largely ignored. He gives as an example the prohibitions against usury. But second, Milbank, a committed socialist himself, objects that the search for some common religious platform in support of these causes will actually obscure their character and undermine their effectiveness. They have, he argues, an "ineradicable relation to specifically Western culture" (Milbank 1990a, 185).

As an example of the confusion he has in mind, Milbank points to Marjorie Suchocki's identification of a common principle of liberation, feminist, and pluralistic theologies as the prohibition on making one mode of humanity normative for others. This is simply wrong in his view. Wrong, first, because liberation movements, feminism, and pluralistic theories certainly do make some modes of humanity normative. Wrong, second, because this attempt to assimilate feminist concerns to interreligious ones has resulted only in granting primary normative weight to modern secular categories above both, categories which are in fact only ambiguously supportive of these causes themselves. Milbank argues it is the deeper roots of socialism and feminism in the Western and particularly Christian traditions that must be acknowledged, along with the nature of the universal and particularistic claims that these movements share with Christianity (see Milbank 1990b).

In Knitter's liberation theology of religions the sharp dualism we have seen in Hick and Smith returns in a "soteriocentric" form. As Milbank puts it, "Insofar as salvation is 'religious,' it is formal, transcendental and private; insofar as it is 'social,' it is secular" (Milbank 1990b, 245). When Knitter or Suchocki talk of salvation, they do not intend attention to the varying views of ultimate human fulfillment, but to some historical, instrumental, minimal human enablement. Suchocki, for instance, suggests attention to the religions' ideals solely because one might find there more readily abstractable common elements of human physical well-being. In fact, advocating "justice" as the interreligious imperative assumes just such a meeting place of "foundational" human well being, upon which religions may go on to add divergent versions of "higher" beatitude.

For example, in arguing that the liberation starting point is agreeable to the various traditions, Knitter offered a justification in the case of Christianity. He argued it is not beliefs, worship, or practice that should constitute Christian identity but action on behalf of Jesus' vision of justice. A crucial disjunction occurs here, however. By "the kingdom" or "Jesus' vision of justice" Knitter does not mean to refer to actual material attributed to Jesus or norms modeled on Jesus narratives. Instead it is clear that "justice" has become a quantity arrived at by other means, primarily certain modern types of social analysis. Jesus sought justice, by his lights. We know what justice is by social analysis that is not religiously confessional. In pursuing it we are following Jesus. The crucial mediation is carried out by social analysis, which is presumed to be neutrally situated as regards the religions. It is this analysis, whether Marxist, Weberian, Durkheimian, which at root enables the claims for a "soteriocentric" norm across faiths, a norm that is supposedly nonconfessional.

We have already seen the way in which religions are treated as private, spiritual forces, detached from their content. Now we see how that matches up with the proposal of a justice norm. *What* religion is intrinsically becomes a commitment to love the neighbor, or an unrestricted openness to freedom, or some such formulation. But "true religion" as so defined is radically detached from the traditions' concrete prescriptions of the substance of what it means to love, or what freedom is. Insofar as they offer such prescriptions, the religious traditions are expressing only cultural influences, applicable at best to a lost time and place. If this dualism is rigidly enforced, then the connectability of the religions to modern social analysis can be assured. The social analysis provides the simple account of "the way things are," the prescription for what ought concretely to be done to act in authentic furtherance of the religious impulse; the religions need only supply the impulse itself.

One interesting and admirable aspect of this appeal to social analysis is that it can clearly be used to cast into question the religious or theological preferences of its advocates. To social analysis we have appealed; to its results we must defer. Soteriocentric theologians argue that religions must take responsibility for the social effects of their doctrines and practices; therefore their proposals can fairly be evaluated on these same terms. This evaluation presumably must include more than a comparison of the professed aims of religious groups. It should deal directly with the roles they actually play in social process. For instance, if we take the starting point suggested by Paul Knitter, the social interests of the poor, which Christian groups in Latin America would we judge most favorably by this standard: liberation theology base communities or pentecostal movements?

There is little doubt that the liberation communities would agree more readily with Knitter's formulations than the pentecostals would. But Knitter has made it clear that it is not words but effects that are crucial: effective *praxis*. Here on many counts there is increasingly acknowledgment of the achievements of the pentecostal communities (e.g., see Martin 1990). The collapse of the Soviet empire leaves fresh in our minds the image of cases where the language of liberation and *praxis* had been absolutely monopolized by one party, bearing little relation with their actual exemplification. It will require several more decades before a full answer can be given about Latin America. But if it is social effects that are the standard, one can hardly decree now what the result will be. In other words, a plausible case can be made according to the soteriocentric standard that some who do not endorse it may meet it more effectively than those who do. This highlights again the ambiguity of an interreligious dialogue that insists on the sole priority of "justice." It may seal itself off from those with special strengths to advance concrete human well being although they do not articulate their religious end in the same way.

This movement toward the authority of social scientific categories has long been underway in Western Christianity, without any special reference to religious diversity. It has to do with the apologetic strategy of borrowing credibility from secular method. Milbank suggests that the continuation of this strategy in pluralistic theologies is now somewhat anachronistic: "The alliance of theology with the modernist legacy of social theory from the nineteenth century, which is at once 'scientific' and 'humanist,' appears all the more curious in light of recent developments within social theory itself" (Milbank 1990b, 2). His point is that the notion of an autonomous secular reason, operating without necessary grounding in any particularistic "mythical" structure, is increasingly contested within the field of secular social theory itself.

This critique comes from several incompatible directions, including deconstructionists on the one hand and defenders of classical virtue like Alasdair MacIntyre on the other (Milbank 1990b, chaps. 5 and 7). As Milbank says:

> An extraordinary contrast therefore emerges between political theology on the one hand, and postmodern and post-Nietzschean social theory on the other. Theology accepts secularization and the autonomy of secular reason; social theory increasingly finds secularization paradoxical and implies that the mythic-religious can never be left behind (Milbank 1990b, 3).

The presumption of an objective, universal rationality which is ingrained in the Western social sciences is contested by "genealogical" analyses that trace the exercise of these disciplines back to specific interests and social locations. Thus the whole area of social analysis finds itself torn in a manner analogous to the tension we examined earlier in philosophy between rationality and evaluative orientation. The genealogical assertion that theology is disguised social theory is balanced out by the realization that social theory is disguised theology. This suggests that the religious dimensions of society cannot be relegated to its "superstructure," for there is no socioeconomic reality which is more basic than that of religion. Social readings of the world are inescapably "mythic" from this perspective. Theological reliance on these categories of social analysis to provide a noncontroversial definition of what it means to carry out Christian ethics in cooperation with those of various faith traditions thus ironically leads us back to religious difference, encoded in the social analysis itself. The attitudes, practices, and beliefs of the traditions are not "forms" somehow entirely created by a culture to clothe some essential religious disposition or interaction—an interpretation that comprehensively rules out significant *reciprocal* influence between form and content—but are themselves constitutive religious elements that also contain an impetus toward a certain range of social structures and possibilities.[3]

The power of Milbank's argument lies in its judo-like response to the genealogist's critique of theology. Theology has rightly become aware, he says, of the "degree to which it is a contingent, historical construct emerging from, and reacting back upon, particular social practices conjoined with particular semiotic and figural codings. It is important to realize that my entire case is constructed from a complete *concession* as to this state of affairs, and that the book offers no proposed restoration of a pre-modern Christian position" (Milbank 1990b, 2). Having agreed

---

[3] See, for instance, Stackhouse's *Creeds, Society and Human Rights* for an extensive argument to this effect around the question of human rights.

that Christian tradition and theology constitute an encoded vocabulary of social practice, Milbank proceeds to defend it (in revised Augustinian form) as by far the superior such vocabulary precisely because it offers a way to accept difference in peace.

In Milbank's view, this is precisely what the genealogical versions of post-modernity cannot do. They speak of justice, but have no categories for difference except those of power and suspicion. Augustine in the *City of God* argued that eternal life was the only possible fulfillment of the aim of human good that philosophy had rightly intimated. In similar fashion, Milbank argues that Christian theological discourse itself contains the "social theory" for which modern sociological thought rightly specifies a need, a need it cannot meet. Christian particularity contains resources capable of fulfilling the desire for peace which pluralistic theories express, but which pluralistic attempts to subordinate that particularity necessarily frustrate. "With an extreme degree of paradox, one must claim that it is only through insisting on the finality of the Christian reading of 'what there is' that one can both fulfill respect for the other and complete and secure this otherness as pure neighborly difference" (Milbank 1990a, 189).

The presumed certainty and neutrality of the mediation provided by social theories are deeply shaken. To presuppose dogmatically such certainty is no longer even a matter of implicitly requiring that other religions accept the modern West's dominant norm. It is to insist that all religions be judged according to one *among* contending Western views of social theory. There certainly will be no global interreligious dialogue structured around a common starting point of "justice" if no such common starting point exists even in the West. The developments within Western social theory which Milbank stresses help to clarify the status of the "liberation theology of religions." To become frank advocates of one orientational view of justice is to take up a stand among the religions, not on some common ground between them. The possibilities for cooperation and alliance are very real, but they require an honesty about one's own particularistic "mythic" grounds and their constitution of different social projects.

Such questions may seem far removed from passionate calls for interreligious dialoguers to leave their air-conditioned hotel halls and face instead life in the festering *fabellas*. But such calls are issued with equal or greater regularity by persons within various traditions who do not hold pluralistic views. Indeed, many an exclusivist or inclusivist Christian lives a life of poverty and oppression alongside those of diverse faiths, and would share a distaste for those of any theological stripe who would pass by on the other side of the road to attend a conference rather than offer a cup of water. The liberation theology of religions does not deny that the various traditions address poverty and injustice. The key to its claim to offer a new interreligious norm is the presumption of a new systemic insight into these subjects, functional knowledge of causes and remedies that supersedes any substantive approach to these issues in any of the traditions themselves. If this were not the case, then those practicing the liberation theology of religions would be ready to lay aside or provisionally to suspend their feminist commitments, or their class analysis, and so on, as Knitter earlier insisted Christians should lay aside their convictions about the universal decisiveness of Christ. These would be commitments whose validity could only be affirmed much later as a result of dialogue that would take up the widest range of other possible commitments. Yet the "soteriocentric" approach can be constituted as something distinct from the prior dialogue agenda only by insistent advocacy of just such particularistic commitments.

Liberation has many meanings in various religious traditions. "Liberation" in "the liberation theology of religions" would appear to deal distinctively with structural organization in a modern secular state. It presupposes economic and political analysis that itself makes little sense without reference to such societies. Therefore its mandatory if implicit prescription for justice in any social order that does not already conform to this model is for it to be transformed until it does. To take a very simple example, a society with a significant part of its material production set within a clan structure which merges economic, legal, family, and religious dimensions and rigidly prescribes social roles for its various members is not compatible with economic autonomy for individual women. The preconditions for such autonomy include a system of private property ownership, an exchange economy, a legal structure prioritizing the individual over communal or family groups, and so on.

Thus Milbank, who is particularly concerned with socialism, finds it telling that Christian socialists prior to the contemporary period almost unanimously identified secularization with free-market economy, centralized state sovereignty, and bureaucratic structures (Milbank 1990b, 243). These Christian socialists sought to derive their socialism directly from Christianity, both in terms of principles and in terms of historical precedents. Milbank argues that liberation theologians are correct when many of them state that they have not elected Marxism over Christianity. The decision was of a quite different order: to embrace secular social analysis as the normative account of the way things work. This is a movement that was made before the rise of liberation theology by large numbers of Western theologians whose political orientations may have been quite different. Liberation theologians are correct to point out that their critics are often disingenuous in attacking "sociological theology" when in fact they are only objecting to a divergent form of a theology they have long practiced themselves. Given such a prior commitment to modern social analysis, Marxism was secondarily attractive to some of these theologians as the path *within* such social theory that could lead back to socialist conclusions that resembled those earlier grounded in Christian tradition.

For our purposes, the significance of this exchange has to do with the interreligious context. Whether or not one entirely agrees with Milbank's analysis, it is itself an example of the arguments over modernity and post-modernity that now exercise us in the West. And the mere existence of these arguments is fatal to the implicit attempt to give social theory neutral normativity. Increasingly our conventional liberal ideas of justice cannot be simply presumed as universals on which to scaffold religious cooperation and by which to reinterpret religious traditions. Those ideas themselves stand in need of a convincing "religious" grounding. Recent discussions of "public theology" highlight this concern.[4] There is of course no necessity for any individual liberation theologian to grant secular social theory the unquestioned mediating role Milbank suggests they do. Many—for example, Leonardo Boff, José Míguez Bonino, and Enrique Dussel—argue strongly that they do not, that their notions of liberation are primarily biblically based and that social analysis is shaped and utilized by those standards. If so, then they are appealing to particularistic Christian grounds and in fact are close to Milbank's position. Those, liberation theologians or not, who make such social theory determinative must defend its normativity. They must make a straightforward case for the universality of a particular Western standard. In either case, the "justice" norm is decidedly not neutral in religious terms.

In chapter 3 we reviewed an apparent convergence between a normative emphasis on the *praxis* of dialogue and a normative emphasis on the *praxis* of justice. In the first case, the principle was that whatever conditions made interreligious dialogue possible were, for that reason, binding on the various traditions. This led to a recognition that for authentic communication to take place, justice would have to be established. Otherwise, not all parties could speak with the same freedom and power. In the second case, the imperative for all faiths to be held accountable to the oppressed led to the question of what norm of justice could be enforced on them without itself exercising illegitimate domination. The answer seemed to be that a fully inclusive dialogue would be necessary to arrive at such a definition of justice. This "chicken or egg" problem at least seemed to point to a mutually reinforcing process, where dialogue about justice and critique of the traditions on the basis of justice dialectically alternated.

---

[4] See, for instance, Ronald Thiemann's *Religion in American Public Life: A Dilemma for Democracy* and Max L. Stackhouse's *Public Theology and Political Economy*. Both these books take the specific character of the various religious traditions with great seriousness.

What I maintain, borrowing Milbank's analysis, is that this entire process has a much more particularistic and even confessional location than that description indicates. The "dialogue about justice" it envisions is severely restricted. In fact it translates into a dialogue about details of a very specific social theoretical approach, one increasingly not even dominant in the West where it originates. Therefore, to reverse the supposed convergence of dialogue and justice, I would claim that if we are serious about an inclusive dialogue, we must recognize that "justice" is already a significantly exclusivistic way of framing the question. M. M Thomas tells the story of planning an interfaith study session on the topic of creation and history. A Hindu pundit invited to take part declined with the observation that the subject had already been thoroughly defined in Christian theological categories. He saw no space in the proposal to receive his positive religious convictions, since in his view creation and history were metaphysical evils to be overcome (Thomas 1990, 57). At the very least, dialogue involves recognition of "other-rationality" which entails consideration of alternative ways of constituting the very questions that "justice" addresses.

On the other hand, it is perfectly appropriate for some to insist on justice as the starting place and norm, a justice given substance by just such particularistic commitments as we have reviewed. Dialogue in this case has a decidedly subordinate role to that of witness and mission on behalf of the universal norms of human well-being we propound. The primary priority is action and cooperation in that mission with those in other traditions who most closely approximate our understanding, a thoroughly inclusivist agenda. This particularistic "mission to the world" is what the various forms of the liberation theology of religions are truly about. The perspective that I have outlined regards such missions as defensible, so long as they are honest about their universal claims and their standing among rather than above the religions.

Orientational pluralism and my more pluralistic hypothesis in fact argue that these two "divergent" elements are the keys to a consistent and fruitful treatment of religious diversity. Authentic dialogue about justice must point beyond "justice" as the sole theme of dialogue, because we recognize there are alternative orientations from which the issues are framed quite differently. Commitment to liberation will inevitably place action and witness in a higher priority than dialogue as the pure search for understanding, since we are inevitably committed to maintaining that our view of justice is preferable to others.

To put it another way, understanding is always an intermediate good. One of the questions I posed in the introduction was what the "thick" description of a religious tradition is *for*. I suggest that such sympathetic understanding, the appropriate goal of academic study of religion per se, is never fully sufficient in itself. It leads to consideration of two kinds of alternativeness in the faiths. The first has to do with truth. We seek to understand in order to arrive at some judgment of the truth of the matter, a process that can be continually repeated. At one level this is an alternative of true and false. But at another level, we may recognize the truth—that is, the descriptive accuracy and the religious validity—of another tradition. This raises a question that has to do not simply with truth or error but with fullness and the greatest possible coherence, with how we are to understand the mutual relations among truths and authentic experiences. The second kind of alternative has to do with practice. Even two truths that are mutually consistent may not be practicable by the same person at the same time in the same depth. Understanding in this sense is always at the service of practice and always leads us to a choice about our own behavior.

In summary, I believe that recognition of an actual diversity of religious ends offers a sounder basis on which to overcome oppression of one faith by another and to explore the distinctive contribution religious traditions can make to the resolution of other human conflicts. In terms of the conflict between faith traditions, my hypothesis is that actual religious difference, eschatological or historical, is not a root evil. The material recognition of difference, coupled with the affirmation of diverse religious ends, allows more substantive mutual affirmation among the faiths and a firmer basis for peaceful interaction than other approaches. Of course there are real differences which are not in practice reconcilable; a Buddhist, a Muslim, and a Christian may each have his or her own grounds for concluding that National Socialism or Stalinism involve human aims that must be flatly opposed. It seems that pluralistic theories want to exclude such a possibility in the relations between religions themselves, as well as the possibility that they can appropriately "rank" each other according to internal criteria. I exclude neither. The primary interreligious challenge is to acknowledge authentic human options that are truly distinct and yet seek the most integrated understanding possible of their relations, an understanding that should itself be a frankly particularistic one. There is a basic divergence between those who see the source of interreligious conflict in the illusion of diverse faith fulfillments—an illusion to be overcome by dispelling the distinctions—and those who see the problem not in actual differences but in our capacity to integrate difference into a rich and peaceful whole. I hold the latter view, suspecting that the claims to "see beyond" the distinctive life of each tradition are sandy foundations for mutual respect.

In terms of the religions' impact on social evils, I have argued that we are best served by the same two elements I emphasized earlier: advocacy of the universal relevance of our convictions, and recognition of the integral otherness and universal scope of varying approaches. Thus it is appropriate for the universal mission of Christian liberation theologies to express itself in straightforwardly normative ways, but crucially important, even in terms of the justice norm it affirms, for there to be dialogue with religious perspectives on the human condition that configure its social and ethical elements quite differently than Western norms of justice. Milbank's analysis brings home the fact that to affirm a soteriocentric priority which has any substantive content is precisely to affirm one particular religious conviction among others. It is mission and evangelism in an inclusivist mode. As such, it is entirely in order.

8

Wisdom and Witness

An overworked image in discussion of religious pluralism is that of several blind persons examining an elephant. One, feeling the trunk, believes it to be a snake. Another, feeling the leg, believes it to be a tree. Yet another, touching the elephant's flank, insists it is a wall. The story classically illustrates the way apparently conflicting conclusions stem from various limited perspectives on the same reality. The story of course is told from the point of view of the sighted person among the blind. But that assumed perspective is plainly untenable. The claim to be sighted in the world of the religiously blind cannot be rationally confirmed; there is no perspective "above" the faiths and the unfaiths in that sense.

We are all in a similar position. Here there is a very real parity among the adherents of all faiths and none. We each have our own religious experience, which is continuous for us with the media of that experience. We are also each able to conceive and even to stress the distinction between that which we encounter in our religious experience and the means through which we come to the encounter or interpret it. We have some knowledge of the reported and practiced faiths of others, within and without our traditions. We reach some tentative judgments about which of these elements appear valid and truthful, even though they are not identical to those of our own faith and may not have been part of our direct experience. In an interplay of all these factors, we shape and receive a sense of the whole.

The parable's choice of an elephant as the object makes it laughably obvious that the blind persons could dispel their naive dogmas in a few moments, quickly accumulating all of each other's relevant experience of trunk, legs, and side, and then assimilating them to the same description. But the world is not an elephant. The parable would be more apt if we supposed we were speaking of a continent or a city, if we supposed that the blind persons themselves all came from continents and cultures of radically different types and times, and if we put ourselves not in the place of an omniscient observer but among the seekers. Exchange of experience is much more difficult in this context; a single life can gather only one very small thread of the whole. How one spends that life, in what modes of seeking, will inevitably affect what one finds and will shape how all other information is construed to form some integral vision of the whole. We are not in the place of the sighted observer in the parable of the elephant. We cannot claim a "God's-eye view." We may, indeed we should, seek the most adequate reading of the world we can attain, based on the orientation through which we see it, our direct experience, and the most extensive integration possible of the warranted claims of others.

THE LIMITS OF PLURALISTIC THEOLOGIES

Naive realism in religion thinks of God as geographically "up there" or pictures Jesus as sitting on top of a palpable right hand of the divine. Critical realisms on the other hand acknowledge fully that religious concepts and practices involve human projection, and still hold that these human projections may "fit" something external to them. There are many varieties of such critical realism. Some are vanishingly close to the border with religious non-realism. They hold that these projections do not actually contact an "outside" reality, and yet that such projections are among the most valuable human resources we have. The difference in human life that comes from acting *as if* these projections had correlatives is real enough, and it is this "outside" reality that can be taken as the critically realistic content of religious affirmations.

Hick, for one, rejects such a view. The fundamental difference between realists and non-realists boils down in his eyes to a question about the nature of the universe in relation to us. Is there any hope for persons crushed in history as we know it? (see Hick 1993, 13). The religious realist answers that the universe is such that it is reasonable to entertain an unrestricted hope for such people. The religious non-realist by contrast regards the universe as offering no grounds for such a hope, and can only "rejoice with the elite few whose heredity or environment or both are such that they are able to attain to personal blessedness . . . before death extinguishes them" while the mass of humanity churns its way through misery to nothingness (Hick 1993, 14). This great question is in Hick's view indifferent to any of the specific religious "objects" or ends of the diverse traditions. I argued that his attempt to claim a highly generic fulfillment of this hope as the *distinctive* feature of his "pluralistic hypothesis" proves to be incoherent, because Hick fails to specify a future possible state of affairs predicted by his hypothesis that is distinguishable from concrete religious fulfillments envisioned by the traditions. He refuses to address what would *count* as "blessedness." He is careful, for instance, to treat the moral qualities of his "soteriological criterion" as signs that transformation toward a better possibility is taking place, not as constituting the content of that possibility.

But there are many critically realistic possibilities other than Hick's. I have argued that the supposition of a diversity of concrete religious fulfillments is both reasonable and on many counts preferable to Hick's hypothesis. I maintain that this approach makes sense philosophically, historically, and ethically. Theologically, I have argued that though it is a challenge for Christian thought to come to terms with this possibility, it is an approach with deep grounds in fundamental Christian sources and convictions.

In outlining my view I have leaned heavily on some "post-modern" critiques by way of illustration, for instance, LaFargue in chapter 5 and Milbank in chapter 7. I have done this in order to point up the fact that the radical recognition of conditioning which pluralistic writers try to make serve as exclusive support for their conclusions can be deployed even more convincingly in another way. This is the weight, for instance, of Milbank's insistence that he fully concedes the historical contingency of Christian theology and *on those terms* commends its distinctive truth. What such post-modern critiques make clear is the increasingly problematic nature of the typical pluralistic move: because we are radically conditioned knowers/experiencers, it must be an object/experience separate from such conditioning that is the true referent in religion. The two halves of this assertion are at war with each other, and the more strongly one is stressed, the weaker the other becomes.

This reflects the dilemma that thinkers of all sorts face today: the need to move beyond enlightenment assumptions and yet to stop short of the totally relativistic types of post-modernism. Pluralistic theories often simply bundle together the two extremes. On the one hand, there is the enlightenment understanding of religions as sets of propositions about a universe which is descriptively univocal. On such terms, the religions will be distilled to their cognitive content. On the other hand, one can go the full Nietzschean route to insist that all "truths" are rooted not in one reality, but in the myths and wills of the human knowers themselves. Religious unity in the first case comes by focusing on some core of rational propositions of a metaphysical and moral nature. In the second case it comes by identifying not the substance but the *function* of the faiths, to claim not that they believe the same thing but that they share the same character. If the first stresses the reference of religion, the second stresses the disposition of the religious.

Hick's thesis combines the sparest possible form of enlightenment deism (in the "thin" common cognitive content of all the religions) with a thoroughgoing view of all "actually existing" religion as culturally determined forms. The shared cognitive content of the religions is the proposition that ultimate reality is such that humans can adapt to it in a way that will achieve a limitlessly better possibility. The mythological complexes of the faiths are the dispositional ways in which this is done. Thus an assertion of a universal truth about what is objectively so is coupled with a purely functional interpretation of the role of all concrete historical religious phenomena: they serve simply to induce an experiential disposition in believers. These two are so isolated from each other that the connection between them is thin to the point of invisibility. But this is precisely the issue post-modern critiques press upon us. Yes, on the one side it is implausible to suppose that the transcendent has been *literally* described in particular conditioned terms. Pluralistic writers stress this point tirelessly. But equally it is implausible, perhaps even incoherent, to speak of a transcendent that is not continuous with conditioned existence. The attempt to strain all cultural content from some sole religious object or attitude is as suspect as the fundamentalist totalizing of it. I have argued that my approach is an advance over such pluralistic strategies because it offers a much more consistent treatment of this fundamental question.

In chapter 1 and in chapter 5 I pointed out that the *type* of perspective Hick and others represent is in fact characteristic of all the religious traditions themselves.[1] On this point, the attempt to find support for the pluralistic strategies in the religions themselves succeeds rather better than its advocates intend. The religions must be recognized at a fundamental level not only as subjects of pluralistic interpretation but alternatives to it and to each other. That is, the religions require to be interpreted in a manner which recognizes their power to interpret the interpreter: a requirement I maintain can only be met by frankly acknowledging alternative religious aims. This recognition at the same time offers us the way to understand how salvific states could be significantly affected by historical experience, and yet need not be constricted in a flat right/wrong dichotomy.

Without such a recognition, the religions disappear as what they are—ultimate world-making contexts of understanding—to be replaced not, as often claimed, by an appreciation of their diversity but rather by a competing mythos. In the pluralistic case the mythos is a modern, Western one, as I argue in chapter 4. I do not mean in any way to suggest that one cannot argue for the universal superiority of the particularly modern Western mythos. Insofar as the pluralists do so, I have noted that I have no methodological quarrel with them. I contend that this is appro-

---

[1] In the sense, first, that any religious practice or life can be taken to evince philosophical presumptions about the world, whether these are elaborated or not, and second, that even "scholastic" traditions make clear that the benefits of practice cannot depend upon exhaustive or literal knowledge of its object, for this is impossible to the seeking devotee. The "apophatic" stream in Christian theology and the treatment of avyakata or "unanswered questions" in Buddhism are not anticipations of the pluralistic view but testimony that these traditions have perceived and addressed the issues in their own ways.

priate behavior, as is the correlative argument by Buddhists, Christians, or others.

The *scope* of this alternativeness between the religions is clearly a second question: Does it hold only within the experiential dimension by which humans construe the world or is it also a metaphysical feature of the universe? I argue that it certainly holds within the historical frame, so that the diversity of religious options which exist within and among the traditions is religiously significant because it determines the nature of the fulfillments that human communities and individuals achieve. There is also good reason to believe that this diversity endures in eschatological fulfillments. If these varied religious aims are actualized, the universe must be such as to support these alternative human fulfill-ments. Among the various religions, one or several or none may pro-vide the best approximate representation of the character of that cos-mos, explaining and ordering these various human possibilities within it. It is appropriate then for each to argue for and from its own universal view, so long as the diversity and actuality of religious ends are recog-nized.

Within the experiential-historical frame, I differ from Hick in stress-ing the distinctiveness of religious experiences and practices taken in their wholeness rather than some abstract similarity in their effects. The distinctive thing about the depths of Jewish religious fulfillment, for instance, is not "transformation toward a limitlessly better human pos-sibility." Such a phrase abstracts from what *is* distinctive about such fulfillment: the particular sets of relation, obligation, joy, transforma-tion, concepts, and mystery that grow out of Jewish sources and consti-tute forms of life that could not exist without them. *This* love of God, delight in the law, respect for wisdom, passion for justice; *these* images of the divine, structures of community, traditions of interpretation are what enrich and fill up particular human lives and communities.

My view does not rule out an eschatological convergence of some religious goals, particularly since many faith traditions themselves tes-tify to such a possibility in inclusivist terms. But I insist that this is a contention that must be proposed and defended on the basis of specific cases. A primary pluralistic contention is that an eschatological sce-nario in which one religion would be revealed to be the true one and all others false is not merely offensive to our sensibilities but defective in exhibiting insufficient *continuity* with this life. There should be some integral relation between future human states and present ones, else the universe is organized neither in accord with principles of equity we rec-ognize nor with processes of development we can conceive. I agree with this contention, and suggest that my hypothesis meets its concern much more effectively than the pluralistic ones do. It is pluralistic theories, as I have outlined, that dramatically deny this continuity by denying to salvation any determinate qualities.

This question of continuity carries us naturally into issues of history. The seamless web of religious history which W. C. Smith describes to us is a reality. But it is not a spectrum whose infinite shades reflect only the secondary forms of a primordial religious reality, faith. Smith has largely dropped the cognitive concerns that so exercise Hick in favor of an attitudinal or existential quality. But on this ground he replicates the dichotomy we have already seen. For Smith it is the connection between faith and its forms that becomes the vanishing point. The forms flow together in one human "religious quest" for faith which, once found, comes in varying intensities but one flavor.

I have already expressed my objections to this grand scheme. Like the rest of history, the human religious story is a field within which there are thresholds of all sorts. The borders between the watersheds are indeed rarely sharp, but the regions they separate are often decisively different. Surely this is one of the fascinations of the study of history. What ingredients, however minor they might seem, if added or subtracted in a given situation would have led to dramatically different social results? We know that many natural systems exhibit this hair-trigger sensitivity to initial conditions, in which the "butterfly effect" of a tiny variation in one part of the system explodes into an extreme divergence in the later behavior of its entire ecology. But such sensitivity does not exist for every variation of a similar amount, only for those that take place around certain "ridges" or thresholds.

I commend a similar perspective on religious diversity, both at the level of individuals and communities. This seems consistent with the traditions' own self-description, with serious affirmation of the validity of their ends, and with emphasis on the significance of the differences between them. The religious dimension of human history does present us with a seamless garment, in which not only the traditions themselves but other dimensions—political, moral, economic—intermingle. I argued in chapter 6 that within even one faith tradition it is possible to move toward alternative religious ends. Individual traditions are juxtaposed not as neat geometric shapes but rather as large "basins of possibility" with long, spidery fractal regions spread through each other's "territory." As anyone who has looked at such a fractal image can imagine, one is never very far from thresholds. Likewise, within a religious tradition one is never far from choices that can lead deeper into the distinctive religious life that religion seeks or toward divergent possibilities. The watersheds these thresholds separate are distinct, and their characters different, corresponding to the diverse religious ends I have discussed. We can be grateful to writers like Smith for illustrating so eloquently the inadequacy of a "block" view of religious traditions. To put it another way, none of us is ever far from the edges of our tradition. But the inclusivist views of the various religious traditions themselves had already taken this insight far. And far from diminishing the importance of religious change and development, such an understanding should heighten it.

I have suggested that religious traditions are like trade winds that bear devotees and nominal adherents alike in a general direction. But persons always "tack" within this prevailing current. It is the seamless interconnection of the traditions that widen the possibilities and sharpen the significance of this individual response. I maintain that it is consistent with the historical data to believe that even without leaving one major religious tradition a person has full opportunity to incline effectively toward a variety of religious fulfillments. Such a perspective tallies with the consistent testimony of the different traditions that daily progressions in practice or transitions even from one portion of a tradition to another can have far-reaching consequences. The significance of all such changes must, on pluralistic theories, be radically discounted as issues of outward form and expression only. Recurrent admonitions within the various traditions about the crucial role of regular and intense practice in differentiating us as members of a tradition and setting us on the path to a distinctive end make good sense. As most great spiritual teachers have advised us, the religious quest is not one in which each incremental application on our part produces an identical incremental result. And yet such regular practice is an integral element to see us up to or through crisis points or thresholds. There is no such thing as the situation imaged by the picture of a religious tradition as a large circle, with a person standing at rest in its center, passive, far from encounter with or response to any but one possibility. In the religious field the thresholds lie close at hand at nearly every point.

I have found much substance in the pluralistic discussion of religious diversity and justice. The moral revulsion against imperialism and religious arrogance, the passion for peace and mutual respect, the unsparing awareness of one's own limited perspective: these make a necessary claim on any theory or theology of the religions. I have not been convinced, however, either that those espousing pluralistic doctrines practice such commitments in a manner superior to those who may hold some other perspectives or that the moral commitments themselves lead exclusively to pluralistic conclusions. But I have found that "soteriocentric" writers like Knitter are significantly more interested in addressing the dualism I criticize in other pluralistic views. They do not have the problem of continuity between the radically transcendent and historical dispositions toward it or between the radically existential attitude of faith and cultural expressions of it, for they stress precisely the unity of form and content. It is justice as human, historical well-being that they see as the effective content of religion and only those religious concepts and practices that serve it are affirmed. The tension between the two poles in our earlier writers here is emphatically collapsed around the imperative to serve the suffering and the poor. The continuity problem, the issue of whether concrete historical religious behavior or belief has anything to do with religion qua religion, is thus addressed in a much more direct manner: the two are virtually identified.

I have indicated the ways in which I feel this is a refreshing change. But in collapsing the dualistic tension which other pluralists use as the primary basis to validate the variety of traditions, ethical pluralists raise new difficulties about diversity. Indeed, I identified several tensions that preclude making the "liberation theology of religions" a shortcut to pluralistic assumptions which cannot be adequately grounded in philosophy or history. One of these is the tension between "justice" as the common imperative to action which the religions face and open dialogue as the means to formulate any notion of justice that can claim to be justly arrived at. Once the historical shape of religion is admitted to be integral to religious fulfillment, the diversity of the religions precisely as historical and social projects would seem to require a strong recognition of difference and choice. I suggested that ethical pluralists attempt to meet this problem by seeking some way of defining justice in at least a minimal way without leaning on traditions of a particularistic religious sort. The primary candidate for this task is modern Western social theory and the modes of analysis that have flowed from it. Here we ran into the problem that some of these modes of analysis themselves (to say nothing of criticism coming from "traditional societies") radically question the neutrality, and even the nonreligious character, of this social theory itself. That is, a good deal of post-modern social theory suggests that "the critique of social, political and economic reality depends on theology, not the other way around" (Stackhouse 1991, 19). This can only point us back to the religions as varying ways of posing and answering the question of human well-being. That hardly rules out an imperative toward cooperation in those already manifest areas where differing perspectives lead to consistent conclusions. But it requires also a certain respect for and attention to alternative practices and approaches.

Though ethical pluralism closes the gap between transcendence or subjectivity and history, it opens a different one, between content and vitality. Oddly enough, the "soteriocentric" emphasis upon justice as the basis of religious unity tends to lead to a denial that religions have their distinctive, substantive contributions to make to any public discussion of justice. The power of the religions is much coveted for enlistment in just causes, but there is little if any cogent account of what distinctive agency a particular religion might add to such causes. Faith becomes a private motive force for public action whose nature and rationale must be given in terms that supersede the religions themselves rather than being a residue of them. Despite these concerns, ethical pluralism consistently presents itself as the most enduring and important form of the pluralistic perspective.

Pluralistic theory in the forms we have examined is static. It has no future and no depth. It does not lack a future in the sense that it can be expected to disappear. It may even dominate much of our intellectual environment in periods to come. Rather I mean that it is committed to believing it has nothing to learn and no alternatives to consider. The specifics of existing traditions and the changes of religious life to come hold nothing but further confirmations of a theory. Even the most exclusivist of past missionaries did not rule out the possibility of discovering among unbelievers an original way to be wrong! But pluralists are unshakable in their expectation to find only the same ways of being wrong (identifying *forms* of the Real with the Real itself, or confusing faith with the medium through which faith is expressed) which are helplessly also ways of being right. As to depth, consistent pluralists would seem able to dive into the riches of the particular traditions only to return with an abstract kind of typological interpretation which hardly seems worth the trip. They focus on "a limitlessly better possibility," seeing that life has "a cosmic point," or the most generic notions of "human well-being." Each of these seems similar to the genie's lamp of fairy tales: a gift one could ardently desire only with some concrete notion about what to wish for with it.

MANY TRUE RELIGIONS . . .
AND EACH THE ONLY WAY

In contrast to these pluralistic theologies, I have attempted to illustrate an alternative approach to religious pluralism by suggesting another theory of religious diversity (orientational pluralism), commending a particular *class* of views within this theory (inclusivist pluralisms), and outlining one Christian instance of such a view. Each of these three arguments has a certain independence, but I believe their mutual consistency and enrichment make the whole even more compelling than the parts. I can only close by summarizing briefly the virtues of such an approach.

First, we can now answer one of the questions with which I began the book, and which I suggested was a nagging embarrassment to pluralistic theories. Why do we study religions at all? What is the significance for us of the distinctive, constitutive *othernesses* of the faiths? In various ways, pluralistic theories insist that the real and one significance of these othernesses is to be found not in what properly belongs to each but in their collectivity. *That* there are religious differences tells us that moral transformation can take place in varying contexts, that diverse mythological complexes can evoke dispositions with some generic similarities, that culture, time and psyche surely condition faith. Any particular religious difference tells us something only as an instance of these principles.

It is as if we were faced with a number of different tickets (train, boat, plane, bus), each with distinctive maps and itineraries attached. Those who favor a pluralistic theory like those examined in the first part of this book could interpret each of these separate travel plans as another repetitive piece of evidence in favor of that hypothesis. They could maintain that because travel of any sort involves some constant generic elements (tickets have a price; some representation of the path is needed; we will never depart if we don't show up on time) it is false and arrogant to suppose that we would miss something on one trip we might find on another or that we don't all have the same destination. There is, after all, only one world. And these trips are all ways of relating to it. The ship passenger who exclaims "This is the only way to travel!" would be a fool to mean the statement literally, for legions are at that moment journeying in other vehicles on other routes.

On such grounds, only the ignorant would take the specifics of the ocean itinerary to Sri Lanka to describe a decisive *alternative*, whose implementation might make of my life something fundamentally other than it would be on some other expedition. It will be relentlessly (and rightly) insisted that none of the maps or itineraries provides a "literal" representation of its destination or of the trip itself. Instead we will be told it is "travelling" as a human condition, "arrival" as the subjective realization of a sense of completion, and "the Destination" as the ultimate ground of the possibility of any arrival which are truly real. Jaffna, Kyoto, Santiago de Compostela are mythical forms of "The Destination." These forms involve certain literal or metaphorical sets of beliefs . . . even true ones. Some people might even literally arrive at such places! None of this should distract the enlightened traveller from the insight that these places and their features are all quite secondary. The apparent differences in these journeys will resolve themselves under the right kind of analysis: you could find in each of the destinations a Hilton hotel with all the Western amenities. If you have time only for one of these trips, you haven't missed much.

To continue the metaphor, I read the situation differently. I regard these cities as sites within a single world, whose global mapping has a determinate character. Jaffna is a place I will never arrive at inadvertently at the same time I get to London. I regard information about it as highly relevant regarding possibilities and experiences that I will never actualize unless I strike out in that direction and which others can actualize whether I strike out or not. My significant choices are not exhausted in the single global decision whether to regard all these tickets reductionistically or realistically—that is, deciding whether the tickets to these places are mere pieces of paper, illusions, with neither vehicle or destination of any generic description to back them up, or whether they are all valid tickets, each an express instance of the general truth that human life can truly go somewhere.

A great deal hinges on where I want to go. The ship passenger who exclaims "This is the only way to travel!" is certainly correct in that this is the only way to travel—if one intends to stick to water transport and so to the sites that can be reached by that means. The passenger is further correct if he or she means to designate a particular end for the journey and to imply that the only way to arrive there is to take *some* one of the limited number of various vehicles that is going there. And depending on the nature of the specific destination (say it is an island) the passenger is further correct in implying that some ways—bus, for instance—will not serve for this trip at all.

The point I am making with the metaphor is that the specifics of another religious tradition are deeply significant on a number of counts. They provide me my only ground for considering what is a crucial and alternative possibility for me—an alternative not only of form but of substance. In this sense, the call of every faith's devotees for others to attend to its witness as a crucially important word or way is fully justified. The specifics of the traditions also provide me my only ground for understanding so far as I can—in their actual integrity—the differing goals and realizations of my neighbors. Even further, their testimony provides powerful warrants for insights and practices whose validity I can come to recognize and which I must then struggle to integrate into my particular integral grasp of the whole. Both the attentiveness to the specificity of another tradition's elements on its own terms and the struggle toward integration are sustained by the conviction that these specifics cannot be "gotten over" in any of the standard pluralistic ways.

Second, the approach I have outlined allows for a much more nuanced understanding of the relations between religious traditions and the various kinds of judgment and dialogue that are possible. The exclusivist-inclusivist-pluralistic typology is inadequate, not only for description (diagnosis, as it were) but even more for prescription. In dialogue or interreligious relation, at least the following forms of judgment are appropriate at varying times. *Judgments of error:* evinced assumptions or specific claims of a religious tradition may be judged to be wrong, and at the extreme a particular religious end may be judged illusory. *Judgments of alternativeness:* the religious fulfillment of another tradition is recognized as actual, its claims to constitute the way to that fulfillment are accepted as valid, and the status of this fulfillment is placed in some penultimate relation to one's own. *Judgments of convergence and even identity:* another faith may be judged to seek an end which is either historically or eschatologically the same as the aim of one's own tradition. When there is also understood to be essential convergence in the *means* to this fulfillment, this could move toward a kind of parity of the traditions (for instance, a Christian view of Judaism which understood God's covenant with Jews and with Gentiles as parallel and irreducible but both rooted in the same triune God). *Classically inclusivist judgments:* another faith may be judged to contain resources which can lead some of those within it toward the fulfillment sought in the "outsider's" tradition instead of that predominant in the "home" tradition. As I have suggested earlier, often possibility for the most virulent religious conflict rests where devotees perceive the closest links with other traditions.

In short, an appreciation of the diversity of effective religious ends provides the best ground on which to achieve the difficult and delicate task of affirming the validity of differences while still maintaining that the alternatives are importantly different. This approach offers the widest scope for religious particulars to be recognized for what they are and not what some absolute axioms decree they must be. It opens the space for religious traditions to be grasped as alternatives, defining a form of life which is capable of relativizing other options. While it impels us toward this fundamental openness to traditions other than our own, it also impels us to grant validity to the missionary witness of the various religious traditions, not only in nurturing their own members but in presenting their faith to others as of universal relevance and unique content. Witness to others and attentive openness to their witness turn out to be intimately related. The possibility of the first is inextricably bound up with the possibility of the second. The two can hardly fit together without an appreciation of the true complexity of the religious picture. A healthy attempt to practice either one—openness to others' distinctive claims or authentic witness to our own—will increasingly lead us to respect the necessity of the other. A move "beyond inclusivism" is impossible and the attempt counter-productive.

This is not unrelated to the continuing discussion about the place for different kinds of study and teaching of religion in our culture. Religious studies is increasingly caught between two assumptions. The first presumes that truly analytical study of religion fits the particular traditions into the same supervening academic categories, whether psychological or historical or anthropological. This practice is regarded as legitimate so long as the categories to which the traditions are subordinated are not themselves religious in any particularistic way. The second presumes that one has only truly begun to study a religion when one is able to see and understand the world as constituted through its specific resources. This is a task which in theory could require the lifetime of the student, just as well as full practice would require the lifetime of the devotee. Pluralistic theories of religion come down sharply on the side of the first assumption and therefore have difficulty knowing what to do with the many interfaith studies that emphasize the second. The first assumption involves an indefensible dichotomy between categories of interpretation that are religiously particularistic and those that are not. Once this dichotomy is relaxed, the two types of approach to the study of religion are no longer so much at odds. Though this implies that theology should gain a rightful footing within the field of religious studies, it does not imply that so-called objective methods of study are devalued. Such methods, largely enlightenment-derived, have made crucial contributions to our understanding. All that is required is that such study be expected to give the same particularistic account of itself that other religious views must. The characteristic feature of religious studies in a pluralistic culture should be the capacity for two-way deconstruction and two-way construction. It would be a poor teacher of Islam, for instance, whatever his or her own faith, who could not impress vividly on students the implausibility and inconsistency of a modern Western academic approach to religion from most Muslim perspectives, as well as indicating the way in which such academic methods could reinterpret Muslim tradition on Western assumptions.

A third advantage of the approach I suggest is its treatment of the significance of religious change and development. A full appreciation of the possibilities for "tacking" within religious traditions moves us beyond the simple dogmatism that identified universal religious truth with a privileged specific culture and the equally simple dogmatism which absolutized the doctrine that the concrete contents of religion were locked in separate cultural compartments. Only some coordination of these two assumptions—that true religious fulfillments span cultural differences and that all such fulfillments indelibly bear cultural marks—can be viable. That we are likely to follow the religious tradition we are born into—though this is in fact increasingly less likely in many parts of the world, and what we are "born into" increasingly becomes rather equivocal in many areas—has long been an argument against the universal truth of any particular faith. Such an argument is dramatically diminished when these traditions are seen as less monolithic, the ways toward other faiths' religious aims lying at hand even within a single tradition. Pluralists correctly point to a widespread fear of interreligious relations that is felt by believers in many faith groups. They are right that the hesitancy of many Christians to take up issues of religious diversity is a tacit admission that the crude common categories their religious formation has given them to apply to such issues would rapidly break down in the face of greater familiarity. A framework such as the one I have suggested provides the room for this necessary development. But it also avoids the serious failing of pluralistic theories, the failure to grant religious change any substantive meaning.[2]

---

[2] To consider only one concrete example, we may take interfaith marriages. As even limited experience demonstrates, there is no single format for interfaith families. In some cases the title is a euphemism for a religious vacuum. In others it reflects a unified "syncretistic" practice in which there is a religious unity in the family around convergent interpretations of two traditions. This usually involves an "inclusivistic" strategy toward one or even both of the traditions. In still others it designates a situation where two distinct religious practices are carried on by different persons in the family. There are further possibilities as well. The perspective I have outlined would indicate that these variations represent real and crucial religious choices. This perspective offers grounds for understanding that a family's sense of struggle among these options is entirely justified, for the issues involved are substantive and not simply personal or practical.

Surely we further the goal of a "religious interpretation of religion" which Hick calls for if we find that there is a consistent way to affirm the long-standing inclusivist theories of the various religions, theories which affirm precisely that there are within other religions, as a kind of minor key, crosscurrents that may be "crowned" with the fulfillment the "home" religion seeks. In this respect, the pluralistic claim that all the paths of all the religions are "crowned" with the fulfillment of the pluralistic religious goal can be seen not as a new level of religious theory but simply as one more in a chain of permutations that lie in the same field.

I will close this review of my argument by briefly comparing it with another perspective that questions the current treatments of religious diversity. In *Is There Only One True Religion or Are There Many?* Shubert Ogden proposes a fourth way beyond exclusivism, inclusivism, and pluralism (Ogden 1992). The key to his perspective is a distinction between representation and constitution. He holds that neither Christ nor any historical event can be taken to constitute or cause human salvation; this can only be attributed to God. Exclusivists and inclusivists agree that the Christ event constitutes salvation and deny that others can have access to salvation except through that constituting event. Both, in Ogden's view, assert there is only one true religion. Pluralists deny that any particularistic event can be constitutive of salvation and insist that there necessarily are many true religions.

In brief, Ogden's argument is that if the Christian religion itself is correct, this necessarily implies that some others may be. If Christianity is true, "then any and all religions can also be true in the very same sense, because or insofar as they give expression to substantially the same religious truth" (Ogden 1992, 102). He maintains that religions do have distinctive constitutive elements, and the truth or falsity of the religion is determined by whether these constitutive elements truly *represent* the divine. As opposed to the pluralists, then, Ogden recognizes a unique constitutive and representational element in each religious tradition which may *not* be a true representation of the divine. The "representational" aspects of a religious tradition fall in two tiers: those that are constitutively representative, and those that are derivatively representative. Within Christianity, for example, Ogden uses the example of the sacraments. All Christian sacraments represent Christ and the believer's relation to Christ, while Christ as the primal sacrament represents God. "They [the sacraments] represent God's love by representing him, he represents God's love by *constituting* them" (Ogden 1992, 98). But, Ogden says, Christ manifests or expresses a salvation that is already given as a possibility. It is not Christ who makes salvation possible but the love of God, which occasions the Christ event as its expression.

Against the pluralists, Ogden argues, as I have, that there is no metalanguage of a higher order than the religions' languages to express that which is authentically represented by the religions. This is why he speaks of this strictly ultimate reality that alone constitutes salvation as "the love of God." He is a Christian, and to "be a Christian and to take Christianity to be the formally true religion are one and the same thing" (Ogden 1992, 100). Thus he must speak in these "inclusivist" terms, while recognizing the appropriateness of others' inclusivisms. The Christian must regard the Buddhist as an anonymous Christian, insofar as Buddhism is regarded as true, while the Buddhist reciprocally sees the Christian as an anonymous Buddhist to the extent that the Christian is on a valid path. "Provided the self-understandings made explicit in the two explanations are substantially the same, both explanations can be true even though only Christians have reason to offer the one and only Buddhists have reason to offer the other" (Ogden 1992, 102). The pluralists are thus right in claiming that there can be more than one independently true religion. But they are wrong to claim to know already that there are many or to have any other avenue to affirm their truth than the inclusivist one.

Ogden is arguing that the relation of religions can only be approached in the specific. If, for instance, the situation is reached where Buddhists regard Christians as anonymously being *fully* Buddhist and Christians regard Buddhists as anonymously being *fully* Christian, then that is the most perfect form of agreement we can seek. There is no reason for adherents of either to give up their frame of reference—constituted by its unique representation of salvation—for the other or for some new or intermediate representation. Ogden thus avoids the parable of the elephant's presumption to stand in the place of the sighted among the blind. And, because he avoids any a priori assumptions about all religions, even those that manifest certain moral effects, he retains a crucial urgency for attention to religious particulars. Only in this way can one learn if the same self-understanding is manifested in a specific religion as in another one known to be true.

I travel a good way with Ogden. But we diverge at significant points as well. Like the pluralistic writers I have discussed, Ogden accepts a unitary notion of salvation: there can be only one salvation, no more than one thing or condition can legitimately be meant by this word. He also accepts a simple dichotomy of true and false religions. Although no one can rightly claim to have a transtheological description of that which true religions truly represent, we can formally conceive of it. And Ogden holds that we can laboriously and tentatively work out the rough equivalence of one set of representational specifics to another set, without positing some middle terms between them. By contrast, I insist salvation can be understood in the plural. Religions may be seen as both true and alternative rather than necessarily either true or false, and thus two "true" religions need not be assumed to represent the same thing. All religions that are true do not have to be true "in the very same sense." And it does not necessarily follow that the adherents of two true religions must each regard the other as anonymous members of its own tradition.

Salvation, for Ogden, is constituted by something entirely beyond the human plane, and each tradition's unique representation of that something constitutes an irreducibly distinct religion. Christ is this constituting event for Christians. But salvation itself is apparently not constituted by these unique representations, according to Ogden. God constitutes salvation. The constitutive events of true religions represent God's love. Their representations constitute the distinctive features of the religious traditions. Here I differ, arguing that this dualism between true representations of God's salvation and the salvation that is represented cannot be so absolutely enforced. The Christian affirmations about incarnation and Trinity mean that while salvation as a possibility cannot be attributed solely to "the Christ event," apart from God's other creative and sustaining actions, neither can Christ as the Word-in-humanity be excluded from the constitution of our salvation.

Ogden is right that Christ represents God's love to us by constituting signs which then represent God by representing Christ. But this is not the limit of the constitutive power of the Christ event. It surely constitutes "Christian salvation" insofar as that phrase describes a human condition within history shaped by all the signs constituted by the Christ event. I argue that it is significantly (though again not exclusively) constitutive of the transhistorical salvation Christians seek and achieve as well.

Although I do not agree with all of Ogden's conclusions, I believe that he is correct in pointing us beyond the limits of the pluralistic agenda. Once the boundaries of the narrow typology of exclusivist-inclusivist-pluralistic are burst, there is room for a more exciting discussion in which the encounter between faiths will recover an expectant attentiveness to their particulars. This brief comparison is intended both to clarify my own views and to point to the fact that a "post-pluralistic" conversation will involve varied voices. It will be wider and not more limited. This book has focused on distinguishing some alternative approaches to pluralistic theologies. Another work could focus more extensively on conversation among some of these alternative voices, writers like Ogden, Panikkar, DiNoia, and Clooney.

I have done my best to make clear the sense in which any religious tradition's "exclusivist" dimension, its presumption that it constitutes a "one and only" path toward a distinctive—rather than generic—religious end is valid. I defend a claim which in the current climate is seen as highly paradoxical: respect for these exclusivist dimensions is the necessary correlative of respect for the diversity of faith traditions in their concrete, historical actuality. The paradox has more to do with the current intellectual climate than with intrinsic consistency. Only if it is possible to acknowledge this exclusivistic alternativeness in the religions is it possible to claim that there is distinctive truth or insight available in any one or several of them that is not available elsewhere. In this sense, belief in a distinctive, universal witness to be made on the behalf of one's own faith is a crucial contributory factor in even conceiving the possibility of receiving such a witness from others. Any religion's claim to be *the* true religion deserves the cautionary reprimand pluralists offer, as does the claim to be the sole path to any religious fulfillment or salvation. But the conviction that one follows the most inclusive true religion, the superior true religion, with a distinctive fulfillment, is not only defensible but inescapable. The semblance of denying such a conviction is achieved only by shifting the nature of the inclusivism from one based in a specific traditional mythos to one based in a specific modern Western mythos.

The fulfillment we seek need not be everyone's. Ours is not the only salvation: there are others. The "exclusive" witnesses of the various religious traditions are in this sense mutually confirming. Affirmation of a distinctive Christian path and end opens the only space there could be truly to recognize other distinctive paths and ends. To say that a different religious tradition can serve as an ordinary or extraordinary means of attaining the religious aim *my* faith seeks, as my tradition can serve to realize the aim of the other faith, is to say something important. I have sketched the great significance I attribute to this reality. But such "anonymous Christianity" or "anonymous Hinduism" is but one possibility, not the necessity implied in making us all anonymous pluralists. I have argued that a religious tradition may at the same time have its own distinctive religious end and also include within it the means by which people can "tack" toward the achievement of a substantially different one.

In the introduction I suggested that to see nothing ultimately distinctive about one's own religious commitment in relation to others is as serious an impairment as to be ignorant of any religion but one's own. In fact, they are two sides of the same coin. As has been apparent, my own Christian convictions have been engaged in reaching and arguing the views expressed in this work. This engagement is fully consistent with the perspective I have outlined, not a violation of it. Indeed, I think we should reflect very hard on the often facile injunctions that our convictions as Hindus or as Buddhists or as Christians should be excluded from this type of discussion. This is a definitive fork in the understanding of "pluralism": Does one invite the basic religious convictions into the fundamental discussion or *claim* to exclude them until the ground rules and agenda in some way have been set? I opt clearly for the first option.

In this conversation, my Christian faith does not stop being my Christian faith but at the same time it serves as the means for the "tacit knowing" of which Michael Polanyi speaks (Polanyi 1964, esp. 55-65). That is, its very distinctiveness and universal intent serve as a kind of instrument or antenna through which I can register the existence of such distinctiveness and universal intent in other faiths and fathom something of what they may mean. I can only say that in my own relationships of dialogue, such true knowing and being known as I have experienced, depended crucially on this shared identification by contrast.

It is hardly the case that such a view of particularistic religious convictions limits the transformative power of interreligious encounter, or assumes that one's own convictions are fixed in some complacent form. By way of example, I pointed out in chapter 6 that the perspective I am suggesting does not fit easily into traditional Christian theological frameworks. It requires fresh and imaginative thought. And it is precisely the kinds of encounter that pluralistic thinkers speak of that foster this reconstruction. However, I am convinced that the perspective I suggest is fully consistent with biblical and trinitarian convictions, and that this consistency can be more fully worked out. This is important not out of any rote concern for tradition but because to short-circuit the distinctive dimension of Christian faith is to short-circuit continuation of the encounter itself, to destroy, as it were, our primary receptive organ for making contact. This is the same point we made in a different key when speaking of the imperative for justice and raising the question about what distinctive resources or motivation the religions would be thought to bring to such a struggle, once reconceived in pluralistic terms.

I am not so bold as to claim comprehensiveness for the view I have presented. No doubt there are both possibilities and liabilities to which I am still insensible. But I believe that my approach offers a long-term prescription for careful interaction with other religious traditions. Pluralistic theories emphasize for devotees in any tradition a radical and one-time act of renunciation of exclusivism and salvific distinctiveness. I would certainly be the last one to diminish the significance (negative, in my view) of this demand! But were it to be met, it would be a royal charter for isolation among the faiths. There could be only the most practical, instrumental motivations for exploring the details of various traditions, of more or less the same sorts that exclusivists have traditionally allowed. People will struggle across considerable cultural barriers to share something they have tasted as decisively important for human life, or to seek a contribution decisively different from what they may have known before. Travel which is predicated on observing how others do, in their way, the identical thing that we do at home in ours is a form of tourism which is both less dynamic and less serious.

I am convinced that Christianity has the resources to become an active and respectful partner with its religious neighbors. Chief among these resources are the very particularistic confessions which are so much at issue in these discussions. However, the transformation required in the way these confessions are appropriated is nearly as extensive, if not as linear, as pluralistic authors suppose. Christians have grown used to expressing the decisive character of God's act in Christ by contrast with evil, error, and lostness. These expressions are at times appropriate both literally and figuratively. But we have to recognize they have a limited legitimate scope. We need to learn that in relation to living religious traditions the decisive witness to Christ is rightly expressed in relation to the neighbors' *actual* religious aim and practices. There is ample room to commend Christ in such terms. Such witness is consistent with the recognition that my neighbors (pluralistic, Buddhist, Muslim) appropriately also phrase their positive evaluations of my religious life in terms that are fundamentally theirs.

The decisive and universal significance of Christ is for Christians *both* the necessary ground for particularistic witness *and* the basis for recognizing in other religious traditions their own particularistic integrity. We are only beginning to appreciate the ways in which this conviction must be embodied in our theology and our practice. But the way forward lies through this conviction, not around it. Therefore, the way forward lies equally through the distinctive convictions of my neighbors, not around them.

Bibliography

Abhishiktananda, Swami. 1969. *Hindu Christian Meeting Point within the Cave of the Heart*. Bombay.

Almond, Philip C. 1988. *The British Discovery of Buddhism*. Cambridge: Cambridge University Press.

Anderson, Gerald H., and Thomas F. Stransky, C.S.P., eds. 1981. *Christ's Lordship and Religious Pluralism*. Maryknoll: Orbis Books.

Balasuriya. Tissa. 1985. "A Third World Perspective." In Fabella and Torres, *Doing Theology in a Divided World*.

Barrett, David. 1989. *World Christian Encyclopedia*. Oxford: Oxford University Press.

Bauer, Walter. 1971. *Heresy and Orthodoxy in Earliest Christianity*. Philadelphia: Fortress Press.

Berger, Peter. 1992. *A Far Glory*. New York: Free Press.

Brandon, S.G.F., ed. 1962. *The Savior God*. Manchester: Manchester University Press.

Burch, George Bosworth. 1972. *Alternative Goals in Religion*. Montreal: McGill-Queen's University Press.

Chaudhuri, Nirad. 1979. *Hinduism*. London: Chattu and Windus.

Christian, William. 1987. *Doctrines of Religious Communities*. New Haven: Yale University Press.

Clooney, Francis X., S.J. 1990. "Reading the World in Christ." In D'Costa, *Christian Uniqueness Reconsidered*, 63-80.

Cobb, John. 1990. "Beyond Pluralism." In D'Costa, *Christian Uniqueness Reconsidered*.

Conze, Edward. 1962. "Buddhist Saviors." In Brandon, *The Savior God*. Manchester: Manchester University Press.

Costas, Orlando. 1981. "Reply." In Anderson and Stransky, *Christ's Lordship and Religious Pluralism*.

Coward, Harold, ed. 1989. *Hindu Christian Dialogue*. Maryknoll: Orbis Books.

Dalai Lama. 1990. "The Bodhgaya Interviews." In Griffiths, *Christianity Through Non-Christian Eyes*.

Dante Alighieri. 1962. *The Divine Comedy*. Translated by Dorothy L. Sayers and Barbara Reynolds. Baltimore: Penguin.

D'Costa, Gavin. 1986. *Theology and Religious Pluralism*. Oxford: Blackwell.

D'Costa, Gavin. 1990. "Christ, the Trinity, and Religious Plurality." In D'Costa, *Christian Uniqueness Reconsidered*.

D'Costa, Gavin, ed. 1990. *Christian Uniqueness Reconsidered*. Maryknoll: Orbis Books.

Dean, Thomas. 1987. "The Conflict of Christologies," *Journal of Ecumenical Studies* 24 (Winter).

Descartes, Rene. 1968. *Discourse on Method.* Translated by F. E. Sutcliffe. Baltimore: Penguin.

DiNoia, J. A. 1989. "Varieties of Religious Aims: Beyond Exclusivism, Inclusivism, and Pluralism." In Marshall, *Theology and Dialogue.*

DiNoia, Joseph. 1992. *The Diversity of Religions: A Christian Perspective.* Washington: Catholic University Press.

Doniger, Wendy. 1991. "Pluralism and Intolerance in Hinduism." In Jeanrod and Rike, *Radical Pluralism and Truth: David Tracy and the Hermeneutics of Religions.*

Driver, Tom F. 1987. "The Case for Pluralism." In Hick and Knitter, *The Myth of Christian Uniqueness.*

Fabella, Virginia. 1980. *Asia's Struggle for Full Humanity.* Maryknoll: Orbis Books.

Fabella, Virginia, and Sergio Torres, eds. 1985. *Doing Religion in a Divided World.* Maryknoll: Orbis Books.

Gandhi, M. K. 1938. *Hind Swaraj.* Ahmedabad: Navajivan Publishing House.

Gilkey, Langdon. 1987. "Plurality and Its Theological Implications." In Hick and Knitter, *The Myth of Christian Uniqueness.*

Gort, Jerald D., et al., eds. 1992. *On Sharing Religious Experience.* Grand Rapids: Eerdmans.

Griffiths, Bede. 1986. *Christ in India.* Bangalore: Asian Trading Corporation.

Griffiths, Paul, ed. 1990. *Christianity through Non-Christian Eyes.* Maryknoll: Orbis Books.

Griffiths, Paul. 1991. *An Apology for Apologetics.* Maryknoll: Orbis Books.

Griffiths, Paul. 1993. "Stump, Kretzmann, and Historical Blindness," *Faith and Philosophy* 10.

Hamnett, Ian, ed. 1990. *Religious Pluralism and Belief.* New York: Routledge.

Hasluck, F. 1929. *Christianity and Islam under the Sultan.* Oxford: Clarendon Press.

Heim, S. Mark. 1985. *Is Christ the Only Way?* Philadelphia: Judson.

Heim, S. Mark. 1987. "Thinking about Theocentric Christology," *Journal of Ecumenical Studies* 24.

Heim, S. Mark. 1988. "Choosing Roots: The Contexts for Christian Theology in India," *This World* 21 (Spring).

Heim, S. Mark. 1991. "Crisscrossing the Rubicon," *Christian Century* 108, no. 21 (July 10-17).

Heim, S. Mark. 1992. "The Pluralistic Hypothesis, Realism and Post-Eschatology," *Religious Studies* 28.

Hewitt, Harold, Jr., ed. 1991. *Problems in the Philosophy of John Hick.* New York: St. Martin's Press.

Hick, John. 1964. "Theology and Verification." In Hick, *The Existence of God.*

Hick, John. 1964. *The Existence of God.* New York: Macmillan.

Hick, John. 1976. *Death and Eternal Life.* New York: Harper & Row.

Hick, John. 1977. *The Myth of God Incarnate.* Philadelphia: Westminster Press.

Hick, John. 1989. *An Interpretation of Religion.* New Haven: Yale University Press.

Hick, John. 1990. "Straightening the Record: Some Response to Critics," *Modern Theology* 6,2.

Hick, John. 1993. *Disputed Questions in Theology and the Philosophy of Reli-*

gion. New Haven: Yale University Press.

Hick, John, and Paul F. Knitter, eds. 1987. *The Myth of Christian Uniqueness*. Maryknoll: Orbis Books.

Hillman, Eugene. 1968. *The Wider Ecumenism: Anonymous Christianity and the Church*. London: Burns and Oates.

Hodgson, Marshall. 1974. *The Venture of Islam: Conscience and History in a World Civilization*. Vol. 1. Chicago: University of Chicago Press.

Jantzen, Grace M. 1984. "Human Diversity and Salvation in Christ," *Religious Studies* 20.

Jeanrod, Werner G., and Jennifer L. Rike, eds. 1991. *Radical Pluralism and Truth: David Tracy and the Hermeneutics of Religion*. New York: Crossroad.

Kaufman, Gordon. n.d. "Religious Diversity and Theological Meta-thinking." Unpublished paper.

Knitter, Paul. 1985. *No Other Name?* Maryknoll: Orbis Books.

Knitter, Paul F. 1987a. "Introduction." In Hick and Knitter, *The Myth of Christian Uniqueness*.

Knitter, Paul F. 1987b. "Preface." In Hick and Knitter, *The Myth of Christian Uniqueness*.

Knitter, Paul F. 1987c. "Toward a Liberation Theology of Religions." In Hick and Knitter, *The Myth of Christian Uniqueness*.

Knitter, Paul F. 1989. "Making Sense of the Many," *Religious Studies Review* 15.

Krieger, David J. 1991. *The New Universalism*. Maryknoll: Orbis Books.

Küng, Hans. 1987. "Christianity and World Religions: The Dialogue with Islam as One Model," *The Muslim World* 77, 2.

LaFargue, Michael. 1992. "Radically Pluralistic, Thoroughly Critical: A New Theory of Religions," *Journal of the American Academy of Religion* 60,4.

Lindbeck, George. 1984. *The Nature of Doctrine*. Philadelphia: Westminster Press.

Lovejoy, Arthur O. 1974. *The Great Chain of Being*. Cambridge: Harvard University Press.

Marshall, Bruce, ed. 1989. *Theology and Dialogue*. Notre Dame: University of Notre Dame Press.

Martin, David. 1990. *Tongues of Fire*. Cambridge: Basil Blackwell.

McGrane, Bernard. 1989. *Beyond Anthropology: Society and the Other*. New York: Columbia University Press.

McNeill, William H. 1963. *The Rise of the West*. New York: Mentor.

Mesle, C. Robert. 1990. "Review of *An Interpretation of Religion*," *Journal of the American Academy of Religion* 58,4, 710-714.

Milbank, John. 1990a. "The End of Dialogue." In D'Costa, *Christian Uniqueness Reconsidered*.

Milbank, John. 1990b. *Theology and Social Theory*. Oxford: Blackwell.

Nasr, Seyyed Hossein. 1987. "Response to Hans Küng," *The Muslim World* 77, 2.

Netland, Harold. 1991. *Dissonant Voices*. Grand Rapids: Eerdmans.

Newbigin, Lesslie. 1989. *The Gospel in a Pluralist Society*. Grand Rapids: Zondervan.

Newbigin, Lesslie. 1990. "Religion for the Marketplace." In D'Costa, *Chris-*

tian Uniqueness Reconsidered.

Novak, David. 1989. *Jewish-Christian Dialogue: A Jewish Justification.* Oxford. Oxford University Press.

Ogden, Shubert. 1992. *Is There Only One True Religion or Are There Many?.* Dallas: Southern Methodist University Press.

Oxtoby, Willard G., ed. 1982. *Religious Diversity.* New York: Crossroad.

Panikkar, Raimundo. 1973. *The Trinity and the Religious Experience of Man.* London: Darton, Longman, & Todd; Maryknoll, New York: Orbis Books.

Panikkar, Raimundo. 1978. *The Intrareligious Dialogue.* New York: Paulist Press.

Panikkar, Raimundo. 1987. "The Jordan, the Tiber, and the Ganges." In Hick and Knitter, *The Myth of Christian Uniqueness.*

Panikkar, Raimundo. 1989. "The Ongoing Dialogue." In Coward, *Hindu Christian Dialogue.*

Penz, Rebecca. 1991. "Hick and Saints: Is Saint Production a Valid Test?," *Faith and Philsophy* 8,1.

Pieris, Aloysius. 1988. *An Asian Theology of Liberation.* Maryknoll: Orbis Books.

Polanyi, Michael. 1964. *Personal Knowledge.* New York: Harper & Row.

Proudfoot, Wayne. 1985. *Religious Experience.* Berkeley: University of California Press.

Race, Alan. 1982. *Christians and Religious Pluralism: Patterns in the Christian Theology of Religions.* Maryknoll: Orbis Books.

Rahner, Karl. 1966. *Theological Investigations,* Vol. 5. London: Darton, Longman & Todd.

Rawls, John. 1971. *A Theory of Liberalism.* Cambridge: Harvard University Press.

Rescher, Nicholas. 1985. *The Strife of Systems.* Pittsburgh: Pittsburgh University Press.

Rowe, William. 1991. "Paradox and Promise: John Hick's Solution to the Problem of Evil." In Hewitt, *Problems in the Philosophy of John Hick.*

Ruether, Rosemary Radford. 1974. *Faith and Fratricide.* New York: Seabury Press.

Ruether, Rosemary Radford, and Herman J. Ruether. 1989. *The Wrath of Jonah.* San Francisco: Harper & Row.

Sanders, John. 1992. *No Other Name.* Grand Rapids: Eerdmans.

Smith, W. C. 1964. *The Meaning and End of Religion.* New York: Macmillan.

Smith, W. C. 1977. *Belief and History.* Charlottesville: University Press of Virginia.

Smith, W. C. 1979. *Faith and Belief.* Princeton: Princeton University Press.

Smith, W. C. 1981. *Towards a World Theology.* Maryknoll: Orbis Books.

Smith, W. C. 1982. "Is the Qu'ran the Word of God?" In Oxtoby, *Religious Diversity.*

Smith, W. C. 1987. "Idolatry." In Hick and Knitter, *The Myth of Christian Uniqueness,* 53-68.

Smith, W. C. 1988. "Mission, Dialogue, and God's Will for Us," *International Review of Mission* 78 (July).

Smith, W. C. 1992. "Sharing the Qu'ran and the Bible as the Word of God." In Gort, *On Sharing Religious Experience.*

Stackhouse, Max. 1984. *Creeds, Society and Human Rights*. Grand Rapids: Eerdmans.

Stackhouse, Max. 1987. *Public Theology and Political Economy*. Grand Rapids: Eerdmans.

Stackhouse, Max. 1988. *Apologia*. Grand Rapids: Eerdmans.

Stackhouse, Max. 1991. "From the Social Gospel to Public Theology: A Liberal Protestant Perspective," *Lutheran Forum* 25, 4.

Stark, Rodney, and William Sims Bainbridge. 1992. *The Future of Religion*. Berkeley: University of California Free Press.

Suchocki, Marjorie Hewitt, 1987. "In Search of Justice." In Hick and Knitter, *The Myth of Christian Uniqueness*, 149-161.

Surin, Kenneth. 1990a. "A 'Politics of Speech': Religious Pluralism in the Age of the McDonald's Hamburger." In D'Costa, *Christian Uniqueness Reconsidered*.

Surin, Kenneth. 1990b. "Towards a 'Materialist' Critique of Religious Pluralism: An Examination of the Discourse of John Hick and Wilfred Cantwell Smith." In Hamnett, *Religious Pluralism and Unbelief*.

Thiemann, Ronald. 1995. *Religion in American Public Life: A Dilemma for Democracy*. Washington, D.C.: Georgetown University Press.

Thomas, M. M. 1990. "A Christ-Centered Humanist Approach to Other Religions in the Indian Pluralistic Context." In D'Costa, *Christian Uniqueness Reconsidered*.

Thomas, Owen. 1969. *Attitudes toward Other Religions*. New York: Harper & Row.

Troeltsch, Ernst. 1969. "The Place of Christianity among World Religions." In Thomas, *Attitudes toward Other Religions*.

Wainwright, William J. 1984. "Wilfred Cantwell Smith on Faith and Belief," *Religious Studies* 20 (September).

Ward, Keith. 1990. "Truth and the Diversity of Religions," *Religious Studies* 26.

Williams, Rowan. 1990. "Trinity and Pluralism." In D'Costa, *Christian Uniqueness Reconsidered*.

World Council Faith and Order Commission. 1982. *Baptism, Eucharist, and Ministry*. Faith and Order Paper #111. Geneva: World Council of Churches.

World Council Faith and Order Commission. 1991. *Confessing the One Faith*. Faith and Order Paper #153. Geneva: World Council of Churches.

Index

Other Titles in the Faith Meets Faith Series